Security Challenges with Blockchain

Navigate Blockchain Security Challenges, Unveil Vulnerabilities, and Gain Practical Strategies for Secure Application Development

Chintan Dave

www.orangeava.com

First published: April 2024

Published by: Orange Education Pvt Ltd, AVA™

Address: 9, Daryaganj, Delhi, 110002, India

275 New North Road Islington Suite 1314 London,

N1 7AA, United Kingdom

ISBN: 978-81-96862-08-4

www.orangeava.com

Dedicated To

For AVI:

"To my beloved boy AVI, the light of my days and the star of my nights. You are the melody in our hearts and the laughter in our home. Your spirit inspires us, your strength binds us, and your love enriches every moment we share. May you always walk in sunshine, my son, surrounded by love and guided by kindness. With every breath, I dedicate my journey to you, for you are not just a part of my life; you are my whole world."

For *Megha:*

"To Megha, my partner, my confidante, and the love of my life. You are the harmony to my melody, the calm in my storm, and the grace that guides me. Your love is a sanctuary, your wisdom a guiding light, and your strength a foundation upon which I build my dreams. Together, we have woven a tapestry of love, enriched with moments of joy, laughter, and tenderness. I dedicate my every achievement, my every dream, and my every day to you, for you are the essence of my being and the heart of my soul."

About the Author

Chintan Dave stands at the forefront of blockchain innovation, a testament to his deep-seated passion for technology and education. As the esteemed Head of India at AI Certs and Director of Blockchain at NetCom Learning, he orchestrates the integration of blockchain technology into various sectors, wielding a rich tapestry of knowledge gleaned from authoring 18 technical books. His journey is underpinned by a Master of Science in Software Systems from the prestigious Birla Institute of Technology and Science, Pilani, illustrating a lifelong commitment to technological and educational advancement.

An acclaimed Certified Blockchain Expert and Solution Architect, Chintan's professional ethos is characterized by a profound belief in the power of blockchain to transform industries. With over 50 workshops to his name, he has demystified blockchain for countless professionals, outlining its potential beyond the realm of digital currencies. His consultancy work, which spans more than 50 projects, reflects a pragmatic approach to harnessing blockchain for real-world applications. Chintan's expertise covers a broad spectrum of blockchain frameworks, such as Hyperledger and Ethereum, showcasing his versatility and depth of knowledge in the field.

At AI Certs, Chintan leads with a visionary goal: to certify a billion professionals in AI and Blockchain. This ambitious project underscores his dedication to raising the bar for technology certifications worldwide. In his role at NetCom Learning, he champions the cause of lifelong learning, driving the digital transformation agenda through the development of cutting-edge blockchain solutions.

Beyond his professional achievements, Chintan is a prolific author, speaker, and trainer. His publications, which range from Java Programming to Database Programming with VB.Net, serve as critical resources for both novices and seasoned professionals navigating the complex landscape of computer programming and blockchain. His thought leadership extends to major conferences and workshops, where he shares insights on blockchain's security challenges and opportunities.

About the Technical Reviewers

Abhinav Sharma is a Security Researcher with over 1 year of learning experience in blockchain security. He has expertise in building and analyzing comprehensive smart contracts. Currently, he is involved with QuillAudits as a Web3 Security Researcher, uncovering different smart contract attack vectors and analyzing on-chain data. Additionally, he has disclosed various bugs in both public and private blockchain protocols.

Preetam is the CEO and Co-founder of QuillAudits, a leading Web3 security firm committed to securing Blockchain projects. To date, QuillAudits has secured over 850 Web3 protocols with its cutting-edge Web3 security solutions.

Acknowledgements

In the journey of exploring the revolutionary realms of blockchain technology and its profound impact across various industries, the creation of this manuscript has been an enlightening adventure. This endeavor would not have been possible without the collective wisdom, support, and encouragement from numerous individuals and institutions.

First and foremost, I extend my deepest gratitude to Satoshi Nakamoto, whose pioneering work laid the foundation for the decentralized digital future. The insights drawn from Nakamoto's seminal paper have been instrumental in shaping the discussions within these pages. Similarly, the contributions of visionaries such as Vitalik Buterin, whose creation of Ethereum opened new horizons for blockchain applications, have been invaluable.

I am immensely thankful to the academic and professional community for their ongoing research and exploration into blockchain technology. The works of M. Swan, H. Kent Baker, and Hak J. Kim, among others, have provided critical perspectives and frameworks that enrich the narrative of this book.

A special note of appreciation goes to the open-source community and blockchain developers worldwide. Their relentless innovation, collaboration, and willingness to share knowledge have made blockchain technology more accessible and impactful. The discussions on platforms such as Bitcointalk.org and Reddit have been a source of inspiration and insight.

I also wish to acknowledge the support of my peers and colleagues who have provided feedback, critique, and encouragement throughout the writing process. Their diverse perspectives have been crucial in presenting a balanced and comprehensive view of blockchain technology.

To my family and friends, whose patience and understanding have been my stronghold during the countless hours spent researching and writing, I am forever grateful.

Lastly, I extend my thanks to you, the reader, for embarking on this journey with me. It is my sincere hope that this book not only enlightens but also inspires you to explore the potential of blockchain technology in transforming our world for the better.

Together, we stand at the threshold of a new digital era, powered by blockchain. Let us embrace this opportunity with curiosity, courage, and collaboration.

Preface

Welcome to *Security Challenges with Blockchain*, a book dedicated to unraveling the complexities and addressing the pivotal concerns of security within the revolutionary field of blockchain technology. As blockchain continues to carve paths for digital transformation across industries like finance, healthcare, supply chain management, and beyond, it brings with it a new set of security challenges that demand our attention and understanding.

This book embarks on a critical examination of the inherent security risks that accompany blockchain's innovative potential. From its inception as the technology underpinning Bitcoin to its current applications that promise to redefine entire industries, blockchain has been celebrated for its decentralization, transparency, and enhanced security. However, these very attributes also present unique vulnerabilities and challenges that must be navigated carefully to safeguard the technology's integrity and the trust of its users.

Through a comprehensive exploration, readers will gain a profound understanding of the core principles of blockchain technology, including its decentralized nature and the cryptographic protocols that form its backbone. We delve into the technicalities of blockchain to uncover how its security mechanisms work, the types of attacks it faces, and the ongoing efforts to fortify blockchain systems against such threats.

Moreover, we will tackle the broader implications of these security challenges, from scalability and energy consumption issues to the complex landscape of regulatory compliance. This book aims to equip readers with the knowledge to critically assess the security aspects of blockchain technology, understand the challenges at hand, and engage with the ongoing discourse on developing robust solutions.

Security Challenges with Blockchain is more than a guide; it is a call to action for developers, business leaders, policymakers, and enthusiasts to collaborate and innovate in strengthening the security foundations of blockchain technology. As we journey through the chapters, we will not only highlight the challenges but also celebrate the successes and the promising strategies that pave the way for a more secure blockchain ecosystem.

Whether you are deeply involved in the blockchain space or are newly curious about its security dimensions, this book promises to provide valuable insights and foster a deeper understanding of the challenges that lie ahead. Together, let's explore the critical security considerations essential for harnessing the full potential of blockchain technology while ensuring the safety and trust of its users.

Welcome to the exploration of *Security Challenges with Blockchain.*

Chapter 1. Introduction to Blockchain Technology: This chapter provides a foundational understanding of blockchain technology, its evolution, use cases, and key concepts. It covers the definition of blockchain, its decentralized and distributed ledger nature, and how it enables secure and transparent transactions without intermediaries. The chapter explores the structure of a blockchain, consisting of a series of blocks linked through cryptographic hashes, creating an immutable chain of data. Additionally, it discusses the network of computers that store information in a decentralized database, highlighting the permanence and security features of blockchain technology.

Chapter 2. Understanding Blockchain Security: This chapter delves into the essential aspects of blockchain security, particularly in the context of cryptocurrencies and other potential use cases. It emphasizes the decentralized and immutable nature of blockchain technology, which contributes to its high level of security. The chapter explores basic security concepts and terminologies crucial for comprehending the security challenges faced by blockchain networks. It provides an overview of blockchain security, security terminologies, types of security threats, and the potential consequences of security breaches. By examining these key elements, readers gain insights into the security measures necessary to safeguard blockchain networks from various threats and vulnerabilities.

Chapter 3. Security Challenges in Public Blockchains: This chapter explores security challenges in public blockchains, exploring different attack vectors and preventive security measures. It discusses common threats such as double-spending attacks, 51% attacks, Sybil attacks, eclipse attacks, smart contract vulnerabilities, social engineering attacks, malware, and phishing attacks. The chapter also addresses various security measures to mitigate these threats, such as implementing consensus mechanisms, designing network architecture, using cryptographic primitives, multi-factor authentication, access controls, penetration testing, vulnerability assessments, incident response planning, and blockchain forensics. Additionally, real-world case studies on public blockchain security breaches are provided for practical insights.

Chapter 4. Security Challenges in Private Blockchains: This chapter delves into the security challenges faced by private blockchains, including insider attacks and network breaches. It discusses security measures to mitigate these risks. Private blockchains have gained popularity for their control, privacy, and efficiency. The chapter provides an overview of private blockchain security, highlighting their characteristics, benefits, and potential use cases. It further explores common security threats in private blockchains and outlines security measures to enhance protection against these threats, with real-world case studies providing practical insights and lessons learned in securing private blockchain networks.

Chapter 5. Security Challenges in Consortia Blockchains: Consortia blockchains present a unique blend of features from public and private blockchains, offering a controlled environment for organizations to collaborate and share data securely. However, this hybrid nature introduces specific security challenges that must be addressed to safeguard against potential threats like data breaches and financial losses. By understanding the foundational concepts of blockchain technology, identifying common security threats, implementing robust security measures, and learning from real-world case studies, stakeholders in consortia blockchains can navigate the complex security landscape effectively and ensure the secure and efficient operation of their collaborative networks.

Chapter 6. Security Challenges in Decentralized Finance: Decentralized Finance (DeFi) has emerged as a disruptive force in the financial sector, leveraging blockchain technology to offer innovative financial services in a decentralized and transparent manner. The rapid growth of DeFi platforms, particularly on Ethereum, has unlocked new opportunities for users to access lending, borrowing, trading, and earning opportunities without traditional intermediaries. However, the decentralized nature of DeFi also introduces unique security challenges, including smart contract vulnerabilities, decentralized exchange risks, and user-targeted attacks. Addressing these security concerns is crucial to ensuring the trust, integrity, and long-term viability of the DeFi ecosystem.

Chapter 7. Security Challenges in Supply Chain Management: Supply chain management is a critical component of modern business operations, ensuring the efficient flow of goods and services. The integration of blockchain technology in supply chains offers enhanced transparency, traceability, and efficiency. However, this adoption also brings forth new security challenges that organizations must address to safeguard their operations and data effectively. By exploring the role of blockchain in SCM, understanding common security threats, and implementing robust security measures, businesses can fortify the integrity and resilience of their supply chain processes in an evolving digital landscape.

Chapter 8. Security Challenges in Identity Management: This chapter explores the security challenges inherent in identity management, compares blockchain-based systems with traditional approaches, discusses security measures for blockchain-based identity management, and examines privacy-preserving techniques. By addressing these security challenges head-on and leveraging the unique features of blockchain technology, organizations can enhance the security and privacy of identity management processes in the digital age.

Chapter 9. Best Practices for Blockchain Security: This chapter delves into the best practices for enhancing blockchain security to mitigate risks and protect against potential threats. From secure coding practices and smart contract audits to network security and consensus mechanisms, implementing a comprehensive security strategy is essential for maintaining the integrity and trustworthiness of blockchain networks. By following these best practices and staying abreast of emerging security trends, organizations can fortify their blockchain implementations and foster a secure and resilient ecosystem for decentralized applications and digital transactions.

Get a Free eBook

We hope you are enjoying your recently purchased book! Your feedback is incredibly valuable to us, and to all other readers looking for great books.

If you found this book helpful or enjoyable, we would truly appreciate it, if you could take a moment to leave a short review with a 5 star rating on Amazon. It helps us grow, and lets other readers discover our books.

As a thank you, we would love to send you a free digital copy of this book, and a **30%** discount code on your next cart value on our official websites:

www.orangeava.com

www.orangeava.in (For Indian Subcontinent)

☑ **Here's how:**

Leave a review for the book on Amazon.

Take a screenshot of your review, and send an email to **info@orangeava.com** (it can be just the confirmation screen).

Once, we receive your screenshot, we will send you the digital file, within 24 hours.

Thank you so much for your support – it means a lot to us!

Colored Images

Please follow the links or scan the QR codes to download the
Images of the book:

You can find code bundles of our books on our official Github Repository. Go to the following link to and QR code to explore the further:

https://github.com/orgs/ava-orange-education/repositories

Please follow the link to download the Colored Images of the book:
https://rebrand.ly/wupc3wh

In case there's an update to the code, it will be updated on the existing GitHub repository.

Errata

We take immense pride in our work at **Orange Education Pvt Ltd,** and follow best practices to ensure the accuracy of our content to provide an indulging reading experience to our subscribers. Our readers are our mirrors, and we use their inputs to reflect and improve upon human errors, if any, that may have occurred during the publishing processes involved. To let us maintain the quality and help us reach out to any readers who might be having difficulties due to any unforeseen errors, please write to us at :

errata@orangeava.com

Your support, suggestions, and feedback are highly appreciated.

DID YOU KNOW

Did you know that Orange Education Pvt Ltd offers eBook versions of every book published, with PDF and ePub files available? You can upgrade to the eBook version at **www.orangeava.com** and as a print book customer, you are entitled to a discount on the eBook copy. Get in touch with us at: **info@orangeava.com** for more details.

At **www.orangeava.com**, you can also read a collection of free technical articles, sign up for a range of free newsletters, and receive exclusive discounts and offers on AVA™ Books and eBooks.

PIRACY

If you come across any illegal copies of our works in any form on the internet, we would be grateful if you would provide us with the location address or website name. Please contact us at **info@orangeava.com** with a link to the material.

ARE YOU INTERESTED IN AUTHORING WITH US?

If there is a topic that you have expertise in, and you are interested in either writing or contributing to a book, please write to us at **business@orangeava.com**. We are on a journey to help developers and tech professionals to gain insights on the present technological advancements and innovations happening across the globe and build a community that believes Knowledge is best acquired by sharing and learning with others. Please reach out to us to learn what our audience demands and how you can be part of this educational reform. We also welcome ideas from tech experts and help them build learning and development content for their domains.

REVIEWS

Please leave a review. Once you have read and used this book, why not leave a review on the site that you purchased it from? Potential readers can then see and use your unbiased opinion to make purchase decisions. We at Orange Education would love to know what you think about our products, and our authors can learn from your feedback. Thank you!

For more information about Orange Education, please visit **www.orangeava.com**.

Table of Contents

CHAPTER 1
Introduction to Blockchain Technology

Blockchain technology is a revolutionary innovation that has transformed many industries, offering a secure and transparent way to manage transactions without intermediaries. This chapter will provide a detailed understanding of blockchain technology, its evolution, use cases, and key concepts.

Structure

In this chapter, the following topics will be covered:

- Definition of Blockchain
- Evolution of Blockchain
- Blockchain Use Cases
- Key Concepts and Terminologies

Definition of Blockchain

Blockchain technology is a decentralized, distributed ledger that allows for secure and transparent transactions without intermediaries. A blockchain is made up of a series of blocks that store data, with each block linked to the previous block through a unique cryptographic hash. Once a block is added to the chain, it becomes immutable, and the data cannot be altered or deleted.

It is a network of computers that store information in a decentralized database, creating a permanent chain of data that cannot be changed.

To understand how a blockchain works, it's important to break down the definition and look at each part in depth.

Technology Based on Distributed Ledgers

A Distributed Ledger Technology (DLT) is a digital ledger of transactions spread across a network of computers. Unlike a traditional centralized database, a DLT is not run by just one person or group. Instead, it is kept up-to-date by everyone in the network, making it "decentralized."

The fact that a DLT is not centralized makes it safer and easier to understand because there is no single point of failure. If one part of the network goes down, the other parts can still work and keep the ledger up-to-date. This also makes it difficult to change or hack, as there is no single point of entry that malicious actors can use.

Transactions that are Safe and Clear

One of the best things about blockchain technology is that it makes transactions safe and clear. Cryptography is used to protect transactions on a blockchain, which makes it nearly impossible for anyone to change the information in the blocks.

The nodes in the network check each transaction on a blockchain to make sure that the data is correct and that the transaction is valid. This process of checking is called "consensus," and it makes sure that the ledger is always up-to-date and correct.

Also, because a blockchain is open, anyone can see the information stored in the blocks. This makes it easier to track and verify transactions and builds trust and accountability.

Databases in Different Places

A blockchain is a decentralized database, which means that the information is kept on a network of computers instead of in one place. Because there is no single point of failure, it is stronger and less likely to break.

Each node in the network keeps a copy of the blockchain. As new blocks are added, the blockchain is always being updated. This makes sure that the ledger is always up-to-date and correct, even if some nodes in the network go down.

Hashes in Cryptography

In a blockchain, each block has its own cryptographic hash that links it to the previous block. A cryptographic hash is a mathematical formula that turns a piece of data into a string of characters with a fixed length.

Each block's hash includes the hash of the previous block. This makes a chain of data that cannot be broken. If someone tries to change a block in the chain, the hash will change, and the block will no longer be linked to the block before it. This makes it easy to notice if someone tries to change the information in the blockchain.

Chain of Data Unchangeable

Once information is stored in a block on a blockchain, it cannot be changed. This means that it cannot be changed or deleted unless all the nodes in the network agree.

Since the blockchain cannot be changed, the data it stores is reliable and correct. It also keeps a history of all transactions, which makes it easy to track and confirm how assets and goods move around.

Blockchain relies on a system where each block contains a unique fingerprint, linking it securely to the previous block. This creates an unalterable chain of data, resistant to any modifications. By exploring the core components of this technology, we'll unlock its potential applications.

The consensus mechanism is also a very important part of a blockchain. Consensus is the process by which all nodes in the network agree on how the blockchain is right now. In a decentralized system, where there is no central authority to check transactions, consensus is the only way to make sure the blockchain is safe and secure.

There are various methods used by different blockchain systems to reach a consensus. Proof of work (PoW), which is used by Bitcoin and many other cryptocurrencies, is the most well-known and widely used method. In a PoW system, nodes compete to solve hard math problems so that they can add new blocks to the blockchain. The new cryptocurrency units are given to the first node to solve the problem and add the block to the chain.

Proof of Stake (PoS), which is used by several newer cryptocurrencies such as Cardano and Polkadot, is another popular way to reach a consensus. In a Proof-of-Stake system, nodes are chosen to verify transactions based on how much cryptocurrency they hold. This means that nodes with more cryptocurrency have a better chance of being chosen to validate transactions and earn rewards.

In addition to consensus, blockchain also uses cryptography to make sure that the network is safe and private. Hashing is one of these methods. It is the process of turning data into a unique cryptographic hash. This hash is then used to make sure that the data is correct. Any change to the data will change the hash, which will inform the network that the data has been changed.

Public-key cryptography is also used by Blockchain to keep transactions safe. In a system with public keys, each user has two keys: a public key that everyone knows and a private key that only the user knows. When a user wants to make a transaction, they use their private key to sign it. Their public key is then used by the network to check that the transaction is legitimate.

In summary, blockchain is a distributed ledger technology that enables secure and transparent transactions without the need for intermediaries. It is a network of computers that store information in a decentralized database. Each block in a blockchain has a unique cryptographic hash that connects it to the block before it. This makes a permanent chain of data that cannot be changed. Blockchain also uses consensus mechanisms, such as PoW and PoS, and cryptographic techniques, such as hashing and public-key cryptography, to ensure the security and privacy of the network.

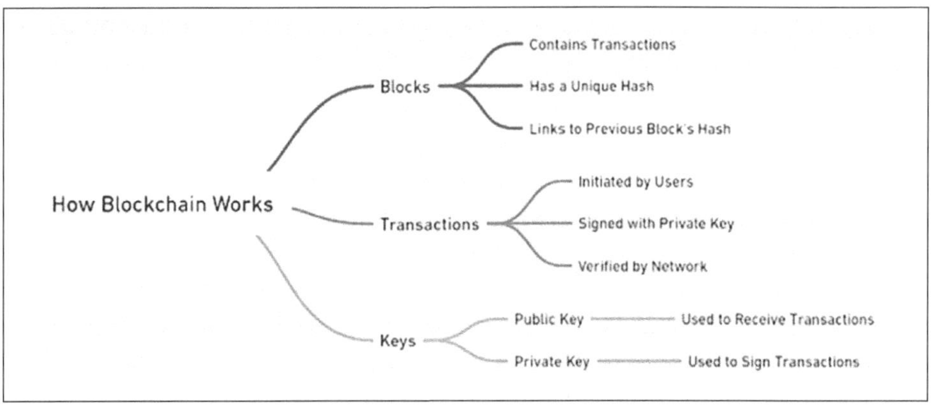

Figure 1.1: *How blockchain works*

Evolution of Blockchain

The concept of blockchain was first introduced in 2008 by Satoshi Nakamoto, who proposed the use of blockchain technology for the creation of a decentralized digital currency, Bitcoin. Since then, blockchain technology has evolved significantly, and several new cryptocurrencies have emerged, each with its unique features and use cases.

While blockchain technology is often associated with Bitcoin, the idea of creating a secure and distributed ledger of data had been explored by various researchers and developers before 2008. For instance, in 1991, Stuart Haber and W. Scott Stornetta proposed a system for timestamping digital documents using a chain of cryptographically secured blocks. In 1998, Nick Szabo introduced the concept of Bit Gold, a decentralized digital currency that used a proof-of-work mechanism to create new units and verify transactions. In 2004, Hal Finney created Reusable Proof of Work (RPOW), a system that allowed the transfer of a token that represented a proof-of-work solution. These and other works laid the foundation for the development of blockchain technology and influenced the design of Bitcoin and subsequent cryptocurrencies. Therefore, it is important to acknowledge the contributions of these pioneers and their role in the history of blockchain.

The second generation of blockchain technology, also known as Blockchain 2.0, emerged with the development of Ethereum. Ethereum introduced the concept of smart contracts, which are self-executing contracts that automatically enforce the terms of an agreement.

The third generation of blockchain technology, also known as Blockchain 3.0, focuses on scalability and interoperability. Blockchain 3.0 projects aim to address the limitations of the previous generations and provide solutions for real-world problems.

The blockchain is an innovative concept that has revolutionized the way we store, verify, and transfer data. In 2008, as part of the process that led to the establishment of the cryptocurrency Bitcoin, the very first blockchain was launched. Since then, blockchain technology has seen significant evolution, spawning new cryptocurrencies and diverse applications. In this chapter, we will discuss the development of blockchain technology, including its various generations, as well as its impacts on a variety of different businesses.

First Generation of Blockchain

Blockchain technology was first launched in 2008, along with the Bitcoin cryptocurrency. Satoshi Nakamoto is regarded as the pioneer of blockchain technology. He also proposed that blockchain technology could be used to create a decentralized digital currency. Security, transparency, and immutability are three key features of the latest version of blockchain technology.

The blockchain achieves its goal of providing a secure ledger for transactions by using cryptographic methods, which prevent the data stored on the blockchain from being altered. The blockchain's inherent transparency allows all parties to see the details of every transaction, and anyone can independently check the validity of the data. The blockchain's immutability means that once data has been added to the blockchain, it cannot be changed or deleted.

Second Generation of Blockchain

The creation of Ethereum marked the beginning of the second generation of blockchain technology, which is often referred to as Blockchain 2.0. Ethereum pioneered the idea of "smart contracts," which are essentially contracts that can carry out their own execution and automatically uphold an agreement's obligations. The necessity for intermediaries such as lawyers or notaries to oversee the execution of traditional contracts is eliminated with the use of smart contracts, which represents a substantial advancement over traditional contracts. Smart contracts are a significant improvement over traditional contracts.

Moreover, Ethereum was the first platform to introduce the idea of decentralized applications, commonly known as DApps. These programs are executed on blockchains. DApps are built from the ground up to be decentralized, which means that their operation does not rely on a single controlling entity. This gives them an advantage over more conventional apps in terms of security and transparency.

Third Generation of Blockchain

The third generation of blockchain technology, also known as Blockchain 3.0, has an emphasis on scalability as well as interoperability across different blockchains. Projects working on Blockchain 3.0 intend to address the limits of earlier versions of the technology and give answers for issues that occur in the real-world. Scalability, interoperability, and governance are three characteristics that stand out most prominently in this new generation of blockchain technology.

As the current generation of blockchains can only process a finite number of transactions in one second, scalability is one of the most important concerns surrounding blockchain technology. In order to solve this problem, the Blockchain 3.0 teams are working on establishing new consensus mechanisms, such as proof of stake, that are capable of managing a greater volume of transactions.

Interoperability is an additional key issue for blockchain technology, as there are now many different blockchains that are incompatible with each other. This makes interoperability an important concern for blockchain technology. Projects based on Blockchain 3.0 have the overarching goal of resolving this issue by creating protocols that will enable various blockchains to communicate with one another.

Governance is also an essential issue for blockchain technology, as there is currently no defined structure for how blockchains should be controlled. This makes governance one of the most important issues surrounding blockchain technology. Blockchain 3.0 projects intend to address this issue by building new governance models that are more participatory and transparent than their predecessors.

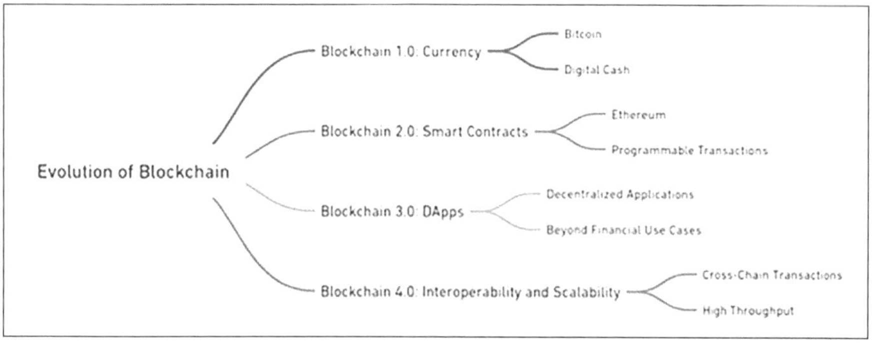

Figure 1.2: *Evolution of Blockchain*

Effects of Blockchain Technology on Different Industries

The application of blockchain technology has the potential to revolutionize many different sectors, including the healthcare industry, the financial sector, and the management of supply chains.

The application of blockchain technology in the financial sector may result in the elimination of the need for middlemen such as banks and payment processors in the processing of transactions. This may result in a revolution in the financial sector. Because blockchain technology can eliminate the need for several middlemen to verify transactions, it can also help boost the efficiency of transactions that take place across international borders.

By giving patients access to their own medical records, blockchain technology has the potential to boost both the effectiveness and the safety of data stored in the healthcare industry. This can lead to an increase in the transparency of healthcare data and make it possible to provide treatments that are more individualized and effective.

Blockchain technology can improve the transparency and efficiency of supply chain management by enabling real-time tracking of items and commodities.

This is one way in which supply chain management might benefit from blockchain technology. This has the potential to aid in the prevention of counterfeiting, fraud, and other forms of supply chain disruption.

Furthermore, real estate, voting systems, and energy management are some of the other areas that stand to gain from the implementation of blockchain technology.

Blockchain technology can streamline the process of purchasing and selling real estate by eliminating the need for middlemen, such as real estate agents and lawyers, thereby facilitating smoother transactions. This can be a significant time saver for buyers and sellers. The immutability and cryptographic protection of property records can both be improved with the help of blockchain technology.

- **Voting Systems**: Blockchain technology has the potential to boost the transparency and security of voting systems by making it possible for voters to remain anonymous while still casting their votes in a secure environment. This has the potential to reduce instances of voter fraud and boost public confidence in the political process.
- **Energy Management**: Blockchain technology can increase the efficacy and transparency of energy management by enabling real-time monitoring of energy production and consumption. This is one of the ways in which the technology can be used, contributing to the optimization of energy utilization and the reduction of waste.

Governance is another issue that must be addressed by blockchain technology. Conflicts and disagreements are possible outcomes of decentralized blockchain networks being managed by user communities rather than a central authority. Many solutions, such as sharding, sidechains, and governance protocols, are now in the process of being developed to address these difficulties.

- Sharding is a process that includes splitting the blockchain network into smaller portions, also known as shards, which are easier to administer. The fact that each shard is capable of independently processing transactions contributes to the increased scalability of the network.
- Sidechains are independent blockchain networks that can be joined to the primary blockchain network. They serve as a useful tool for developing and testing new blockchain features without impacting the primary blockchain network. Sidechains may be used for the development and testing of new blockchain features.
- Governance protocols are a set of rules and processes that regulate the administration and upkeep of a blockchain network. In a community of users, having governance protocols in place can assist prevent the instances of conflicts and disagreements from occurring.

In addition to these obstacles, blockchain technology is also confronted with numerous difficulties in the legal and regulatory spheres. Because blockchain networks are decentralized, it is impossible to implement laws and regulations using these technologies. There is presently no global framework for the regulation of blockchain networks, and governments all over the world are still debating the best way to regulate the blockchain technology that underpins cryptocurrencies.

In spite of these obstacles, the potential advantages offered by blockchain technology are too significant to be disregarded. To capitalize on the opportunities presented by blockchain technology, an increasing number of businesses and sectors are making investments in the research and development of innovative blockchain-based applications and solutions. In the years ahead, we may anticipate seeing widespread implementation of blockchain technology in a variety of industries, which will ultimately lead to improvements in efficiencies, transparency, and security.

One of the most exciting areas of research in blockchain technology is the integration of blockchain with artificial intelligence (AI) and the Internet of Things (IoT). These technologies have the potential to create synergies that can enhance the capabilities and functionalities of each other. For example, blockchain can provide a secure and transparent platform for data sharing and coordination among AI agents and IoT devices, while AI can improve the efficiency and scalability of blockchain networks and applications. IoT can enable the collection and transmission of real-time data from the physical world to the blockchain, where it can be processed and analyzed by AI algorithms. Together, these technologies can enable new forms of decentralized intelligence and automation that can transform various domains, such as healthcare, energy, manufacturing, and transportation.

The future of blockchain technology is full of possibilities and challenges. As the technology matures and evolves, we can expect to see more innovations and applications that can benefit various industries and sectors. Blockchain technology has the potential to create a more efficient, transparent, and secure world, where individuals and organizations can interact and collaborate in a trustless and decentralized manner. However, to realize this potential, there is still a need for more research, development, regulation, and education in the field of blockchain technology. By engaging ourselves in the distributed ledger technology, we can contribute to the advancement and adoption of this revolutionary technology.

Engaging Yourself in the Distributed Ledger Technology

There are several different entry points available for those interested in participating in the blockchain technology space. One option is to educate yourself about blockchain technology and the various uses to which it could be put. You can educate yourself about blockchain technology by making the use of many different online courses, books, and tutorials that are now available.

Participating in blockchain-related forums and events is yet another approach to getting involved in the technology behind blockchains. You can connect with other people interested in blockchain technology and developers by joining one of the many online blockchain forums. Some examples of these communities include Bitcointalk.org and /r/Blockchain on Reddit. You may also learn about the most recent advancements in blockchain technology and network with other blockchain professionals at one of the many blockchain events and conferences that are conducted all around the world.

If you have a background in computer science, another career option you might think about is developing blockchain technology. Blockchain developers are in high demand and are accountable for the creation and maintenance of applications and networks that use blockchain technology.

Lastly, you may also make an investment in blockchain technology by acquiring cryptocurrencies or investing in firms that are directly tied to blockchain technology. Yet, it is essential to keep in mind that investing in cryptocurrencies and firms that are connected to blockchain technology can be dangerous and should be approached with prudence.

Blockchain Use Cases

Blockchain technology has the potential to disrupt many industries, including finance, healthcare, supply chain, and more. Here are some of the most popular use cases of blockchain technology:

- **Cryptocurrencies**: Digital currencies like Bitcoin and Ethereum use blockchain technology to enable peer-to-peer transactions without intermediaries.
- **Smart Contracts**: Blockchain technology can be used to create self-executing contracts that automatically enforce the terms of the agreement.

- **Supply Chain Management**: Blockchain can be used to track the movement of goods and services across the supply chain, ensuring transparency and accountability.
- **Dapps**: Blockchain technology can also be used to create decentralized applications (Dapps) that run on a network of distributed nodes, without the need for a central authority. Dapps can offer various services and functionalities, such as social media, gaming, or e-commerce while ensuring user privacy and control.
- **Healthcare**: Blockchain can be used to securely store and share patient data across different healthcare providers, improving the quality of care.
- **Voting**: Blockchain technology can be used to create secure and transparent voting systems that eliminate the possibility of fraud and manipulation.
- **Identity Management**: Blockchain technology can be used to create a secure and decentralized identity management system, reducing the risk of identity theft and fraud.
- **Gaming**: Blockchain technology can be used to create decentralized gaming platforms that offer transparent and fair gameplay.

Cryptocurrencies

Cryptocurrencies are digital currencies that use blockchain technology to let people trade money directly with each other without going through a middleman. Bitcoin and Ethereum are two of the most well-known cryptocurrencies. They have changed the traditional financial industry by giving people a way to send money that is secure and not controlled by a central authority.

Blockchain technology makes it possible for cryptocurrencies to be decentralized, which means that no government or financial institution can control them. This makes it perfect for people who want to send money without going through banks or payment processors. A network of users checks the validity of transactions, and once they have been checked, they are added to the blockchain. This makes it almost impossible for anyone to change the system or break into it.

Cryptocurrencies also give people a lot of privacy, which is why they are often used for illegal things such as laundering money and selling drugs. However, an increasing number of legitimate businesses are starting to take cryptocurrencies as a form of payment, which is helping to spread their use.

Smart Contracts

When certain conditions are met, smart contracts are computer programs that automatically carry out the terms of a contract. They are often used in fields like real estate, where contracts can be complicated and need a lot of legal oversight.

Smart contracts can be decentralized, thanks to blockchain technology. This means that they are not under the control of any central authority. This makes them safer and easier to understand than traditional contracts, which can be easy to cheat on or change.

Smart contracts can be used to automate a wide range of tasks, from simple payments to complicated legal agreements. For instance, a smart contract could be set up to automatically change who owns a piece of property when certain conditions are met, such as when a sale is made.

Smart Contracts and Decentralized Finance

Decentralized finance, or DeFi, is the use of blockchain technology to create financial services that are open, transparent, and accessible to anyone. DeFi aims to create a more inclusive and efficient financial system that does not rely on intermediaries like banks or governments.

Smart contracts are one of the building blocks of DeFi. They can be used to create various financial applications, such as lending platforms, exchanges, stablecoins, insurance, and derivatives. These applications can offer users more control, choice, and security than traditional financial services.

For example, a smart contract could be used to create a lending platform that allows users to borrow and lend money without involving a bank. The smart contract would automatically match borrowers and lenders, set interest rates, and enforce repayments. Additionally, it would also use blockchain technology to secure funds and ensure transparency and trust among the participants.

Management of the Supply Chain

The process of managing the supply chain involves keeping track of how goods and services move from the supplier to the customer. It is a complicated process that involves many people, such as suppliers, manufacturers, distributors, and retailers.

Blockchain technology can be used to track how goods and services move through the supply chain, making sure that everything is clear and everyone is responsible. Every transaction is added to the blockchain, and once it's there, it can't be changed or taken off. This makes it easy to track where goods come from and where they go, which can help stop fraud and lower the risk of fake goods.

Blockchain technology can also be used to automate payments and inventory management in the supply chain. This can help cut costs and make things work better.

Healthcare

Healthcare is a complicated business that involves many people, such as patients, doctors, hospitals, and insurance companies. Sharing patient information in a safe and effective way is one of the biggest problems in health care.

Blockchain technology can be used by different healthcare providers to store and share information about patients safely, which will improve the quality of care. Each patient would have their own blockchain-based health record with all their medical information, such as test results, diagnoses, and treatment plans.

This would make it easier for doctors to get and share information about their patients, which can help prevent medical mistakes and improve the health of their patients. Patients would also have more control over their information because they would be able to give or take away access to their records.

Voting

Voting is a very important part of a democracy, but it can also be vulnerable to cheating or manipulation. Blockchain technology can be used to make voting systems that are secure, clear, and can't be hacked or changed in any way.

Every vote would be added to the blockchain, and once it is there, it can't be changed or taken away. This makes it almost impossible for anyone to change the results of the vote. The blockchain-based voting system would also be open, so anyone could look at the results of the votes at any time.

This would help people have more faith in the voting system and stop voter fraud. It would also make it easier to hold elections in places that are hard to get to or are not well-developed, where traditional ways of voting might not be available.

Identity Management

In the digital world we live in now, identity theft and fraud are significant problems. Using blockchain technology, you can establish a secure and decentralized system for managing your identity. This will reduce the likelihood of your identity being stolen or falling victim to scams.

Each person would have their own identity record on the blockchain. This record would have all their personal information, such as their name, date of birth, and social security number. This information would be encrypted and stored on the blockchain, making it almost impossible to steal or change.

People would also have more control over their information because they could give or take away access to their identity record. This would make it harder for people to steal someone else's identity because they would have more control over who can see their personal information.

Gaming

Gaming is a huge business that is becoming immensely popular very quickly. However, most traditional gaming platforms are centralized, which means that they are run by either one person or a group. This can lead to cheating, fraud, and unfair games.

Blockchain technology can be used to make decentralized platforms for gaming that are fair and easy to use. Every game would be added to the blockchain, and once it is there, it can't be changed or taken off. This means that no one can cheat or change the game in any way.

Players would also have more control over their in-game assets, as these would be stored on the blockchain and could not be lost or stolen. This would make gaming safer and easier to understand, which could help bring in more people to the industry.

Real Estate

Blockchain technology can also be used to make the real estate market more open and more efficient. Real estate deals often involve more than one person, and they can be complicated and take a long time.

A blockchain-based real estate platform would be more efficient and open, as each transaction would be recorded on the blockchain and could not be changed or deleted. This would make it easier to buy and sell real estate and make it less likely that someone would try to steal your money.

Several companies are already using blockchain technology for real estate. For example, Propy uses blockchain to make it easier for people to buy and sell real estate across borders, and Atlant uses blockchain to make a decentralized real estate platform.

Energy

Blockchain technology can also be used to make the energy industry more efficient and open to the public. There are a lot of problems in the energy industry, such as old infrastructure, rising demand, and the need to switch to renewable energy sources.

A blockchain-based energy platform would be more efficient and open because each transaction would be recorded on the blockchain and could not be changed or deleted. This would help cut down on energy waste and make the energy grid work better.

Several companies are already using blockchain technology for energy. For example, Power Ledger is using blockchain to create a peer-to-peer energy trading platform, and LO3 Energy is using blockchain to create a decentralized energy marketplace.

Government

Blockchain technology can also be used to make government services more open and work better. Governments often have to deal with problems like corruption, inefficiency, and excessive red tapism.

A blockchain-based government platform would be more open and efficient because each transaction would be recorded on the blockchain and could not be changed or deleted. This would help cut down on corruption and red tape, making it easier for the government to do its job.

Several governments are already looking into how to use blockchain technology. For example, Estonia is using it to build a platform for digital identities, and Dubai is using it to build a smart city.

As we have seen, blockchain technology can be used in a various ways, and it is being used across different industries around the world. Even though there are still some problems that need to be fixed, the potential benefits of blockchain technology are immense to ignore, and it's likely that more use cases will come up in the future.

We can expect new applications to emerge across various sectors, transforming how we live and work. From finance (cryptocurrencies) to healthcare, voting, identity management, and even entertainment (gaming), real estate, energy, and governance, blockchain holds the promise of significant disruption. As technology continues to evolve, its impact is poised to grow even stronger.

Blockchain Application in Big Data

Big Data is a large amount of data that needs advanced technologies for storage, processing, and analysis. Blockchain can be used in this situation to make a decentralized, secure, and open system to manage Big Data. The blockchain-based Big Data management system can keep data more secure, make it easier to access, and protect users' privacy. Here is how blockchain technology can help:

- **Data Security**: Blockchain technology provides a safe place to store and manage data, which can lower the risk of data breaches.
- **Data Privacy**: Blockchain technology can be used to make sure that data is only shared with people who are allowed to see it. This can help keep data private.
- **Data Integrity**: Blockchain technology can be used to make a record of data that can't be changed. This can help make sure that the data is correct.
- **Traceability of Data**: Blockchain technology can be used to find out where data came from, which can help stop fraud.
- **Sharing Data**: Blockchain technology can be used to let different organizations share data safely, which can help them work together and come up with new ideas.

Blockchain Application in Land Registration

Land registration is the process of writing down who owns land and what rights and interests go with it. Blockchain can be used in this process to make a secure and clear system for registering land that makes fraud and corruption impossible. The blockchain-based system for land registration can make data more reliable, easy to find, and private. Here is how blockchain technology can help:

- **Secure and Open**: Blockchain technology provides a safe and open way to keep track of who owns the land and what transactions have happened on it. This can lower the risk of fraud and corruption.
- **Eliminate Middlemen**: Blockchain technology can be used to get rid of middlemen like lawyers and notaries, which can save time and money when it comes to registering land.

- **Automated Processes**: Blockchain technology can be used to make self-executing smart contracts that automate the registration, transfer, and ownership of land.
- **Simplified Processes**: Blockchain technology can make it easier for people to buy and sell land by making the complicated process of registering land less complicated.
- **Better Governance**: Blockchain technology can be used to make a decentralized land registration system that is not controlled by a single entity. This can lead to better governance and transparency.

Application of Blockchain in Vehicle Registration

Vehicle registration is the process of writing down who owns a car and what rights and interests go along with that. Blockchain technology can be used to make a system for registering vehicles that is safe, open, and free from fraud and corruption. The blockchain-based system for registering vehicles can make data more reliable, easy to find, and private. Here is how blockchain technology can help:

- Blockchain technology provides a safe and clear way to keep track of who owns a car and who bought it.
- Genomics is the study of genomes, which are the complete set of DNA in a single cell of an organism. Blockchain can be used in genomics. Genomic data can be stored, shared, and accessed by people or groups with the right permissions using blockchain technology. This can make it easier and more accurate to analyze genetic data, which can then be used to make personalized medical treatments and improve health care as a whole.
- Logistics is a complicated process that involves moving goods from one place to another. Blockchain and the Internet of Things (IoT) are used in logistics. With blockchain technology and IoT devices working together, logistics companies can make a safe and clear way to track and trace goods at every step of the supply chain. This can make things run more smoothly, save money, and make customers happier.
- Importers, exporters, customs agencies, banks, and shipping companies all take part in international trade, which is a complicated process involving many different parties. Using blockchain technology can speed up the whole process and make it less likely that mistakes, delays, or fraud will happen. Smart contracts can be used to automate the process and make sure that everyone follows the agreement's terms.

- Customs agencies are in charge of regulating and keeping track of how goods move across borders. Blockchain could be used in this area. With blockchain technology, customs agencies can make a safe and clear way to track and confirm where goods come from and where they are going. This can make customs clearance go faster, save money, and make things safer.
- Blockchain can be used in the auto industry, which is quickly changing, thanks to new technologies like self-driving cars and electric cars. Blockchain technology can be used to make a safe and clear way to keep track of a vehicle's history, including who owned it, how it was maintained, and how it was fixed. This can make used cars easier to sell, cut down on fraud, and make them safer.
- Climate change is a major problem around the world, and reducing carbon emissions is a top priority for many governments and organizations. Carbon credits can be tracked and traded safely with blockchain technology. This gives companies a reason to reduce their carbon footprint. This could make the economy more stable and the environment cleaner.
- The wine industry is highly regulated, and there are strict rules about labeling, quality control, and certification. Blockchain could be used in this industry. Using blockchain technology, the whole process can be streamlined and automated. This makes it less likely that mistakes, fraud, or fake products will happen. People can check to see if the wine they buy is real, and winemakers can make sure that their products are labeled and certified correctly.
- Utility services like electricity, water, and gas are essential to modern life, but the billing and payment process can be complicated and inefficient. This is where blockchain comes in. With blockchain technology, utility companies can make a billing and payment system that is safe, clear, and less likely to have mistakes, delays, or fraud. Smart contracts can be used to automate the process and make sure that customers are charged correctly and on time.
- The art market is notoriously opaque, with little information about prices, ownership, and authenticity. With blockchain technology, art collectors and investors can check that the artworks they buy are real, and artists can make sure they get paid fairly for their work. This could make the art market more open and efficient, which would be good for both artists and collectors.

Application of Blockchain in Industrial IoT Use Cases

The Internet of Things (IoT) connects physical devices with software and sensors so they can talk to each other and share information. IoT devices can be securely connected to the internet using blockchain technology. This creates a decentralized network of devices that can talk to each other and share data in a safe and open way. This can make industrial processes more efficient and automated, which can cut costs and boost productivity.

Blockchain technology is transforming various sectors, including healthcare and finance, by integrating with artificial intelligence (AI). This integration allows for the secure storage of AI algorithms using blockchain technology.

- **Use of blockchain in the telecom industry**:

  Blockchain technology can help the telecom industry in several ways, such as by cutting down on fraud, making payments easier, and making sure data is safe. By using blockchain technology, telecom companies can make a decentralized system for managing customer data. This gives customers more control over their data and makes sure it is safe.

  OmiseGO is an example of how blockchain can be used in the telecom industry. OmiseGO is a payment platform built on the blockchain that lets telecom companies offer their customers safe and clear payment services. With OmiseGO, telecom companies can use blockchain technology to lower transaction costs, speed up, and make transactions more secure.

- **Use of blockchain in the fishing industry**:

  The fishing industry is one of the most complicated and fragmented in the world. There are a lot of different people involved in the supply chain, which is made up of many different links. Blockchain technology can help make the supply chain more efficient and open, lowering the risk of fraud, making people more accountable, and making it easier to track things.

  The Ocean Protocol is one way that blockchain is used in the fishing industry. The Ocean Protocol is a blockchain-based data sharing platform, which lets fishermen share information about their catches with other players in the supply chain, such as processors, distributors, and retailers. Sharing information about catches can make the supply chain more efficient, cut down on waste, and improve the quality of the fish that gets to consumers.

- **Use of blockchain in the power industry**:

  The power industry has to deal with a lot of problems, such as the need to cut carbon emissions and switch to renewable energy sources. Blockchain technology can help make the energy market more efficient and clear, making it easier for renewable energy sources to be added to the grid.

  Power Ledger is one way that blockchain is used in the power industry. Power Ledger is a platform built on blockchain that lets people buy and sell renewable energy directly with each other, without the need for middlemen. With Power Ledger, people can choose where their energy comes from. This lets them support renewable energy sources and reduce their carbon footprint.

- **Use of blockchain in the sharing economy:**

  Companies like Airbnb, Uber, and Lyft are leading the way in the fast-growing sharing economy. Blockchain technology can help make the sharing economy safer and more open, reducing the risk of fraud and making people more accountable.

  Origin Protocol is an example of how blockchain can be used in the sharing economy. Origin Protocol is a platform built on the blockchain that lets people share goods and services directly with each other, without the need for middlemen. With Origin Protocol, consumers can be sure that the goods and services they get are real and of high quality. This builds trust and lowers the risk of fraud.

- **Use of Blockchain in Robotics**:

  The robotics industry is changing quickly, and robots are getting better and smarter every day. Blockchain technology can help make the robotics industry more efficient and open, making it easier for robots to be used in many different fields.

  SingularityNET is an example of how blockchain can be used in the robotics industry. SingularityNET is a blockchain-based platform that lets developers make and share AI algorithms and robotics apps without the need for middlemen. With SingularityNET, developers can work together and share their knowledge, making the robotics industry more efficient and open to new ideas.

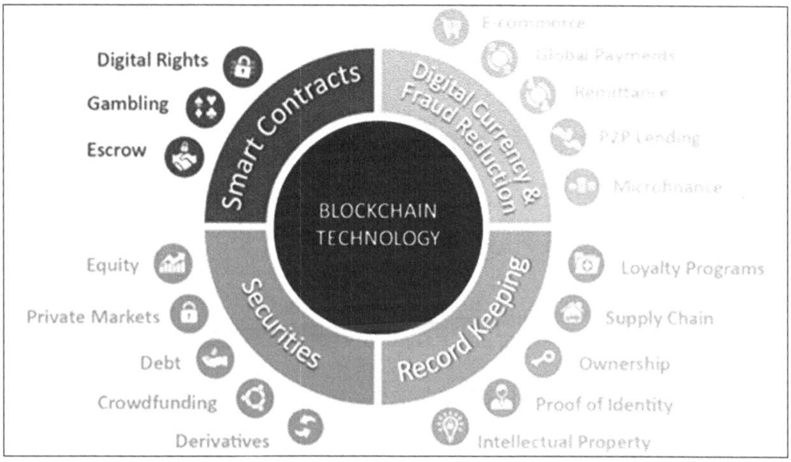

Figure 1.3: *Blockchain applications (source: ACI Worldwide)*

Key Concepts and Terminologies

To understand blockchain technology, it is important to be familiar with its key concepts and terminologies. Here are some of the most important ones:

- **Nodes**: Computers that participate in the blockchain network by validating transactions and creating new blocks.
- **Consensus**: The process by which nodes in a blockchain network agree on the state of the ledger.
- **Mining**: The process of creating new blocks and adding them to the blockchain.
- **Hashing**: The process of converting data into a unique cryptographic hash that can be used to verify its integrity.
- **Private Key**: A secret code that allows users to access their cryptocurrency wallets and make transactions.
- **Public Key**: A code that is publicly visible and used to receive cryptocurrency payments.
- **Fork**: A situation where a blockchain splits into two separate chains, typically due to a disagreement among the network participants.
- **Gas**: A fee paid in cryptocurrency to execute a smart contract on the Ethereum blockchain.
- **Token**: A unit of value created and managed on a blockchain, typically used as a means of exchange or to represent a specific asset.

- **Decentralized Applications (DApps)**: Applications that run on a blockchain network, enabling secure and decentralized solutions.

Terms Used in Blockchain

Airdrop: An airdrop occurs when a cryptocurrency token or coin is sent, usually for free and for marketing purposes, to a large number of wallet addresses.

Atomic Swap: An atomic swap is a type of smart contract that lets people trade one cryptocurrency for another without going through a central authority.

Bitcoin: Bitcoin is a type of digital currency that runs on a peer-to-peer (P2P) network without a central authority or middlemen.

Block: A block is a group of transactions that have not been written down in any other blocks yet.

Blockchain: A blockchain is a public and decentralized ledger that uses cryptography to keep track of transactions between agents in a network. It lets transactions be grouped into blocks and recorded in chronological order using cryptography in chain blocks. The ledger can be viewed by all users in the network. This database is not owned, controlled, or managed by a single entity.

Uses for Blockchain: A blockchain application is a peer-to-peer (P2P) system that verifies, timestamps, and permanently stores transactions and agreements on a shared ledger that is sent to all nodes that are taking part.

Byzantine Fault Tolerance (BFT): BFT is the property of a system that can resist the class of failures that come from the **Byzantine Generals' Problem**. This is a logical problem that shows how a group of Byzantine generals might have trouble communicating when trying to decide on their next move. So, a BFT system can still work even if some of the nodes do not work or do something bad.

Central Bank Digital Currency (CBDC): A CBDC is the paper money of a country or region issued and controlled by the country's monetary authority. So, CBDC is a form of money created and backed by a government through its central bank. This list of words was put together by H. Kent Baker and Hak J. Kim.

Cold Wallet: A cold wallet is a piece of hardware or another type of physical device that lets investors access their crypto-asset holdings.

Consensus Protocol (algorithm or way of doing things): A consensus protocol is a set of rules and tools that are built into a blockchain to bring together the preferences and decisions of users and manage how the network makes decisions. It decides how users on that blockchain can agree on a single data value or a single state of the network, even though they are using different processes.

A Consortium Blockchain: A consortium blockchain is a **semiprivate** system with a controlled group of users that can be used by more than one organization. The protocol layer is run by a group of companies that work together and have to follow laws and agreements that are not part of the blockchain code. A consortium blockchain is a mix of the **low trust** of public blockchains and the **highly trusted single entity** model of private blockchains.

So, a consortium blockchain is private, partly decentralized, and has agreement from more than one party.

Crosschain: A crosschain is when two blockchains that are mostly separate can work together. It makes it possible for blockchains to talk to each other because they are built the same way.

Cryptocurrency: A cryptocurrency is a digital or virtual currency that uses encryption to control the number of units of currency that can be made and to make sure that money is being sent from one person to another. It works without being controlled by a central bank. Blockchain technology is at the heart of many cryptocurrencies, such as Bitcoin, which are decentralized networks.

Not sure about cryptocurrency: Cryptocurrency agnostic means that projects are made to work with a variety of tokens, cryptos, and altcoins. This makes it possible for users from different ecosystems to join, which increases the building capacity of both new and old cryptocurrency projects.

Cryptoeconomics: Incentives and cryptography are used in cryptoeconomics to make new kinds of systems, applications, and networks. It also looks at how the economy works when people are trying to hurt each other.

Cryptographic Hashing: This is the process of putting a random string of digits into a hashing formula over and over again until you get the result you want. It only makes one output of a fixed length. A hash function algorithm is something like MD5, MD4, or SHA-256.

Cypherpunk: A cypherpunk is someone who thinks that technology should help protect privacy.

Cryptography: Cryptography is the use of a mathematical formula to hide and reveal information. It is used in blockchain to make wallets, sign transactions, and check the block.

Crypto tokens: A crypto token, also called a cryptocurrency or a crypto asset, is a special type of virtual currency token that represents an asset or utility and lives on its own blockchain.

dApp: A **decentralized application**, or dApp, refers to a computer program that runs on a distributed computing system.

Decentralized Autonomous Organization (DAO): A DAO is a virtual organization that is made up of computer code and runs on a distributed ledger or blockchain.

Dispersed Network: A decentralized network is one in which anyone can use the ledger to conduct business. The network is decentralized because it is not run by a single organization.

Delegated Proof of Stake (DPoS): DPoS is a consensus protocol that checks and approves transactions in a blockchain in a reliable way.

Distributed Hash Table (DHT): DHT is a key-value store where the keys are hashes. It is often used to coordinate P2P systems and keep track of metadata about them. In a DHT, key-value pairs are kept, and any participating node can quickly get the value that goes with a certain key.

Distributed Ledger: A distributed ledger is a database that can be accessed by many people from different places or sites. It lets the people involved in a transaction see what is going on. Each participant at a network node can access and own a copy of the records that are shared across the network. Any changes or additions to the ledger are shown and sent to everyone who is involved.

Double Spending: When digital currency is spent more than once, this is called **double spending**. By checking each transaction in the network, blockchain stops people from spending the same money twice. It checks to see if the money for the transaction has already been spent.

Encryption: Encryption is the process of changing information into a form that can't be read. It is often used to protect sensitive information so that only people who are allowed to see it can see it.

Encrypting Information: Encrypting information on a blockchain keeps sensitive data from falling into the wrong hands and being misused or made up. So, only people who are allowed to can see the information. Different blockchains use different encryption algorithms, but the Bitcoin blockchain uses the SHA-256 algorithm, which makes a 32-byte hash that has so far been hard to hack.

Block of Genesis: The first block in a blockchain is called the **genesis block**. It is the ancestor of all the other blocks in the blockchain, making it the model for them all. If you follow the chain backward from any block, you will end up at the first block, known as the Genesis block.

Hard Fork: When a cryptocurrency on a distributed ledger goes through a protocol change that leads to a permanent split from the legacy or existing distributed ledger, this is called a **hard fork**. When this major change is made to a blockchain network's protocol, blocks or transactions that were previously invalid become valid or vice versa. So, a hard fork is a change to the blockchain network that can't be used with the old version.

Hashing: Hashing is a mathematical process that miners use to make the network safe. It is a transaction's unique identifier.

Rate of Hash: Hash rate is the amount of computing power that miners give to the network to keep it safe in exchange for block rewards and transaction fees.

Hot Wallet: A **hot wallet** is a website that lets investors or merchants access their cryptocurrency holdings through an online platform or app.

Hybrid Blockchain: A hybrid blockchain is a mix of both public and private blockchains. It can host an app or service on a private blockchain while using a public blockchain for security and transactions.

Proof of Work/Proof of Service (Proof of Stake): A **PoW**/PoS hybrid consensus mechanism uses parts of both the PoW and PoS models to decide who has the right to validate transactions.

Hyperledger: Hyperledger is an open-source blockchain project that aims to help blockchain projects move forward together, instead of using different proprietary systems.

Immutability: Once a block is in the blockchain, it can't be deleted or changed. This is what immutability means.

Initial Coin Offering or ICO: ICO is a way to get money from outside sources by giving away tokens in exchange for cryptocurrencies. ICOs are often a form of crowdfunding, although they can also be conducted privately without seeking money from the public.

Interoperability: Interoperability means that different complex systems can share data and information in a way that is compatible with each other.

InterPlanetary File System (IPFS): IPFS is a protocol and P2P network for storing and sharing files in a distributed file system.

Network Lightning: A lightning network is a group of off-chain payment channels where two people can make a very fast, low-cost transaction or series of transactions that are then settled on-chain. It adds another layer to Bitcoin's blockchain so that users can set up payment channels between any two parties on that extra layer.

Merkle tree: A Merkle tree, also known as a hash tree, is a structure used in blockchain to efficiently and securely organize large amounts of data. It consists of a root, leaves, and the raw data itself, arranged in a tree-like format. The Merkle tree helps in quickly encoding and verifying data through blockchain signatures or hashing. The Merkle root, specifically, is a single hash that represents all the transactions in a block, ensuring the integrity and security of data in a blockchain network..

Miner: A miner is a node on the network that takes part in the consensus process that is used to check transactions before they are put together in blocks. Miners help with the block verification process by checking each transaction to see if it is legitimate. Miners are encouraged to take part in this process because they can get paid for confirming blocks as they are added to the blockchain or for processing transactions.

Mining: Mining is the process of adding new transaction records to a block and checking other miners' blocks to make sure they are correct. It lets nodes come to a safe, hard-to-change agreement. Miners get paid for their work by collecting transaction fees.

Node: A computer, laptop, or server that connects to the blockchain network is called a "node." It stores, shares, and keeps the data from the blockchain. All the nodes in a blockchain network are linked to each other and constantly share the most up-to-date information.

Nonce: A "number only used once," or "nonce," is a "pseudo-random" number that is used during the mining process as a counter. It is a number that is added to a hashed or encrypted block in a blockchain. When the block is rehashed, the number must meet the difficulty level requirements. So, a nonce is the number that miners on the blockchain are trying to figure out.

Not on the Blockchain: Off-chain is a term for a cryptocurrency transaction that does not happen on the main blockchain and is not recorded there.

Transaction on the Chain A cryptocurrency transaction that takes place on the blockchain is called "on-chain."

Oracle: An oracle is a way for a blockchain or smart contract to talk to data from outside of itself. Blockchain oracles are third-party services that connect blockchains to the outside world.

An Orphan Block: An orphan block is a validated block that is not added to the blockchain network because there was a delay in adding the block to the blockchain.

Say, for example, that two blocks are checked at the same time. Once a node accepts one block, the other block is thrown away. This is called an "orphan block." So, an orphan block is a block that is valid and has been checked, but the chain does not want it.

Peer-to-peer (P2P): In blockchain, a P2P network is one where peers can communicate and do transactions directly with other network members without having to rely on an intermediary or third party to perform confirmations or other verification processes.

Private (or by invitation only) Blockchain: A private blockchain is closed and can only be used by people who have been invited. This means that only certain users or entities on a blockchain can give permission to others, allowing them to choose members or validators. It has centralized authority and is often used to run business operations inside the company.

Private Key: A private key is a piece of cryptography that lets a user access his or her own cryptocurrency or transaction. It works like a password and protects the user from theft and unauthorized access to money.

Point of Action (PoA): POA is another combination of PoW and PoS that tries to take the best parts of both.

Proof of Burn (PoB): POB is a different consensus algorithm that tries to solve the problem of a PoW system using a lot of energy.

Proof of Being Able (PoC): POC is a way to come to an agreement that uses a method called "plotting."

Proof of Work Based on a Program (ProgPoW): ProgPow is a blockchain protocol consensus algorithm that is designed to reduce the mining efficiency advantage that specialized hardware like ASIC miners have over less advanced machines like a standard CPU. This means that average crypto participants can mine coins.

Proof that Time Has Passed: Proof of Elapsed Time (PoET) is a consensus algorithm that uses a fair lottery system to make sure that the process doesn't use too many resources and stays as efficient as possible. For example, each node in the network that wants to take part has to wait for a random amount of time, and the first one to wait the full amount of time wins the new block. Each node in the blockchain network picks a random amount of time to wait and then goes to sleep for that long. The one with the shortest wait time adds a new block to the blockchain and tells the whole peer network what it needs to know. The same steps are then repeated to find the next block.

Proof that It Can be Found: Proof of Reserve (PoR) is a short way for a file system (the prover) to show a client (the verifier) that a target file is whole and can be fully recovered by the client.

Storage Proof: Proof of Storage is a consensus protocol that is mostly used to make sure that a remote file is still in good shape.

Work Sample (PoW): PoW is the first algorithm that a blockchain network uses to reach a consensus. In a Proof-of-Work (PoW) algorithm, miners compete to be the first to validate a block. The first miner to validate a block gets paid. For example, a miner puts transaction data (block) and a random string of digits (nonce of block) into a hashing formula over and over again until he or she gets the Proof of Work (PoW).

Other miners can check the PoW by using the supposed input string with the same formula to see if the result is the same as what the first minor showed. Some people think that PoW is a controversial consensus algorithm because it costs a lot of electricity to do the formula calculations.

What's at Stake: Proof of Stake (PoS) is a consensus algorithm that asks users to show that they own a certain amount of currency, which is their stake in the currency. PoS makes it possible for miners who hold coins (like Bitcoin) to mine or verify transactions. In other words, a miner's mining power depends on how many coins he or she has. So, the PoS process gives more power to the bigger players in the network.

Public Blockchain (no permission needed): A public blockchain, also called a permissionless blockchain, is a decentralized ledger that anyone can access.

Users don't need permission from anyone on the network to do things such as joining the network, receiving or sending transaction data, or taking part in the consensus process to decide what blocks get added to the chain.

Public Key: A public key is a cryptographic code or address that is used to make it easy for two parties to send and receive cryptocurrency. It's like an access code, allowing the agent to access certain information.

SHA-256: SHA-256 stands for Secure Hash Algorithm 256-bit and is used to protect cryptography. SHA-256 generates an almost-unique 256-bit signature for a text, which is used to mine Bitcoin and make addresses.

Sidechain: A sidechain is a way for tokens and other digital assets from one blockchain to be used safely in a different blockchain and then moved back to the first blockchain if needed.

Smart Contract: A smart contract is a piece of computer code that runs on the blockchain and moves digital assets automatically based on rules that have already been set. So, smart contracts are codes that are built into software and make it possible for certain tasks or processes to be done automatically.

Soft Fork: A soft fork is a change to the Bitcoin protocol that only affects blocks or transactions that were already valid before the change.

Stablecoin: A stablecoin is a crypto asset that usually takes the form of a coin or token that is linked to or backed by an underlying asset, such as a currency or a basket of commodities. The main goal of stablecoins is to help build an alternative financial system that does not depend on or have control over its currency units by the government or another centralized body.

Old Brick: A stale block is one that is no longer part of the best blockchain because it was replaced by a longer chain.

Tamper-Resistant Ledger: A tamper-resistant or immutable ledger is a record that can't be changed because it is encrypted and has a digital signature.

Wallet: The main way to store crypto assets is in a wallet.

Conclusion

Blockchain security is a complex and evolving field that demands a comprehensive approach involving various technical, social, and legal measures to guarantee the integrity and immutability of the blockchain ledger. To keep blockchain networks secure and trustworthy for all users, a multi-faceted strategy is required, which includes securing private keys, using consensus algorithms to validate transactions, and implementing best practices for smart contract security. Nevertheless, developers and users must remain vigilant and informed about emerging risks and work collaboratively to tackle these challenges as they emerge.

In the next chapter, we will learn about blockchain security. Security breaches in blockchain technology can have severe consequences, including the loss of funds and assets, damage to network reputation, and implications for smart contract execution. Despite the potential risks, legal and regulatory frameworks governing blockchain technology are still in their infancy, making it difficult to ensure adequate protection. It is therefore crucial for all stakeholders to work together to address these challenges and develop effective measures to secure blockchain networks. With ongoing vigilance and collaboration, the blockchain ecosystem can continue to thrive and offer significant benefits to businesses and individuals alike.

References

Nakamoto, S. (2008). Bitcoin is an electronic cash system that operates on a peer-to-peer basis. This can be retrieved from the Bitcoin website at https://bitcoin.org/bitcoin.pdf.

Buterin, V. (2014). A Decentralized Application Platform That Supports the Next Generation of Smart Contracts. White Paper was retrieved from the Ethereum Wiki at https://github.com/ethereum/wiki/wiki/White-Paper.

Swan, M. (2015). A New Economic System Based on Blockchain Technology. The O'Reilly Media, Inc. company.

Tapscott, David, and Andrew Tapscott (2016). The Blockchain Revolution explains how the technology that underpins Bitcoin is transforming not only the financial industry but also the world at large. Penguin.

Antonopoulos, A. M. (2014). Realizing the Potential of Digital Currencies Through Mastery of Bitcoin. The O'Reilly Media, Inc. company.

Cocco, L., Marchesi, M., & Ziccardi, G. (2019). The fundamentals and applications of blockchain technology and smart contracts. Springer.

Understanding Blockchain Consensus Models, authored by M. Swan (2017). 11-26 in the first issue of the Journal of Digital Banking.

Zheng, Z., Xie, S., Dai, H., Chen, X., & Wang, H. (2017). An Explanation of the Blockchain Technology, Including Its Architecture, Consensus, and Prospective Developments Big Data was the topic of discussion at the IEEE International Conference (pp. 557-564). IEEE.

Mougayar, W. (2016). The Blockchain in Business: What It Can Do, How It Can Be Used, and What Its Future Holds is the Subject of This Book. John Wiley and Sons Publishers.

Narayanan, A., Bonneau, J., Felten, E., Miller, A., & Goldfeder, S. (2016). An Extensive Overview of Bitcoin and Related Cryptocurrency Technology. The Press of Princeton University.

CHAPTER 2
Understanding Blockchain Security

Introduction

In recent years, blockchain technology has gained significant popularity, particularly in the context of cryptocurrencies. However, blockchain is not only limited to cryptocurrencies; it has many other potential use cases. One of the most significant benefits of blockchain technology is its ability to provide a high level of security due to its decentralized and immutable nature. However, blockchain technology is not completely immune to security threats. In this chapter, we will explore the basic security concepts and terminologies essential for understanding the security challenges faced by blockchain technology. We will provide a detailed overview of security threats and their potential consequences.

Structure

In this chapter, we will cover the following topics:

- Overview of Blockchain Security
- Security Terminologies
- Types of Security Threats
- Consequences of Security Breaches

Overview of Blockchain Security

Blockchain is a distributed ledger technology that maintains a continuously growing list of records called blocks. Each block contains a cryptographic hash of the previous block, a timestamp, and transaction data. This structure ensures that the blockchain is tamper-evident and secure. The security of a blockchain system relies on several features, including decentralization, consensus mechanisms, and cryptographic algorithms:

- **Decentralization**: A blockchain system is decentralized, meaning that there is no central authority controlling the network. Instead, it is distributed among a network of nodes, each of which holds a copy of the blockchain. This ensures that no single point of failure exists in the system.
- **Consensus mechanisms**: Consensus mechanisms are used to ensure that all nodes on the blockchain network agree on the current state of the ledger. These mechanisms prevent double-spending and ensure that the integrity of the blockchain is maintained. The most commonly used consensus mechanisms are Proof-of-Work (PoW), Proof-of-Stake (PoS), and Delegated Proof-of-Stake (DPoS).
- **Cryptography**: Cryptographic algorithms are used to secure the data on the blockchain. Public and private keys, digital signatures, and hashing algorithms are some of the most commonly used cryptographic tools in blockchain technology.

Introducing Blockchain Technology and its Security Features

Blockchain technology has emerged as a transformative force across various industries, offering unprecedented security, transparency, and efficiency. As a blockchain security expert, it is crucial to understand the fundamental concepts of blockchain and the security features that underpin its operations.

At its core, blockchain is a decentralized and distributed digital ledger that records transactions across multiple computers or nodes. These transactions are grouped into blocks, which are then cryptographically linked together, forming a chain of information. This decentralized nature eliminates the need for intermediaries, such as banks or clearinghouses, and enables peer-to-peer transactions.

One of the key security features of blockchain is immutability. Once a transaction is recorded on the blockchain, it becomes virtually impossible to alter or delete. This characteristic is achieved through cryptographic hashing, where each block is assigned a unique identifier based on the data it contains. Any change to a block's data would require recalculating the hash of subsequent blocks, making tampering evident and practically infeasible.

Another important security feature of blockchain is transparency. Blockchain networks are typically open and accessible to all participants, allowing anyone to view and verify transactions. This transparency fosters trust among participants as they can independently verify the accuracy and integrity of the data on the blockchain.

Furthermore, blockchain leverages advanced cryptographic techniques to ensure the security of transactions and data. Digital signatures are used to verify the authenticity and integrity of transactions, preventing unauthorized modifications. Encryption algorithms protect sensitive information, such as user identities and transaction details, ensuring confidentiality.

To maintain the integrity of the blockchain network, consensus mechanisms are employed. These mechanisms determine how transactions are validated and added to the blockchain. Popular consensus algorithms include Proof of Work (PoW) and Proof of Stake (PoS). PoW requires participants, known as miners, to solve computationally intensive puzzles to validate transactions. PoS, on the other hand, selects validators based on the number of tokens they hold, reducing energy consumption. These consensus mechanisms make it extremely difficult for malicious actors to manipulate the blockchain, preserving its security.

Smart contracts are agreements that run by themselves on the blockchain, which adds more security features. Smart contracts streamline business processes, lowering the reliance on third parties and the possibility of human mistakes. However, it is very important to perform careful security audits and testing to find weaknesses in smart contract code and reduce dangers related to coding mistakes or harmful attacks.

To enhance security further, organizations implementing blockchain should adopt best practices, such as secure key management, encryption, and regular vulnerability assessments. Robust key management practices ensure that private keys used for digital signatures and encryption are stored securely. Encryption adds an extra layer of protection to sensitive data stored on the blockchain. Regular vulnerability assessments and security audits help identify and address potential weaknesses before they can be exploited by malicious actors.

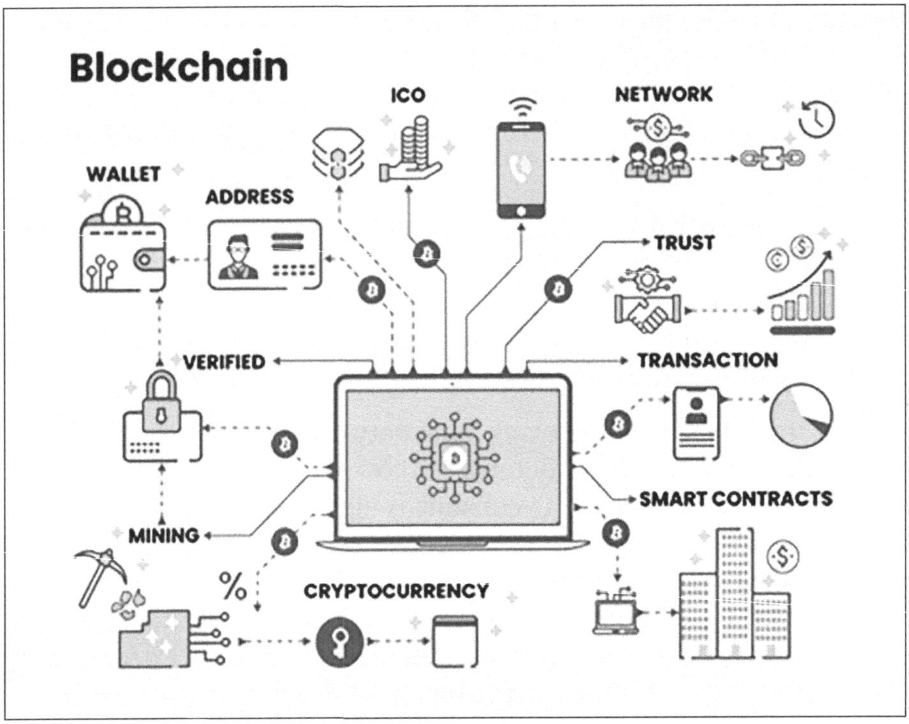

***Figure 2.1**: Blockchain (source: https://mmcgbl.com/how-blockchain-technology-is-transforming-the-cybersecurity/)*

Strong Encryption: Encryption is a Critical Component

A secure blockchain system is built on a foundation of robust security measures and best practices. As a blockchain security expert, it is essential to understand the key characteristics that contribute to the security of a blockchain system. These characteristics are crucial for ensuring the integrity, confidentiality, and availability of blockchain networks:

- **Immutable and tamper-resistant**: A secure blockchain system should be immutable, meaning that once a transaction is recorded on the blockchain, it becomes permanent and cannot be altered or tampered with. The cryptographic hashing of blocks and the decentralized nature of blockchain make it highly resistant to tampering, providing a strong guarantee of data integrity.
- **Encryption**: Transaction details, user identities, and smart contract information in CFC should be encrypted using strong cryptographic algorithms. Encryption ensures that only authorized parties with the

appropriate decryption keys can access and understand the data, thereby protecting confidentiality.

- **Robust identity management**: A secure blockchain system requires a robust identity management mechanism to ensure that only authorized participants can interact with the network. Public Key Infrastructure (PKI) is commonly used to establish digital identities and enable secure communication between participants. PKI relies on digital certificates and cryptographic keys to authenticate and authorize users, mitigating the risk of impersonation attacks.
- **Resilient consensus mechanisms**: Consensus mechanisms play a vital role in maintaining the security and integrity of a blockchain system. Robust consensus algorithms, such as Proof of Work (PoW) or Proof of Stake (PoS), should be implemented to prevent malicious actors from gaining control over the network. These mechanisms ensure that transactions are validated by a distributed network of nodes, making it difficult for any single entity to manipulate the blockchain.
- **Secure smart contracts**: Smart contracts are an integral part of many blockchain systems, automating the execution of agreements and business processes. To ensure security, smart contracts should undergo thorough code reviews, audits, and testing to identify and mitigate vulnerabilities. Additionally, best practices such as adhering to standardized coding guidelines, using formal verification techniques, and implementing secure coding practices should be followed.
- **Secure key management**: Proper key management is crucial in a secure blockchain system. Private keys, which are used for digital signatures and encryption, should be stored securely using hardware wallets or secure key management systems. Multi-factor authentication, access controls, and regular key rotation should be implemented to protect keys from unauthorized access or theft.
- **Continuous monitoring and auditing**: A secure blockchain system requires continuous monitoring and auditing to detect and respond to any security incidents or anomalies. Real-time monitoring tools should be employed to detect suspicious activities, such as unauthorized access attempts or unusual transaction patterns. Regular security audits and vulnerability assessments help identify and address any weaknesses or vulnerabilities in the system.
- **Network and data protection**: To enhance the security of a blockchain system, network segmentation and data protection measures should be implemented. Network segmentation helps isolate different components of the system, limiting the impact of a potential breach. Data protection mechanisms, such as encryption and access controls, ensure that

sensitive data stored on the blockchain is protected from unauthorized access or manipulation.

- **Compliance with legal and regulatory requirements**: A secure blockchain system should comply with applicable legal and regulatory requirements, such as data protection regulations and anti-money laundering (AML) laws. Organizations should implement appropriate measures to ensure data privacy, confidentiality, and compliance with relevant regulations specific to their industry and jurisdiction.

A secure blockchain system encompasses several key characteristics, including immutability, encryption, robust identity management, resilient consensus mechanisms, secure smart contracts, proper key management, continuous monitoring, network and data protection, and compliance with legal and regulatory requirements. By implementing these characteristics and adhering to best practices, organizations can build and maintain secure blockchain systems that foster trust and enable secure transactions and interactions within the network.

Key Components of Blockchain Security

A secure blockchain system should have the following key components:

- **Authentication**: Authentication is the process of verifying the identity of a user. In a blockchain system, authentication is achieved using public and private keys.
- **Authorization**: Authorization is the process of granting permission to access certain resources or perform specific actions on the blockchain. Authorization is enforced using smart contracts.
- **Data Integrity**: Data integrity refers to the accuracy and consistency of data on the blockchain. Cryptographic algorithms such as hashing and digital signatures are used to ensure data integrity.
- **Availability**: Availability refers to the ability of the blockchain network to remain operational even in the face of attacks. Decentralization ensures that the blockchain network remains available even if some nodes are compromised.

Ensuring the security of online transactions has always been a problem for web applications. The traditional solutions adopted by e-commerce sites, as well as by remote banking sites, use the encryption of communications (for example, through the SSL/HTTPS protocol) established by users previously identified by personal authentication credentials. Encryption prevents the possibility of sensitive information (such as credit card numbers) relating to transactions being exposed to prying eyes but does not prevent the possibility of sensitive information leakage due to data breaches affecting the servers.

By leveraging these data breaches, attackers can exploit the user's sensitive data to conduct unauthorized transactions, in place of the unsuspecting user (identity theft). In the case of blockchain, by definition, transactions are public and transparent, allowing the nodes of the network to validate them, thus ensuring the immutability and non-repudiation of the transactions recorded in the ledger.

It should be emphasized that while transactions on a blockchain are public, it does not mean that confidential information relating to users is publicly disclosed. In fact, blockchain users can demonstrate their digital identity (and ownership of assets exchanged in transactions) simply by signing transactions with their private key (which fulfills the same role as personal login credentials on traditional websites).

Public and Private Key Security

It is evident that it is the duty of individual users to protect and properly preserve their private keys since the loss of a private key could result in the loss of all their assets and funds recorded in the blockchain. A private key is a long string of characters that serves as the digital signature for transactions on the blockchain network. Private keys can be generated and stored in software wallets, hardware wallets, or paper wallets.

Storing private keys in a paper wallet is a popular option, as it is immune to cyber-attacks. A paper wallet is a physical document containing the private key printed on it, making it impossible for an attacker to steal the key remotely. This option is, however, susceptible to physical attacks, such as theft or damage to the document.

Hardware wallets are a safer option, as they store private keys on a special device that is protected by advanced security measures, such as biometric authentication and encryption. Hardware wallets are designed to protect private keys from remote and physical attacks.

Software wallets are the least secure option, as they are vulnerable to remote attacks, such as malware or phishing attacks. To secure private keys stored in software wallets, it is advisable to implement multi-factor authentication, which requires additional authentication factors (such as a fingerprint or facial recognition) in addition to the private key. Regularly updating software and firmware on wallets and hardware devices can also keep them secure against known vulnerabilities.

Cryptography and Encryption

Cryptography plays a vital role in ensuring the security and privacy of data in blockchain systems. It encompasses various techniques and algorithms that protect information from unauthorized access, tampering, or interception. Encryption, a fundamental component of cryptography, converts plaintext data into ciphertext, making it unreadable to anyone without the proper decryption key. Let's explore the importance and use of cryptography and encryption in blockchain systems.

- **Importance of Cryptography in Blockchain**: Cryptography forms the foundation of blockchain security by providing the following benefits:
    - **Confidentiality**: Encryption ensures that sensitive information, such as transaction details or user identities, remains confidential and accessible only to authorized parties.
    - **Integrity**: Cryptographic hashing algorithms ensure that data stored on the blockchain remains unaltered and tamper-proof.
    - **Authentication**: Digital signatures verify the authenticity and integrity of transactions, enabling participants to trust the validity of the data.
    - **Non-repudiation**: Through digital signatures, blockchain participants cannot deny their involvement in a transaction, ensuring accountability.
- **Encryption Techniques in Blockchain**: Encryption techniques are used in blockchain systems to safeguard sensitive data:
    - **Symmetric Encryption**: In symmetric encryption, the same key is used for both encryption and decryption. It is efficient but requires a secure method of key distribution among authorized parties.
    - **Asymmetric Encryption**: Asymmetric encryption uses a pair of keys: a public key for encryption and a private key for decryption. This technique offers enhanced security and enables secure communication between blockchain participants.
    - **Homomorphic Encryption**: Homomorphic encryption allows computations to be performed on encrypted data without the need for decryption, preserving data privacy during computations in blockchain networks.
- **Key Management in Blockchain**: Proper key management is critical for maintaining the security of encrypted data in blockchain systems. Key management practices include:

- **Secure Key Storage**: Private keys used for encryption, decryption, and digital signatures must be stored in secure hardware wallets or key management systems to prevent unauthorized access.
- **Key Rotation**: Regular key rotation helps minimize the impact of a compromised key. It involves generating new keys and securely replacing the existing ones.
- **Multi-Factor Authentication**: Adding an additional layer of authentication, such as biometrics or one-time passwords, strengthens key-based access control.

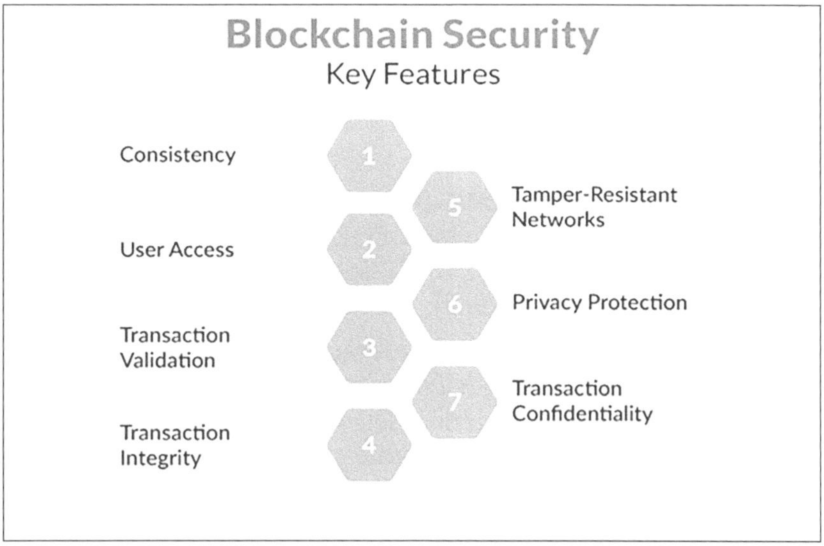

Figure 2.2: *Blockchain security (source - https://www.selecthub.com/endpoint-security/blockchain-security/)*

Consensus Mechanisms

Consensus mechanisms are essential components of blockchain systems that ensure agreement among participants regarding the validity and order of transactions. These mechanisms enable decentralized networks to reach consensus without relying on a central authority. Let's explore the significance of consensus mechanisms in blockchain and the different types commonly employed:

- **Importance of Consensus Mechanisms in Blockchain**: Consensus mechanisms address critical challenges in decentralized networks, such as:
  - **Byzantine Fault Tolerance**: Consensus mechanisms enable blockchain systems to function correctly even in the presence of malicious nodes or actors attempting to disrupt the network.

  - **Double-Spending Prevention**: Consensus ensures that a digital asset or cryptocurrency cannot be spent twice, maintaining the integrity and trustworthiness of the blockchain.
- **Common Consensus Mechanisms in Blockchain:**
  - **Proof of Work (PoW)**: PoW is widely known for its use in Bitcoin. It requires participants (miners) to solve complex mathematical puzzles, verify transactions, and add them to the blockchain. PoW ensures network security through computational work, but it can be energy-intensive.
  - **Proof of Stake (PoS)**: PoS selects validators to create new blocks based on the number of tokens they hold and are willing to "stake" as collateral. It is more energy-efficient than PoW and provides proportional decision-making power based on participants' stake in the network.
  - **Delegated Proof of Stake (DPoS)**: DPoS introduces a voting-based consensus mechanism where stakeholders select a limited number of delegates responsible for block production and validation. DPoS aims to achieve faster block confirmation times and scalability.
  - **Practical Byzantine Fault Tolerance (PBFT)**: PBFT is a consensus mechanism commonly used in permissioned blockchain networks. It relies on a predetermined set of validators who reach consensus through multiple rounds of voting. PBFT ensures high throughput and low latency but requires a trusted set of validators.
- **Practical Applications of Consensus Mechanisms**:
  - **Financial Transactions**: Consensus mechanisms provide secure and reliable validation of financial transactions, eliminating the need for intermediaries like banks and reducing transaction costs.
  - **Supply Chain Management**: Blockchain consensus ensures transparency and immutability in supply chain networks, enabling participants to trace and verify the origins and authenticity of products.
  - **Healthcare Systems**: Consensus mechanisms enhance the security and privacy of patient data, allowing authorized parties to access and update medical records securely.
- **Challenges and Considerations**:
  - **Scalability**: Consensus mechanisms must be designed to accommodate a growing number of participants and transactions without sacrificing security and decentralization.
  - **Energy Efficiency**: Energy consumption associated with certain

consensus mechanisms, such as PoW, is a concern. Developing greener alternatives or transitioning to more energy-efficient algorithms is an ongoing area of research.

- **Security and Attack Resistance**: Consensus mechanisms should be resistant to various attacks, such as Sybil attacks, 51% attacks, and Distributed Denial of Service (DDoS) attacks. Robust security measures and continuous monitoring are necessary to mitigate these risks.

In summary, consensus mechanisms are crucial for establishing agreement and trust in blockchain networks. They provide the necessary security and integrity required for decentralized systems to operate reliably. Understanding the different consensus mechanisms and their applications enables organizations to choose the most suitable mechanism for their specific use cases while considering scalability, energy efficiency, and security requirements.

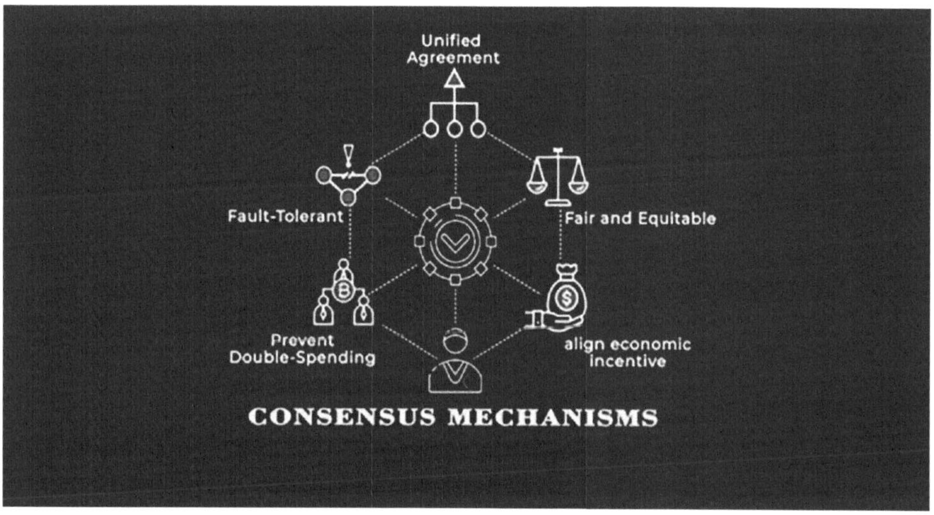

Figure 2.3: *Consensus mechanism (source: https://academy.suncrypto.in/what-is-consensus-mechanism-in-crypto-world/)*

Hashing and Digital Signatures

In the realm of blockchain technology, hashing and digital signatures are integral components that ensure data integrity, authentication, and non-repudiation. Let's delve into the significance and applications of hashing and digital signatures in blockchain systems:

- **Hashing in Blockchain**: Hashing is a process of transforming input data into a fixed-size output, known as a hash value or hash code. It is a one-way function, meaning it is computationally infeasible to derive the original input from the hash value. In blockchain, hashing serves several purposes:

  - **Data integrity**: Hashing verifies the integrity of data stored on the blockchain. Even a minor change in the input data results in a completely different hash value, making tampering evident.
  - **Merkle trees**: Hashing is employed to construct Merkle trees, a data structure that efficiently verifies the integrity of large sets of data. Merkle trees provide an optimized way to verify transactions and efficiently retrieve specific information from a vast amount of data.

- **Digital signatures in blockchain**: Digital signatures play a crucial role in ensuring the authenticity, integrity, and non-repudiation of transactions and messages in blockchain systems. They are created using cryptographic algorithms and involve the following steps:
  - **Private Key Sign**: The sender of a message uses their private key to generate a unique digital signature for the message.
  - **Public Key Verify**: The recipient of the message uses the sender's public key to verify the digital signature's authenticity and integrity.
- **Importance and Applications of Digital Signatures**: Digital signatures provide several essential benefits in blockchain systems:
  - **Authentication**: Digital signatures verify the identity of the sender, ensuring that the message or transaction is genuine and not tampered with.
  - **Non-repudiation**: Once a digital signature is generated, the sender cannot deny their involvement in the transaction. This property enhances accountability and prevents fraudulent activities.
  - **Secure Transactions**: Digital signatures secure transactions by providing cryptographic proof of the sender's consent and the integrity of the message.
- **Public key infrastructure (PKI) in blockchain**: PKI is a framework that facilitates the secure management of digital certificates and cryptographic keys in blockchain systems. It establishes trust between participants and enables secure communication. PKI consists of the following elements:
  - **Certificate authorities (CAs)**: CAs issue digital certificates that bind an entity's identity to its public key.
  - **Public and private keys**: Public keys are shared openly, while private keys are kept confidential and used to generate digital signatures.

- **Practical use cases**:
  - **Financial transactions**: Hashing and digital signatures ensure the security and integrity of financial transactions in blockchain-based cryptocurrencies, providing tamper-proof records and preventing double-spending.
  - **Smart contracts**: Digital signatures authenticate the identities of participants in smart contract interactions, ensuring that only authorized parties can execute and validate the contract terms.
  - **Supply chain management**: Hashing and digital signatures are used to verify the authenticity and integrity of product information and ensure the traceability of goods across the supply chain.
- **Security considerations**:
  - **Key management**: Proper key management practices, including secure storage and regular key rotation, are essential to maintain the security of digital signatures.
  - **Algorithm selection**: Choosing strong and well-vetted cryptographic algorithms is crucial to ensure the resilience and security of hashing and digital signatures.
  - **Secure channels**: Digital signatures should be transmitted through secure channels to prevent interception or tampering during transmission.

Hashing and digital signatures play pivotal roles in ensuring data integrity, authentication, and non-repudiation in blockchain systems. By employing these cryptographic mechanisms, blockchain networks can achieve secure and trustworthy transactions, smart contracts, and data storage, fostering transparency and accountability in various industries.

Transaction Validation

Once a transaction is initiated and signed with a private key, it is broadcast to the nodes of the blockchain network. These nodes are responsible for validating the transaction and adding it to the blockchain ledger.

To ensure transaction security, nodes use a consensus algorithm to confirm the validity of each transaction. Different blockchain networks use different consensus algorithms, but the most commonly used are Proof of Work (PoW) and Proof of Stake (PoS).

In a PoW consensus algorithm, nodes compete to solve complex mathematical puzzles in order to validate transactions and earn rewards in the form of cryptocurrency. The first node to solve the puzzle adds the transaction to the blockchain ledger, and the other nodes verify the validity of the solution. This process is computationally intensive and requires significant amounts of computing power, making it difficult for attackers to manipulate the blockchain ledger.

In a PoS consensus algorithm, nodes are selected to validate transactions based on the amount of cryptocurrency they hold. Nodes with larger holdings have a greater chance of being selected, and their holdings serve as collateral to ensure their honesty in validating transactions. This consensus algorithm is less computationally intensive than Proof of Work (PoW), making it more energy-efficient.

Another risk for smart contracts is the possibility of a contract becoming "stuck" or "frozen" due to unforeseen circumstances. This can happen when a smart contract is programmed to execute a specific set of instructions under certain conditions, but those conditions are not met, or the contract becomes unable to execute due to external factors such as network congestion or bugs in the contract's code. In these cases, it may be necessary to "hard fork" the blockchain network, which involves creating a new version of the blockchain with different rules to resolve the issue.

In addition to the technical risks associated with blockchain security, there are also social and legal risks that must be considered. For example, while blockchain technology is designed to be decentralized and immutable, it is still subject to the laws and regulations of the countries in which it operates. In some cases, these laws may conflict with the principles of decentralization and anonymity that are central to blockchain technology, leading to legal challenges and regulatory uncertainty.

Another social risk associated with blockchain security is the possibility of centralization. While blockchain networks are designed to be decentralized, there are concerns that large mining pools or other groups could gain too much control over the network, leading to centralization and potentially undermining the security and integrity of the blockchain ledger.

To address these risks, it is important for blockchain developers and users to stay informed about legal and regulatory developments in the countries in which they operate, and to work towards maintaining the decentralization and security of the blockchain network.

Security Terminologies

Here are a few security terminologies explained:

- **Public and private keys**

Public and private keys are cryptographic tools used to secure transactions on the blockchain. Public keys are a user's public identifier on the blockchain, while private keys are used to sign transactions and prove ownership of assets. The public key is used to verify the signature on a transaction, while the private key is used to generate the signature. Private keys should always be kept confidential, as anyone who gains access to them can spend the assets associated with them.

- **Cryptography and encryption**

Cryptography is the practice of securing communication through the use of mathematical algorithms. Encryption is the process of converting plaintext into ciphertext to protect sensitive information from unauthorized access. The use of cryptography is critical to securing blockchain transactions, as it ensures that only the intended recipient can access the information.

- **Consensus mechanisms**

Consensus mechanisms are the protocols used by blockchain networks to validate transactions and maintain the integrity of the blockchain. They enable all participants on the blockchain to agree on a single version of the truth, without the need for a central authority. There are different consensus mechanisms, including proof of work, proof of stake, delegated proof of stake, and others.

- **Hashing and digital signatures**

Hashing is the process of converting data of any size into a fixed-length string of characters, which is called a hash. Digital signatures are used to ensure the integrity of transactions and prove ownership of assets. They are created by taking a hash of the transaction data and then encrypting it with the private key of the sender.

Types of Security Threats

Let's know about various types of security threats:

51% Attacks

In the world of blockchain, a 51% attack is a potential security threat that can compromise the integrity and trustworthiness of a blockchain network. It refers to a situation where a single entity or a group of collaborating entities controls more than 50% of the total computational power (hashrate) in a blockchain network. Let's explore the concept of 51% attacks, their implications, and preventive measures:

- **Understanding 51% Attacks**:
  - **Consensus Manipulation**: A 51% attack allows the controlling entity to manipulate the consensus mechanism of a blockchain network. They can potentially reverse transactions, double-spend coins, exclude specific transactions from being confirmed, or even halt the network's operations.
  - **Potential Threat**: Although rare, 51% attacks pose a significant risk, particularly in smaller or less secure blockchain networks. Attackers may target networks with lower hashrates, aiming to exploit vulnerabilities and gain control.
- **Implications of 51% Attacks**:
  - **Double Spending**: An attacker can spend the same cryptocurrency multiple times by creating a longer private chain that conflicts with the main blockchain's history.
  - **Transaction Reversal**: Transactions that have already been confirmed can be reversed, leading to potential financial losses for individuals or businesses.
  - **Loss of Trust**: 51% attacks undermine the trust and credibility of a blockchain network. They can discourage users and investors, leading to a loss of confidence in the system.
- **Preventive Measures against 51% Attacks:**
  - **Increased Hashrate Distribution**: The distribution of hashrate across a blockchain network is crucial. By encouraging more participants to join and contribute computational power, the risk of a single entity gaining majority control decreases.
  - **Consensus Algorithm Considerations**: Different consensus algorithms have varying susceptibility to 51% attacks. For example, Proof of Work (PoW) networks with higher hashrates are generally more resistant to such attacks.
  - **Network Monitoring and Detection**: Continuous monitoring of network hashrates and suspicious activities can help identify potential 51% attack attempts. Early detection allows for timely intervention and mitigation measures.
  - **Network Fork Resistance**: Implementing mechanisms that increase the cost and complexity of creating a forked chain can deter attackers. Longer confirmation times and additional consensus rules can make it more challenging to carry out successful 51% attacks.
  - **Decentralization and Network Growth**: Encouraging a diverse and decentralized network by attracting more participants can enhance

network security and reduce the likelihood of a single entity gaining majority control.

- **Real-World Examples**:
    - **Ethereum Classic (ETC)**: In 2019, the ETC blockchain experienced a 51% attack, resulting in double-spending and transaction rollbacks.
    - **Bitcoin Gold (BTG)**: In 2018, Bitcoin Gold suffered a 51% attack that allowed attackers to double-spend coins and manipulate the blockchain.

It is important to note that larger and more widely adopted blockchain networks, such as Bitcoin and Ethereum, have significantly higher hashrates, making it extremely challenging for an attacker to accumulate enough computational power to execute a successful 51% attack. However, smaller or newer networks with lower hashrates remain vulnerable and need to implement stringent security measures.

Thus, 51% attacks represent a potential security risk in blockchain networks, where a single entity or a collusion of entities controls more than 50% of the network's hashrate. Implementing preventive measures, such as increasing hashrate distribution, choosing robust consensus algorithms, and implementing network monitoring, is crucial to mitigate the risk of 51% attacks and maintain the integrity and trustworthiness of blockchain systems.

Sybil Attacks

In the realm of blockchain and decentralized networks, a Sybil attack is a type of security threat where a malicious actor creates multiple fake identities or nodes to gain control or influence over the network. This attack is named after the famous book "Sybil," which portrays a person with dissociative identity disorder. Let's delve into the concept of Sybil attacks, their implications, and possible mitigation strategies:

- **Understanding Sybil Attacks**:
    - **Creation of Fake Identities**: In a Sybil attack, an attacker creates multiple fake identities, often referred to as Sybil nodes, and distributes them across the network.
    - **Influence and Control**: By controlling a significant portion of the network's nodes, the attacker can manipulate the network's operations, disrupt consensus, and potentially launch other attacks.

- **Implications of Sybil Attacks**:
  - **Manipulation of Consensus**: Sybil attacks can undermine the consensus mechanism of a blockchain network. The attacker can create a false majority or skew the decision-making process to their advantage.
  - **Double Spending**: By controlling multiple identities, the attacker can attempt to execute double-spending attacks, where the same digital assets are spent more than once.
  - **Eclipse Attacks**: Sybil attacks can be used to isolate or eclipse honest nodes, making them unaware of the true state of the network and potentially enabling further attacks.
- **Mitigation Strategies against Sybil Attacks**:
  - **Identity Verification**: Implementing mechanisms to verify the identity and authenticity of network participants can help prevent Sybil attacks. This may involve KYC (Know Your Customer) procedures or other forms of identity validation.
  - **Reputation Systems:** Implementing reputation-based systems can help identify and isolate potential Sybil nodes. By evaluating the behavior and interactions of nodes over time, suspicious or malicious nodes can be flagged or excluded.
  - **Proof-of-Work (PoW) and Proof-of-Stake (PoS) Combinations**: Combining PoW and PoS mechanisms can provide additional security against Sybil attacks. PoW can act as a deterrent, requiring computational resources to create multiple identities, while PoS can restrict influence based on the number of tokens held.
  - **Sybil Resistance Protocols**: Developing protocols specifically designed to be resistant to Sybil attacks can help mitigate their impact. These protocols may introduce additional consensus rules or reputation-based mechanisms.
  - **Decentralization and Peer Diversity**: Promoting a diverse and decentralized network with a large number of independent nodes reduces the effectiveness of Sybil attacks. This makes it harder for attackers to control a significant portion of the network.
- **Real-World Examples**:
  - **Steemit**: Steemit, a blockchain-based social media platform, faced Sybil attacks in its early stages. Attackers created numerous fake accounts to exploit the reward system and gain undue influence.
- **Ongoing Research and Development**: Sybil attacks remain an active area of research, with ongoing efforts to develop new mitigation techniques

and explore the potential vulnerabilities in different consensus mechanisms.

Sybil attacks pose a significant threat to blockchain networks by exploiting the ability to create multiple fake identities. Implementing robust identity verification measures, reputation systems, combining PoW and PoS, and promoting network decentralization are crucial steps to mitigate the impact of Sybil attacks. By safeguarding against these attacks, blockchain networks can maintain trust, security, and integrity in their operations.

Smart Contract Vulnerabilities

Smart contracts, being self-executing agreements stored on the blockchain, bring automation and efficiency to various industries. However, they can be susceptible to vulnerabilities and coding errors, which may lead to significant security risks. As a blockchain security expert, it is crucial to understand common smart contract vulnerabilities and take preventive measures. Let's explore some of the key vulnerabilities and best practices for securing smart contracts:

- **Reentrancy attacks**: Reentrancy is a vulnerability where a contract's code allows an attacker to repeatedly call back into the contract before the previous execution completes. This can lead to unauthorized access to contract funds or manipulation of contract state. Preventive measures include using the "Checks-Effects-Interactions" pattern, where state changes are made before interacting with external contracts and implementing proper safeguards to limit external calls.
- **Integer overflow/underflow**: Integer overflow/underflow occurs when a variable exceeds its maximum or minimum value due to incorrect arithmetic operations. Attackers can exploit this vulnerability to manipulate contract logic or gain unauthorized access to funds. Mitigation techniques involve using safe math libraries or applying proper range checks and validations in the contract code.
- **Unchecked external calls**: Smart contracts can interact with external contracts or send funds to external addresses. Failure to perform proper checks and validations when making external calls can lead to unauthorized transfers or the execution of malicious code. The use of the "Checks-Effects-Interactions" pattern, input validation, and strict adherence to secure coding practices help prevent this vulnerability.
- **Time manipulation**: Smart contracts rely on timestamps for various purposes, such as time-based conditions or lock periods. Attackers can exploit timestamp manipulation to bypass time-based restrictions or execute actions prematurely. Implementing secure timestamp

mechanisms and considering potential time-based attack vectors during contract design and development can help mitigate this risk.

- **Denial of Service (DoS)**: Smart contracts are susceptible to DoS attacks, where an attacker exploits contract logic or resource limitations to exhaust computational resources, causing the contract to freeze or become unresponsive. Proper resource allocation, gas limits, and code optimization techniques can help mitigate the risk of DoS attacks.
- **Solidity compiler vulnerabilities**: Solidity, the most popular language for writing smart contracts on Ethereum, is subject to its own set of vulnerabilities. Regularly updating the Solidity compiler to the latest stable version, implementing code audits, and following best practices recommended by the Solidity team can help address potential compiler-related vulnerabilities.
- **Lack of input validation**: Failure to properly validate and sanitize user inputs can lead to security vulnerabilities, such as injection attacks or unexpected behavior. Implementing input validation checks, using secure parameterized functions, and following secure coding guidelines help mitigate input validation vulnerabilities.
- **Code audits and security testing**: Regular code audits and security testing, including static analysis tools and manual reviews, play a crucial role in identifying and mitigating smart contract vulnerabilities. These processes help uncover coding errors, vulnerabilities, and potential attack vectors before deployment.
- **Continuous monitoring and upgrades**: Once deployed, continuous monitoring of smart contracts is essential to detect any anomalies or potential security breaches. Additionally, smart contracts should have the ability to upgrade or patch vulnerabilities through well-defined upgrade mechanisms while maintaining backward compatibility.

Securing smart contracts requires a comprehensive approach that includes secure coding practices, code audits, continuous monitoring, and adherence to best practices specific to the chosen smart contract language. By addressing common vulnerabilities and adopting preventive measures, blockchain systems can enhance the security and trustworthiness of their smart contract implementations.

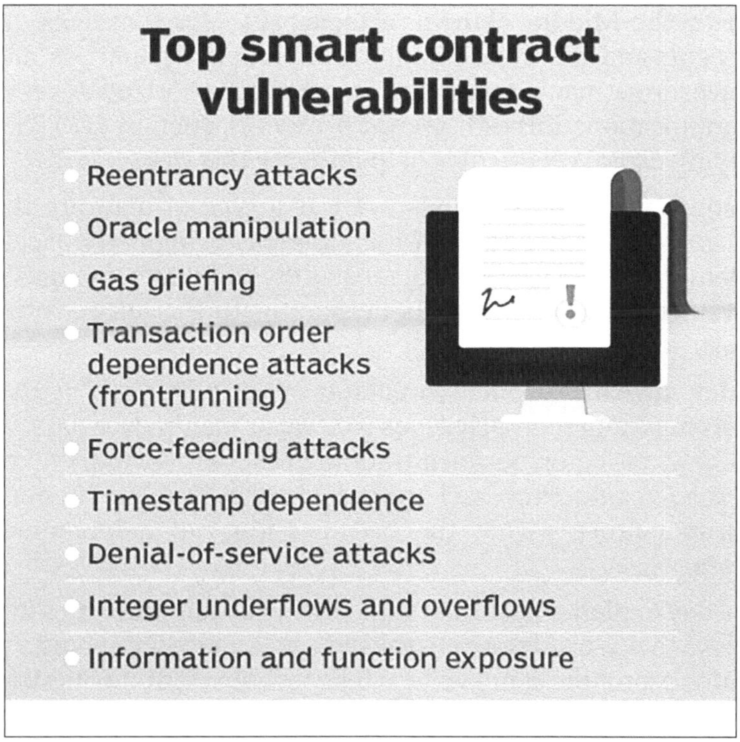

Figure 2.4: *Smart contract vulnerabilities*

Malware and Hacking Attacks

In the digital landscape, malware and hacking attacks pose significant threats to the security and integrity of various systems, including blockchain networks. As a blockchain security expert, it is essential to understand common types of malware and hacking attacks, as well as employ robust preventive measures. Let's explore some prevalent malware and hacking attack vectors and strategies to mitigate their risks:

- **Phishing attacks**: Phishing attacks involve deceptive techniques, such as fake websites or emails, to trick users into revealing sensitive information like usernames, passwords, or private keys. Preventive measures include user education, employing email filters, and adopting multi-factor authentication to prevent unauthorized access.
- **Distributed denial of service (DDoS) attacks**: DDoS attacks aim to overwhelm a system by flooding it with an excessive amount of requests or network traffic, rendering it inaccessible. Implementing DDoS mitigation solutions, such as traffic filtering and rate limiting, helps protect blockchain networks from such attacks.

- **Man-in-the-Middle (MitM) attacks**: In MitM attacks, an attacker intercepts and alters the communication between parties, allowing them to eavesdrop, manipulate data, or gain unauthorized access. Protecting communications through secure protocols, such as HTTPS or TLS, and verifying digital certificates help mitigate this risk.
- **Ransomware attacks**: Ransomware is a type of malware that encrypts data and demands a ransom for its release. Regularly backing up data, implementing robust security measures, and educating users about safe browsing and email practices help mitigate the impact of ransomware attacks.
- **Insider threats**: Insider threats involve individuals with authorized access misusing their privileges to steal or manipulate data, compromise system security, or perform fraudulent activities. Implementing access controls, conducting background checks, and maintaining a strong security culture within the organization can help minimize insider threats.
- **Zero-day exploits**: Zero-day exploits target vulnerabilities in software or systems that are unknown to the vendor. Employing security patches and updates promptly, using vulnerability scanners, and conducting security audits are essential in reducing the risk of zero-day exploits.
- **Social engineering attacks**: Social engineering attacks manipulate individuals into revealing sensitive information or performing actions that compromise security. Educating users about social engineering techniques, practicing skepticism, and implementing strict security protocols help mitigate the impact of such attacks.
- **Malware infections**: Malware, including viruses, worms, and Trojans, can infect systems and compromise security. Employing robust antivirus and anti-malware solutions, regularly updating software, and avoiding suspicious downloads or attachments help protect against malware infections.
- **Intrusion and brute-force attacks**: Intrusion attacks involve unauthorized access to systems, while brute-force attacks attempt to crack passwords or encryption keys through exhaustive trial-and-error methods. Implementing strong passwords, using multi-factor authentication, and employing intrusion detection and prevention systems help protect against such attacks.
- **Regular security audits and testing**: Conducting regular security audits, vulnerability assessments, and penetration testing helps identify vulnerabilities, assess system weaknesses, and implement appropriate security measures to mitigate risks.

Protecting blockchain networks from malware and hacking attacks requires a multi-layered approach. Implementing preventive measures, educating users, keeping software up-to-date, and conducting regular security assessments contribute to maintaining the security, integrity, and confidentiality of blockchain systems. By staying vigilant and proactive, organizations can mitigate the risks associated with malware and hacking attacks.

Consequences of Security Breaches

Blockchain technology has been touted as the future of finance and a key driver of the fourth industrial revolution. With its decentralized and transparent nature, it has the potential to revolutionize various industries, from finance to healthcare, by ensuring secure and efficient transactions. However, like any other technology, blockchain is not immune to security breaches, and the consequences of such breaches can be severe. In this section, we will explore the various consequences of security breaches in blockchain technology.

Loss of Funds and Assets

One of the most immediate consequences of security breaches in blockchain technology is the loss of funds and assets. Since blockchain transactions are irreversible, once an attacker gains access to a user's private keys, they can easily transfer the funds to their own wallet, and the victim has little or no recourse to recover their lost funds. The loss of funds not only affects individual users but can also have a significant impact on the reputation of the blockchain network. For example, the DAO attack on the Ethereum blockchain in 2016 resulted in the loss of over $50 million worth of Ether, leading to a significant drop in Ethereum's market value and a loss of confidence in the network.

Damage to Network Reputation

In addition to the loss of funds, security breaches can also damage the reputation of the blockchain network. Blockchain technology relies on trust and transparency, and any security breaches that compromise these principles can erode the confidence of users and investors in the network. A high-profile security breach can lead to negative media coverage and a loss of trust in the network, which can take years to rebuild. The impact of a security breach on a network reputation can be severe, especially in the case of public blockchains that rely on a large user base to maintain their security and decentralization.

Implications for Smart Contract Execution

Smart contracts are self-executing contracts that run on blockchain technology. They are used to automate various transactions, from financial contracts to supply chain management. Smart contracts are designed to be tamper-proof, but a security breach in the underlying blockchain can compromise the integrity of smart contracts. An attacker can exploit vulnerabilities in the blockchain to alter the state of a smart contract, leading to unintended consequences. For example, an attacker can manipulate the code of a smart contract to steal funds or redirect them to a different address. Such a security breach can have severe implications for the execution of smart contracts, leading to financial losses and damage to the reputation of the blockchain network.

Legal and Regulatory Implications

Blockchain technology operates in a regulatory grey area, and the implications of security breaches on legal and regulatory frameworks are still unclear. While some countries have recognized cryptocurrencies and blockchain technology as legitimate forms of currency and assets, others have banned their use altogether. A security breach in a blockchain network can lead to legal and regulatory scrutiny, especially if the breach involves the loss of significant amounts of funds or assets. The lack of clear regulations and laws governing blockchain technology can make it challenging for victims of security breaches to seek legal recourse.

Recent Developments in Regulations by Governments

Another aspect of security breaches in blockchain technology is the reaction of governments and regulators to these incidents. Some governments have taken a proactive approach to regulate and monitor blockchain technology, while others have adopted a more restrictive stance. For example, some countries have launched or announced plans to launch their own central bank digital currencies (CBDCs), which are digital versions of their national currencies that run on blockchain technology. CBDCs aim to provide a secure, efficient, and transparent alternative to traditional payment systems, as well as to counter the influence of cryptocurrencies. However, CBDCs also pose challenges to the security and privacy of users, as they may be subject to surveillance and censorship by central authorities. On the other hand, some countries have imposed bans or restrictions on the use of cryptocurrencies and blockchain technology, citing concerns over security, money laundering, terrorism financing, and tax evasion. These measures can limit the innovation and development of blockchain technology, and also create difficulties for users who want to access or transfer their funds or assets. Therefore, security breaches in blockchain technology can have significant implications for the regulatory environment, as well as affecting the adoption and acceptance of blockchain technology by governments and users.

Impact on User Trust and Adoption

One of the most significant consequences of security breaches in blockchain technology is the impact on user trust and adoption. Blockchain technology relies on a large user base to maintain its security and decentralization. If users lose confidence in the security of the blockchain network, they are less likely to use it for their transactions, leading to a loss of adoption. A high-profile security breach can also deter new users from joining the network, leading to a slowdown in growth and development. The loss of user trust can have long-term implications for the blockchain network, leading to a decline in its value and relevance.

Protecting Yourself from Potential Breaches

Blockchain is a distributed ledger technology that offers secure and transparent transactions. However, like any other technology, blockchain is not immune to security breaches. Security breaches in blockchain can result in financial loss, data theft, and reputational damage. Therefore, it is essential for users to take steps to protect themselves from security breaches in blockchain. In this section, we will discuss the steps that users can take to protect themselves from security breaches in blockchain.

Using a Reputable Wallet Provider

Users should use a reputable wallet provider with a strong security track record. A wallet provider is a software application that allows users to store, send, and receive digital assets such as cryptocurrencies. There are various wallet providers in the market, and it is important to choose one that has a strong reputation for security. Users should research wallet providers and choose one that has a history of keeping user funds safe. Additionally, it is important to ensure that the wallet provider uses strong encryption to secure user data. Encryption is a method of encoding data so that only authorized users can access it. A strong encryption method makes it difficult for attackers to access user data.

Another important feature that users should look for in a wallet provider is two-factor authentication (2FA). 2FA is a security feature that requires users to provide two forms of identification before accessing their accounts. This could be a password and a verification code sent to a user's mobile device. 2FA provides an extra layer of security that makes it difficult for attackers to gain access to a user's account even if they have the password.

Using Strong Passwords

Users should use strong passwords that are difficult to guess or crack. A strong password is a combination of upper and lowercase letters, numbers, and special characters. A strong password makes it difficult for attackers to guess or crack the password. Users should avoid using easily guessable passwords such as "password" or "123456". Additionally, users should avoid using the same password for multiple accounts. If an attacker gains access to one account, they can use the same password to access other accounts. Therefore, users should use a unique password for each account.

Keeping Private Keys Safe

Private keys are used to access and manage a user's digital assets. Private keys should be kept safe and secure and never shared with anyone. Users should consider storing private keys offline, such as on a hardware wallet, to reduce the risk of theft or loss. A hardware wallet is a physical device that stores a user's private keys offline. This reduces the risk of theft or loss compared to storing private keys on a computer or mobile device. Hardware wallets are also less vulnerable to malware and phishing attacks.

Being Cautious of Phishing Scams

Phishing is a type of cyber attack where attackers try to trick users into giving up their private keys or other sensitive information. Phishing attacks can be in the form of emails, text messages, or phone calls. Attackers create fake websites or emails that look similar to legitimate ones to trick users into providing sensitive information. Users should always double-check the URL of any website they visit and never click suspicious links or download attachments from unknown sources. Additionally, users should never share their private keys with anyone.

Staying Up-to-Date on Security Best Practices

Users should stay up-to-date on the latest security best practices and be aware of common threats and vulnerabilities. This includes keeping software and operating systems up-to-date, using anti-virus software, and regularly backing up important data. Software and operating system updates often include security patches that address vulnerabilities that can be exploited by attackers. Anti-virus software can detect and remove malware that can steal private keys or other sensitive information. Regularly backing up important data ensures that users can restore their data in case of data loss due to a security breach or other reasons.

Conclusion

Blockchain security is a complex and evolving field that requires a range of technical, social, and legal measures to ensure the integrity and immutability of the blockchain ledger. By taking a multi-faceted approach that includes securing private keys, using consensus algorithms to validate transactions, and implementing best practices for smart contract security, blockchain networks can remain secure and trustworthy for all users. However, it is important for developers and users to stay informed about emerging risks and to work together to address these challenges as they arise.

Security breaches in blockchain technology can have severe consequences, ranging from the loss of funds and assets to damage to network reputation and implications for smart contract execution. Legal and regulatory frameworks governing blockchain technology are still in their infancy, making it challenging. The next chapter explains the security challenges faced by public blockchains and the various attacks that can compromise their security.

References

- Narula, N. (2018). Cryptocurrency Security Threats and Countermeasures. In S. S. Choudhary, & S. K. Jena (Eds.), Security, Privacy and Anonymity in Computation, Communication and Storage (pp. 315-327). Springer.
- Reed, J., & Storace, D. (2018). Smart Contract Security: Vulnerabilities, Attacks, and Mitigations. IEEE Security & Privacy, 16(6), 20-27.
- Antonopoulos, A. M. (2014). Mastering Bitcoin: Unlocking Digital Cryptocurrencies. O'Reilly Media, Inc.
- Alharby, M. H. (2019). Blockchain security and privacy: a survey. IEEE Access, 7, 67876-67906.
- Böhme, R., Christin, N., Edelman, B., & Moore, T. (2015). Bitcoin: Economics, technology, and governance. Journal of Economic Perspectives, 29(2), 213-238.

- Grigg, I. (2019). Triple-entry accounting. In D. D. Friedman, R. Reuveny, & M. J. Clark (Eds.), Oxford Handbook of Computational Economics and Finance (pp. 103-124). Oxford University Press.
- Swan, M. (2015). Blockchain: Blueprint for a new economy. O'Reilly Media, Inc.
- Tapscott, D., & Tapscott, A. (2016). Blockchain revolution: how the technology behind Bitcoin is changing money, business, and the world. Penguin.
- "Mastering Blockchain" by Imran Bashir - This book provides a comprehensive overview of blockchain technology, its components, and how it works. It also covers security and privacy issues in blockchain and how to mitigate them.
- "Blockchain Basics: A Non-Technical Introduction in 25 Steps" by Daniel Drescher - This book is an excellent resource for beginners who want to learn the basics of blockchain technology. It covers key concepts, including security and privacy, in simple language.
- "Blockchain Security: A Comprehensive Guide for Beginners" by Vipin Bharathan and Venkata Harish Kalluri - This book provides an overview of the security threats and vulnerabilities in blockchain and how to protect against them. It covers topics such as cryptography, digital signatures, and secure key management.
- "Blockchain for Dummies" by Tiana Laurence - This book is a beginner's guide to blockchain technology, including security and privacy. It covers topics such as digital wallets, private and public keys, and smart contracts.
- "Blockchain: Blueprint for a New Economy" by Melanie Swan - This book provides an in-depth analysis of blockchain technology and its potential impact on various industries. It also covers security and privacy issues in blockchain and how to address them.
- "The Basics of Bitcoins and Blockchains" by Antony Lewis - This book provides an overview of blockchain technology and its applications, including security and privacy. It covers topics such as cryptography, digital signatures, and public and private keys.
- "Blockchain and the Law: The Rule of Code" by Primavera De Filippi and Aaron Wright - This book explores the legal and regulatory aspects of blockchain technology, including security and privacy. It covers topics such as smart contracts, digital identity, and intellectual property.
- "The Blockchain Revolution: How the Technology Behind Bitcoin Is Changing Money, Business, and the World" by Don Tapscott and Alex Tapscott - This book provides an overview of blockchain technology

and its potential impact on various industries. It also covers security and privacy issues in blockchain and how to address them.

- "Blockchain Technology and Applications" by Vigna and Casey - This book provides an overview of blockchain technology and its applications, including security and privacy. It covers topics such as cryptography, digital signatures, and public and private keys.
- "Blockchain and Cryptocurrency: International Legal and Regulatory Challenges" by Maria D. Garana - This book provides an in-depth analysis of the legal and regulatory challenges of blockchain technology, including security and privacy. It covers topics such as digital identity, data protection, and cybercrime.

Chapter 3

Security Challenges in Public Blockchains

Introduction

This chapter delves into the security challenges faced by public blockchains, exploring various attack vectors and security measures to prevent them.

Public blockchains possess unique characteristics, such as decentralization and transparency, which create a distinct security model. However, these features also pose challenges in maintaining security. Common threats include double-spending attacks, 51% attacks, Sybil attacks, eclipse attacks, smart contract vulnerabilities, social engineering attacks, malware, and phishing attacks.

To counter these threats, the chapter discusses several security measures such as implementing consensus mechanisms, designing network architecture and topology, using cryptographic primitives and algorithms, multi-factor authentication, access controls, penetration testing, vulnerability assessments, incident response planning, and blockchain forensics.

Finally, the chapter provides case studies on public blockchain security breaches to illustrate real-world examples and lessons learned.

Structure

In this chapter, we will discuss the following topics:

- Public Blockchain Security Overview
- Common Security Threats in Public Blockchains

- Security Measures for Public Blockchains
- Case Studies on Public Blockchain Security Breaches

Public Blockchain Security Overview

Public blockchains have emerged as a groundbreaking technology that offers decentralized, transparent, and tamper-proof records of transactions. However, the security of these networks remains a crucial concern. In this exploration, we will discuss an overview of security mechanisms, common threats, protective measures, and case studies of security breaches in public blockchains.

Public blockchains employ cryptographic techniques and consensus mechanisms, such as Proof of Work (PoW) or Proof of Stake (PoS), to maintain data integrity and user authentication. Despite their inherent security features, public blockchains are still susceptible to attacks.

Common security threats in public blockchains include 51% attacks, where a malicious actor gains control of over 50% of the network's hashing power, enabling them to manipulate transactions. Sybil attacks involve creating multiple fake nodes or accounts within the network to disrupt its functioning. Phishing and social engineering exploit human vulnerabilities to deceive users into revealing sensitive information. Lastly, smart contract vulnerabilities can be exploited by malicious actors, resulting in theft or manipulation of contract outcomes.

To protect public blockchains, several security measures can be implemented. These include robust consensus mechanisms, such as Delegated Proof of Stake (DPoS) and Byzantine Fault Tolerance (BFT), network monitoring and anomaly detection to identify potential threats, secure coding practices for smart contracts and other blockchain-related software, and user education to raise awareness about potential risks and best practices.

Notable public blockchain security breaches serve as valuable lessons. The DAO hack in 2016, where a hacker exploited a smart contract vulnerability and stole $50 million worth of Ether, highlights the importance of thorough smart contract auditing. The 2010 Bitcoin value overflow incident emphasizes vigilant monitoring and timely updates. The 2016 Bitfinex hack, which resulted in the loss of 120,000 bitcoins, underscores the need for robust security measures at the exchange level. Finally, the Verge 51% attack in 2018 demonstrates the risks associated with lesser-known cryptocurrencies and the importance of robust consensus mechanisms.

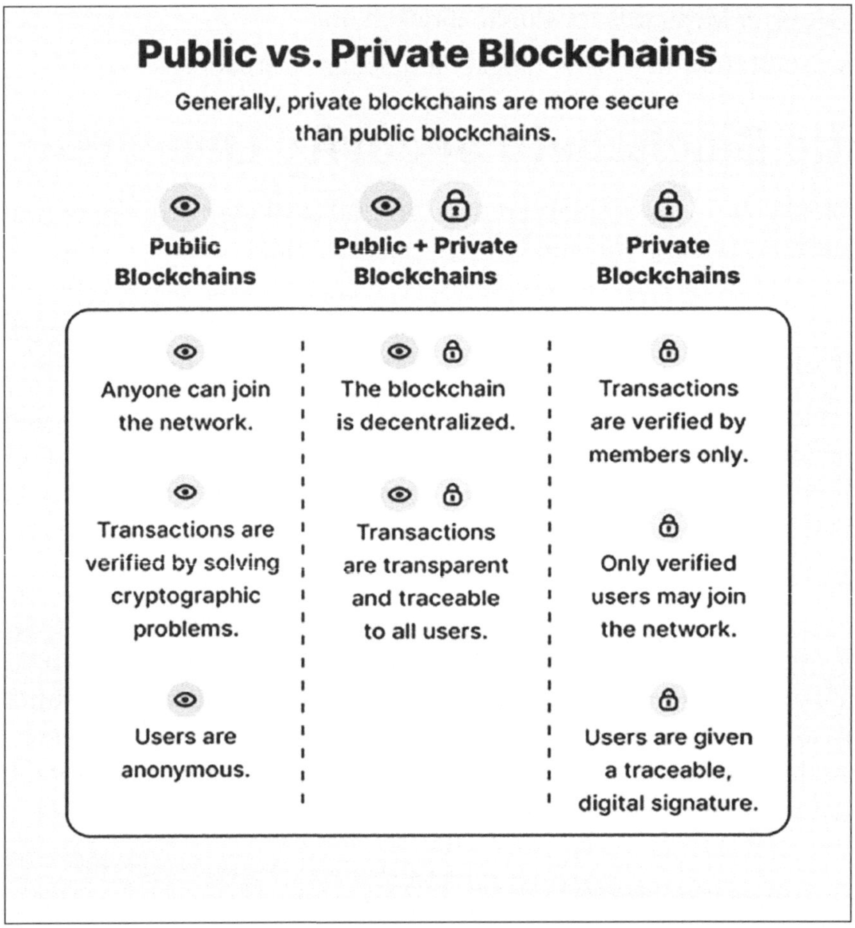

Figure 3.1: *Public versus private blockchains (source - https://us.norton.com/blog/privacy/blockchain-security)*

Public blockchain security is a critical concern for organizations and individuals who use public blockchains, such as Bitcoin and Ethereum, for their transactions. Public blockchains are decentralized networks where anyone can join and participate in the network without any restrictions. This open nature of public blockchains makes them susceptible to cyberattacks, frauds, and data breaches.

The decentralized nature of public blockchains, which makes them more secure than centralized systems, also makes them vulnerable to various types of attacks. For instance, the 51% attack, a type of attack where a group of miners controls more than 50% of the network's computing power, can be used to take control of the blockchain network and manipulate transactions. Other types of attacks that public blockchains are susceptible to include Sybil attacks, DDoS attacks, and mining pool attacks.

To ensure the security of public blockchains, organizations and individuals need to implement various security measures and best practices. These include:

- **Use secure wallets**: A wallet is a digital storage device that is used to store cryptocurrency. It is essential to use a secure wallet that is designed to protect against hacking attempts, malware, and phishing attacks.
- **Use two-factor authentication**: Two-factor authentication is a security measure that requires users to provide two forms of identification to access their accounts. It is essential to use two-factor authentication to protect against unauthorized access to the blockchain network.
- **Use strong passwords**: Strong passwords are critical to protecting against brute-force attacks. A strong password should be at least 12 characters long and include upper and lowercase letters, numbers, and special characters.
- **Use multi-signature transactions**: Multi-signature transactions require multiple parties to sign off on a transaction before it can be executed. This security measure helps to protect against unauthorized transactions.
- **Regularly update software**: It is essential to regularly update the software used to access the blockchain network. These updates often include security patches that address known vulnerabilities.
- **Conduct regular security audits**: Regular security audits can help identify security vulnerabilities and weaknesses in the blockchain network. These audits can help organizations and individuals take proactive measures to prevent cyberattacks and data breaches.
- **Implement encryption**: Encryption is a security measure that helps protect data from unauthorized access. It is essential to implement encryption for all transactions and data stored on the blockchain network.
- **Use decentralized exchanges**: Decentralized exchanges are designed to operate on public blockchains and offer enhanced security features such as multi-signature transactions and non-custodial trading.

One of the challenges of public blockchain security is that not all blockchains are equally secure. Some blockchains, such as Bitcoin and Ethereum, have high levels of security due to their large and diverse network of nodes and miners. However, other blockchains may have lower levels of security due to their smaller or centralized network, which makes them more vulnerable to attacks. Therefore, it is important to conduct regular security audits for decentralized blockchains, especially those that are new or less established. Security audits can help assess the security level and performance of a blockchain network, as well as identify and resolve any potential issues or risks. Security audits can also help verify the compliance and validity of the smart contracts and protocols running on the blockchain network. By conducting regular security audits, organizations and individuals can ensure the security and reliability of their decentralized blockchains.

Public blockchain security is a critical concern for organizations and individuals who use public blockchains for their transactions. The open nature of public blockchains makes them susceptible to various types of attacks, including 51% attacks, Sybil attacks, and DDoS attacks. To ensure the security of public blockchains, organizations and individuals need to implement various security measures and best practices, including using secure wallets, two-factor authentication, multi-signature transactions, regular software updates, security audits, encryption, and decentralized exchanges. By following these best practices, organizations and individuals can protect themselves against cyberattacks and data breaches and ensure the security of their transactions on public blockchains.

Common Security Threats in Public Blockchains

Public blockchains are decentralized networks that allow anyone to participate and transact on the network without any restrictions. While public blockchains offer several benefits such as transparency, immutability, and decentralization, they are also susceptible to various security threats that can compromise the security of the network and its users.

In this section, we will discuss some of the common security threats in public blockchains:

- **51% Attack**

A 51% attack is a type of attack on a blockchain network where a group of miners or nodes control more than 50% of the network's computing power. With this control, the attackers can manipulate the transactions, reverse transactions, and prevent new transactions from being added to the blockchain. The 51% attack is also known as a majority attack, and it is more prevalent in smaller blockchains where it is easier to obtain a majority of the computing power.

The 51% attack is a significant security threat to the blockchain network as it allows the attackers to control the network and compromise its security. With the ability to manipulate transactions, attackers can double-spend, which is the process of spending the same cryptocurrency twice. In a double-spend attack, the attackers can send a transaction to purchase a product or service, and then quickly reverse the transaction before it is confirmed, allowing them to keep their cryptocurrency and get the product or service for free.

The 51% attack can also lead to a fork in the blockchain network, where the network splits into two or more branches, resulting in a loss of consensus. The fork can create confusion among users, and it can cause significant financial losses for investors and traders.

To protect against a 51% attack, blockchain networks can implement various security measures such as multi-algorithm mining, which makes it more difficult for attackers to control the network. The network can also implement checkpoints, which are predetermined points in the blockchain where the network validates the transactions, making it difficult for attackers to manipulate the transactions.

- **Sybil Attack**

A Sybil attack is a type of attack where an attacker creates multiple fake identities or nodes to gain control of the network. With multiple identities, the attacker can manipulate the consensus mechanism and control the network. The Sybil attack is named after the book Sybil, which tells the story of a woman with multiple personalities.

In a Sybil attack, the attacker creates multiple fake identities or nodes and uses them to overwhelm the network. By controlling a large number of nodes, the attacker can manipulate the consensus mechanism, which is the process that the blockchain network uses to validate transactions and create new blocks.

The Sybil attack is a significant security threat to the blockchain network as it can compromise the security of the network and the privacy of its users. The attacker can manipulate the transactions and control the network, which can lead to financial losses and a loss of trust in the blockchain network.

To protect against a Sybil attack, blockchain networks can implement various security measures such as proof-of-work, proof-of-stake, or proof-of-authority consensus mechanisms. These mechanisms make it more difficult for attackers to create multiple identities and control the network.

- **Distributed Denial of Service (DDoS) Attack**

A Distributed Denial of Service (DDoS) attack is a type of attack where an attacker floods the network with a massive amount of traffic to overwhelm the system and make it inaccessible to legitimate users. DDoS attacks can disrupt the network and cause significant financial losses.

In a DDoS attack, the attacker uses multiple devices to send a large amount of traffic to the network, making it difficult for legitimate users to access the network. The DDoS attack can cause the network to crash, resulting in a loss of consensus and a loss of data.

To protect against DDoS attacks, blockchain networks can implement various security measures such as firewalls, intrusion detection systems, and load balancers. These measures can help detect and block malicious traffic, protecting the network from DDoS attacks.

- **Smart Contract Vulnerabilities**

Smart contracts are self-executing programs that run on the blockchain. Smart contracts are vulnerable to coding errors, which can be exploited by attackers to steal funds or cause other types of damage.

Smart contract vulnerabilities can lead to significant financial losses for users and investors, and they are a significant security threat to the blockchain network. Smart contract vulnerabilities can occur due to coding errors, such as buffer overflows, integer overflow, and logical errors.

To protect against smart contract vulnerabilities, blockchain networks can implement various security measures such as formal verification, which is the process of verifying the correctness of the smart contract code. Formal verification can help detect and eliminate vulnerabilities in smart contracts, making the network more secure.

- **Wallet Vulnerabilities**

Wallets are digital storage devices used to store cryptocurrencies. Wallets are vulnerable to hacking attempts, malware, and phishing attacks. Attackers can steal funds or access sensitive information stored in wallets.

Wallet vulnerabilities can lead to significant financial losses for users and investors, and they are a significant security threat to the blockchain network. Wallet vulnerabilities can occur due to hacking attempts, malware, and phishing attacks.

To protect against wallet vulnerabilities, users can implement various security measures such as using a hardware wallet, which is a physical device that stores the private keys used to access cryptocurrency. Hardware wallets are more secure than software wallets, as they are not connected to the internet and are more difficult for attackers to hack.

- **Social Engineering Attacks**

Social engineering attacks are a type of attack where an attacker manipulates individuals into divulging sensitive information or performing actions that compromise the security of the network. These attacks can be used to gain access to wallets, private keys, and other sensitive information.

Social engineering attacks can lead to significant financial losses for users and investors, and they are a significant security threat to the blockchain network. Social engineering attacks can occur due to phishing attacks, where the attacker sends a fake email or message to the user, asking them to provide their login credentials or other sensitive information.

To protect against social engineering attacks, users can implement various security measures such as using two-factor authentication, which requires the user to provide two forms of identification to access the account. Two-factor authentication makes it more difficult for attackers to gain access to sensitive information, protecting the network from social engineering attacks.

- **Malicious Software**

Malicious software such as malware, viruses, and ransomware can infect nodes and wallets, compromising the security of the network. Malicious software can steal funds, corrupt data, and compromise the privacy of users.

Malicious software is a significant security threat to the blockchain network, as it can compromise the security of the network and the privacy of its users. Malicious software can occur due to hacking attempts, phishing attacks, and other types of cyberattacks.

To protect against malicious software, users can implement various security measures such as using antivirus software, which can detect and remove malware from the system. Antivirus software can help protect the network from malicious software, making it more secure.

- **Lack of Regulation**

Public blockchains are not regulated by any government or authority, which makes them susceptible to scams, fraud, and other illegal activities. Lack of regulation can lead to significant financial losses for users and investors, and it is a significant security threat to the blockchain network.

To protect against lack of regulation, blockchain networks can implement various security measures such as implementing Know Your Customer (KYC) and Anti-Money Laundering (AML) policies. KYC and AML policies can help prevent illegal activities on the network, making it more secure.

In conclusion, blockchain security is a critical component of the blockchain network that protects it from various security threats such as 51% attacks, Sybil attacks, DDoS attacks, smart contract vulnerabilities, wallet vulnerabilities, social engineering attacks, malicious software, and lack of regulation. To protect against these security threats, blockchain networks can implement various security measures such as multi-algorithm mining, proof-of-work, proof-of-stake, or proof-of-authority consensus mechanisms, formal verification of smart contracts, hardware wallets, two-factor authentication, antivirus software, and KYC and AML policies.

Security Measures for Public Blockchains

It is essential for organizations and users to understand the various security threats to the blockchain network and implement appropriate security measures to protect against them. Regular security assessments such as penetration testing and vulnerability assessments can also help identify and address security weaknesses in the network.

Overall, blockchain technology has the potential to revolutionize various industries by providing a secure and decentralized platform for transactions and data storage. However, to realize its full potential, it is crucial to ensure the security of the network and protect it from various security threats. By implementing appropriate security measures and staying up-to-date with the latest security trends and threats, organizations and users can ensure the security of the blockchain network and take advantage of its numerous benefits.

Ensuring the security of blockchain-based solutions is essential to prevent cyber-attacks and data breaches. Following best practices for building secure blockchain solutions is critical to achieving this goal. In this section, we will discuss the best practices for building secure blockchain solutions and the process of blockchain penetration testing.

Best Practices for Building Secure Blockchain Solutions

- **Define and Enforce Endorsement Agreements in the context of Business Contracts**

  Endorsement agreements ensure that only authorized parties can participate in the network. This ensures the integrity and security of the network.

- **Enable Identity and Access Management (IAM)**

  IAM helps manage user access and authentication. By implementing IAM, organizations can control access to sensitive data and protect against unauthorized access.

- **Execute Suitable Tokens such as OAUTH, OIDC, and SAML2 for User Authentication, Verification, and Authorization**

  Tokens help ensure secure user authentication and authorization. By using suitable tokens, organizations can protect against unauthorized access and control who can access sensitive data.

- **Securely Store Identity Keys**

  Storing identity keys securely is essential to ensure the security of the network. By using secure storage methods, organizations can prevent unauthorized access and protect against data breaches.

- **Use Privileged Access Management (PAM) Solution to Secure Blockchain Ledger Entries After Suitable Business Logic**

  PAM helps ensure that only authorized personnel have access to sensitive data. By implementing PAM, organizations can control access to sensitive data and prevent unauthorized access.

- **Safeguard API-based Transactions with API Security Best Practices**

  APIs are a critical component of blockchain-based solutions. By using API security best practices, organizations can protect against unauthorized access and prevent data breaches.

- **Use a Data Classification Approach to Safeguard Data or User Information**

  Data classification helps organizations identify and protect sensitive data. By using a data classification approach, organizations can ensure that sensitive data is protected and prevent data breaches.

- **Use Privacy-Preserving Technologies for Sensitive Information**

  Privacy-preserving technologies help protect sensitive information. By using privacy-preserving technologies, organizations can ensure the confidentiality and integrity of sensitive data.

- **Use Standard TLS for Internal and External Communications**

  TLS helps secure communication between nodes in the network. By using standard TLS, organizations can prevent data breaches and protect against unauthorized access.

- **Implement Multi-Factor Authentication**

  Multi-factor authentication adds an extra layer of security to user authentication. By implementing multi-factor authentication, organizations can protect against unauthorized access and prevent data breaches.

- **Keep Strong Cryptographic Key Management**

  Cryptographic key management is essential to ensure the security of the network. By keeping strong cryptographic key management, organizations can prevent unauthorized access and protect against data breaches.

- **Leverage Hardware Security Module (HSM) and Security Incident and Event Management (SIEM)**

  HSM and SIEM help ensure the security of the network. By leveraging HSM and SIEM, organizations can prevent data breaches and protect against unauthorized access.

- **Regular Vulnerability Assessment and Penetration Testing (VAPT)**

  Regular VAPT helps organizations identify and address security weaknesses in the network. By conducting regular VAPT, organizations can prevent data breaches and protect against unauthorized access.

- **Patch Security Loopholes to Protect Blockchain-Based Applications from Vulnerabilities and Data Breaches**

  Patching security loopholes helps organizations prevent data breaches and protect against unauthorized access. By patching security loopholes, organizations can ensure the security of the network.

- **Get an Industry-Recognized Security Certification for Your Blockchain Solution**

  Getting an industry-recognized security certification helps organizations ensure the security of the network. By getting a security certification, organizations can demonstrate their commitment to security and protect against data breaches.

- **Enforce Compliance and Other Security Controls for the Solution**

  Enforcing compliance and other security controls helps organizations ensure the security of the network. By establishing clear guidelines, implementing appropriate controls, and fostering a culture of security awareness, organizations can contribute to a more secure and trustworthy blockchain ecosystem.

Security Testing Tools for Blockchain

Blockchain technology has taken the world by storm, and with the increasing adoption of blockchain, the security of blockchain applications has become a crucial concern for individuals and organizations. Blockchain security testing is an essential process that helps identify vulnerabilities and weaknesses in the blockchain application and ensures its security.

Several blockchain security testing tools are available in the market to help organizations in identifying security loopholes and weaknesses in their blockchain applications. In this section, we will discuss some of the most popular blockchain security testing tools:

SWC-registry

- The Smart Contract Weakness Classification Registry (SWC-registry) is a tool that helps developers identify potential vulnerabilities in their smart contracts. It provides a list of test cases for each vulnerability, making it easier for developers to fix the issue.

MythX

- MythX is an API that provides smart contract security analysis for Ethereum, Quorum, Vechain, Roostock, Tron, and other EVM-compatible blockchains. It uses a combination of static and dynamic analysis to identify vulnerabilities in smart contracts.

Echidna

- Echidna is a Haskell program designed for fuzzing/property-based testing of Ethereum smart contracts. It generates test cases automatically to find vulnerabilities in the smart contract.

Manticore

- Manticore is a symbolic execution tool for the analysis of smart contracts and binaries. It is a tool that is used for vulnerability analysis and finding security bugs.

Oyente

- Oyente is a static analysis tool that is used for smart contract security. It provides a report that identifies potential vulnerabilities in smart contracts.

Securify 2.0

- Securify 2.0 is a security scanner for Ethereum smart contracts. It is an open-source tool that is used to identify vulnerabilities in smart contracts.

SmartCheck

- SmartCheck is a static smart contract security analyzer. It uses an advanced static analysis technique to detect vulnerabilities in smart contracts.

Octopus

- Octopus is a security analysis framework that is used for the WebAssembly module and blockchain smart contract. It can detect vulnerabilities in smart contracts and provide a report that identifies the vulnerability.

Surya

- Surya is a utility tool for smart contract systems. It provides a report that identifies the potential vulnerabilities in the smart contract code.

Solgraph

- Solgraph generates a DOT graph that visualizes the function control flow of a Solidity contract and highlights potential security vulnerabilities. It is a useful tool for developers to identify potential vulnerabilities in their smart contracts.

Solidity Security Blog

- The Solidity Security Blog provides a comprehensive list of crypto-related hacks, bugs, vulnerabilities, and preventative measures. It is a useful resource for developers to learn about potential vulnerabilities and how to prevent them.

Awesome Buggy ERC20 Tokens

- Awesome Buggy ERC20 Tokens is a collection of vulnerabilities in ERC20 smart contracts with tokens affected. It is a useful resource for developers to learn about potential vulnerabilities in ERC20 smart contracts.

In conclusion, blockchain security testing is essential to ensure the security of blockchain applications. Several blockchain security testing tools are available in the market that help identify potential vulnerabilities and weaknesses in blockchain applications. By using these tools, developers can ensure that their blockchain applications are secure and can prevent security breaches.

Case Studies on Public Blockchain Security Breaches

Public blockchain security breaches have become increasingly common in recent years, with attackers exploiting vulnerabilities in smart contracts, wallets, and other blockchain components. These security breaches have led to the loss of millions of dollars in cryptocurrency and have raised concerns about the security of public blockchains.

In this section, we will examine 10 case studies of public blockchain security breaches and the lessons learned from them:

- **Ronin Bridge breach - $612M**: On March 23, 2022, the largest cyberattack of the year occurred when Ronin Bridge, an Ethereum sidechain built for Axie Infinity, was exploited for around $612 million in cryptocurrencies. The hackers accessed private keys, compromised validator nodes, and approved transactions, draining funds from the bridge. The U.S. Treasury Department updated its SDN list on April 14, suggesting Lazarus Group may have been responsible for the exploit. The Ronin Bridge hack remains the largest cryptocurrency exploit to date.
- **FTX Wallet breach – $477M:** During FTX's bankruptcy proceedings on November 11-12, unauthorized transactions resulted in the theft of roughly $477 million worth of crypto. Sam Bankman-Fried suspected either a former employee or malware on a former employee's computer to be involved. By December 27, the U.S. Department of Justice had initiated an investigation into the location of approximately $372 million of the stolen funds.

  The root cause of the FTX wallet breach was a combination of human error and poor security practices. According to a report by Chainalysis, the hackers gained access to the FTX hot wallet through a compromised employee email account that was used to reset the password of the wallet provider, BitGo. The hackers then used phishing emails and social engineering to trick FTX staff into approving the withdrawal requests. The report also found that FTX did not have adequate multi-factor authentication, encryption, or monitoring systems in place to prevent or detect the breach.

  - FTX has since implemented more stringent security measures, such as rotating passwords, enforcing 2FA, and using hardware wallets for cold storage.

  - The hackers have laundered some of the stolen funds through various mixers, decentralized exchanges, and over-the-counter brokers, making it difficult to trace them.
  - FTX has offered a $10 million reward for any information that leads to the recovery of the funds or the arrest of the perpetrators.

- **Wormhole Bridge breach – $321M:** On February 2, Wormhole token bridge suffered a $321 million exploit due to a vulnerability in its smart contract. An attacker was able to mint 120,000 unbacked wETH tokens on Solana (SOL) and swap them for ETH. This breach was the largest of 2022 at the time and ranked third for the year.

  The root cause of the Wormhole Bridge breach was a coding error in the smart contract that implemented the token bridge. The error allowed an attacker to bypass the normal verification process and mint arbitrary amounts of wETH tokens on Solana without locking any corresponding ETH on Ethereum. The attacker then used various decentralized exchanges to swap the unbacked wETH for ETH, draining the liquidity pool and making the bridge insolvent. The Wormhole team said they had audited the code internally but did not use any external security firms. They also claimed that the vulnerability was introduced by a recent update and was not present in the original version of the bridge. The team has since paused the bridge and is working on a recovery plan.

- **Nomad Token Bridge breach – $190M:** On August 2, multiple attackers exploited the Nomad token bridge, a platform that facilitates cross-chain swaps, stealing $190 million. A smart contract vulnerability allowed the attack, and roughly 88% of participants were identified as copycats. White hat hackers managed to recover about $32.6 million in funds.

  The Nomad token bridge breach was caused by a faulty implementation of the secure remote password (SRP) protocol, which is used to authenticate the users and verify the cross-chain transactions. The SRP protocol requires both parties to agree on a large prime number and a generator as parameters, but the Nomad bridge used a fixed and small prime number that was hardcoded in the smart contract. This made it easy for the attackers to brute-force the secret keys and forge valid signatures for any amount of tokens they wanted to transfer. The Nomad team admitted that they did not follow the best practices for the SRP protocol and that they had not audited their code before launching the bridge. They also said that they were working on compensating the affected users and improving the security of their platform.

- **Wintermute breach – $160M:** UK-based crypto market-maker Wintermute experienced a compromised hot wallet, resulting in the loss of around $160 million in 70 different tokens. Blockchain cybersecurity firm CertiK attributed the breach to a vulnerable private key generated by Profanity, an app with a known exploit.

  The root cause of the Wintermute breach was a flaw in the Profanity app, which is a tool that helps users generate and manage private keys for their crypto wallets. Profanity claims to offer a secure and user-friendly way to create and store private keys using mnemonics, passwords, and biometrics. However, according to CertiK, Profanity has a critical vulnerability that allows anyone to derive private keys from the mnemonics by exploiting a weak hashing function and a predictable salt value. The attackers were able to use this exploit to access the Wintermute hot wallet and drain its funds. CertiK warned that any users who have used Profanity to generate their private keys are at risk of losing their assets and advised them to move their funds to new addresses as soon as possible. Profanity has not responded to the allegations or issued any updates on the issue.
- **BNB Chain Bridge breach – $100M:** On October 6, BNB Chain was paused due to suspicious activity, which was later revealed to be a $100 million exploit on its cross-chain bridge, the BSC Token Hub. Initially, it was believed that the attacker stole $600 million, but they had over $400 million in assets frozen on the blockchain, with more possibly trapped in cross-chain bridges on the BNB blockchain side.
- **Wintermute hack – $160M (repeat):** Wintermute, a UK-based crypto market-maker, had a compromised hot wallet, resulting in a loss of approximately $160 million across 70 tokens. Blockchain cybersecurity firm CertiK claimed a vulnerable private key, likely generated by Profanity, was attacked. Conspiracy theories suggesting an inside job were debunked by BlockSec, which stated that the allegations were not convincing.

The Ronin Bridge hack illustrates the risks of using cross-chain bridges, which are often complex and prone to human errors. Cross-chain bridges are designed to enable interoperability between different blockchains, but they also introduce new attack vectors and security challenges. Users should be careful when using cross-chain bridges and only trust reputable and audited ones.

DAO Hack Case Study

Blockchain technology is becoming more popular and widespread, as it provides a secure and decentralized way of storing and transferring digital assets. However, blockchain technology is not immune to hacking attempts, and there have been numerous high-profile blockchain hacks in recent years. In this section, we will examine a detailed case study of a public blockchain hack and explore the steps that led to the hack, the impact of the hack, and the aftermath of the attack.

Figure 3.2: DAO (*source - https://cdn.ttgtmedia.com/rms/onlineimages/how_daos_work-h_half_column_mobile.png*)

Case Study: The DAO Hack

The DAO was a decentralized autonomous organization built on top of the Ethereum blockchain. It was designed to act as a venture capital fund for the blockchain community, allowing investors to pool their resources and invest in promising blockchain projects. The DAO raised over $150 million in funding from thousands of investors in just a few weeks, making it one of the largest crowdfunding campaigns in history.

The DAO was designed to be entirely autonomous, with no central authority or human management. Instead, it relied on smart contracts to manage its operations and investments. Investors could purchase DAO tokens with their Ethereum, giving them the ability to vote on investment proposals and receive a share of the profits.

Hack

In June 2016, the DAO was hacked, resulting in the theft of over 3.6 million Ether, worth around $50 million at the time. The hack was possible due to a vulnerability in the DAO's smart contract code, which allowed the attacker to repeatedly withdraw Ether from the DAO without the proper authorization.

The attacker exploited a flaw in the code that allowed them to create a recursive call, which meant that the attacker could repeatedly request funds from the DAO before the previous transaction had been completed. This allowed the attacker to accumulate a significant amount of Ether before anyone noticed.

Impact

The DAO hack was a significant blow to the Ethereum community, and it had a significant impact on the value of Ether. The value of Ether dropped by over 30% in just a few days following the hack, and it took several months for the price to recover fully.

The hack also led to a split in the Ethereum community, with some members advocating for a hard fork to reverse the hack and return the stolen funds to investors. Others argued that this would violate the principles of decentralization and blockchain immutability, and that the hack was simply a part of the learning process for the blockchain community.

Aftermath

In the aftermath of the hack, the Ethereum community decided to conduct a hard fork to reverse the hack and return the stolen funds to investors. This led to the creation of Ethereum Classic, a separate blockchain that did not include the hard fork and the reversal of the DAO hack.

The hard fork was controversial, with many members of the blockchain community arguing that it violated the principles of decentralization and blockchain immutability. However, the hard fork was ultimately successful, and the stolen funds were returned to investors.

What is a hard fork?

A hard fork is a change in the rules or protocol of a blockchain network that creates a permanent divergence from the previous version. It requires all nodes to upgrade to the new version and results in two incompatible chains that do not recognize each other's transactions. A hard fork can be initiated by developers, miners, or users who want to implement new features, fix bugs, or resolve disputes.

What happened in the Ethereum hard fork?

The Ethereum hard fork was a response to the DAO hack, which exploited a vulnerability in the smart contract code of the DAO, a decentralized autonomous organization that raised $150 million in a crowdfunding campaign. The hacker drained about a third of the funds by creating a recursive function that repeatedly called the withdraw function. The hard fork proposed by the Ethereum Foundation aimed to revert the hack and return the stolen funds to investors by altering the state of the blockchain before the attack. However, not everyone agreed with this decision, and some nodes refused to upgrade to the new version. They continued to follow the original chain, which became known as Ethereum Classic. The hard fork created a split within the Ethereum community and the network, raising questions about the immutability and security of blockchain technology.

Lessons Learned

The DAO hack was a significant wake-up call for the blockchain community, and it highlighted the need for more robust security measures and smart contract auditing. The following are some of the key lessons learned from the DAO hack:

- **Smart contracts are not infallible**: The DAO hack demonstrated that even the most well-designed smart contracts can be vulnerable to attack. Smart contracts must be thoroughly audited and tested to identify any potential vulnerabilities.
- **The importance of community consensus**: The DAO hack highlighted the importance of community consensus in the blockchain space. The decision to conduct a hard fork to reverse the hack was controversial, and it ultimately divided the Ethereum community.
- **The need for regulation**: The DAO hack also highlighted the need for more robust regulatory frameworks to protect investors and prevent similar hacks from occurring in the future.

The DAO hack was a significant event in the history of blockchain technology, and it highlighted the need for more robust security measures to be implemented in public blockchains. While the Ethereum community was able to recover most of the stolen funds through a hard fork, the incident remains a cautionary tale for developers and users alike.

One of the key takeaways from the DAO hack is the importance of thorough testing and auditing of smart contracts before deployment. This can help identify potential vulnerabilities and prevent exploitations like the one that occurred with the DAO.

Another lesson learned is the importance of community involvement and consensus when dealing with security breaches in public blockchains. The decision to implement a hard fork was controversial, but ultimately the majority of the Ethereum community supported it as a way to recover the stolen funds and prevent similar attacks in the future.

Finally, the DAO hack underscores the need for users to take responsibility for securing their own assets. While public blockchains offer a high degree of transparency and decentralization, they also require users to take an active role in protecting their funds. This includes using secure wallets and strong passwords and staying vigilant for potential phishing scams and other security threats.

In conclusion, the DAO hack was a watershed moment in the history of public blockchains, highlighting both the potential of decentralized systems and the risks associated with them. While the incident was a setback for the Ethereum community, it also served as a catalyst for improvements in blockchain security and the development of new tools and protocols to prevent similar attacks in the future. By continuing to learn from the lessons of the DAO hack and other security breaches, we can build a more resilient and secure blockchain ecosystem for years to come.

The Mt. Gox Hack: A Lesson in Cybersecurity for the Crypto Industry

The Mt. Gox hack is considered one of the biggest cryptocurrency hacks in history. Mt. Gox was a Japanese Bitcoin exchange platform foundcd in 2010 that, at its peak, handled over 70% of all Bitcoin transactions worldwide. However, in 2014, the exchange filed for bankruptcy, citing a loss of 850,000 bitcoins worth approximately $450 million at the time. This case study will explore the events that led to the hack, its impact, aftermath, and lessons learned.

Impact

The Mt. Gox hack had a significant impact on the cryptocurrency industry, causing widespread panic and loss of confidence in Bitcoin. The hack resulted in the loss of approximately 850,000 bitcoins, which accounted for around 7% of all bitcoins in circulation at the time. The value of Bitcoin plummeted, and its reputation was severely tarnished.

Aftermath

After the hack, Mt. Gox filed for bankruptcy, and the Tokyo District Court was appointed to oversee the process. The court appointed a trustee to oversee the distribution of the remaining assets, including bitcoins, to the affected customers. In 2018, the trustee announced that all creditors would be repaid in bitcoins, and the process was completed in 2019.

The impact of the Mt. Gox hack was far-reaching, and the repercussions of the event are still being felt today. It led to the development of stricter regulations and security measures within the cryptocurrency industry to prevent future hacks.

Lessons Learned

The Mt. Gox hack taught the cryptocurrency industry several valuable lessons. First, it highlighted the importance of security measures and the need for exchanges to implement robust security protocols to protect customer funds. It also emphasized the need for transparency and open communication with customers in the event of a security breach.

Furthermore, the Mt. Gox hack showed that centralization can be a significant risk factor in the cryptocurrency industry. Exchanges that hold large amounts of cryptocurrency in one central location are more vulnerable to attacks, making it essential for the industry to develop decentralized solutions to mitigate this risk.

Another lesson learned from the Mt. Gox hack is the importance of independent auditing and regulatory oversight. Exchanges must be held accountable for their actions and required to adhere to industry standards to protect their customers.

The Mt. Gox hack was a watershed moment in the cryptocurrency industry, highlighting the need for improved security measures, transparency, and independent oversight. It led to the development of stricter regulations and security protocols, which have made the industry safer for investors. Although the hack was a significant setback for the industry, it ultimately led to its evolution, paving the way for a more secure and resilient future.

Conclusion

Public blockchains face various security challenges due to their unique characteristics and inherent vulnerabilities. By understanding the common threats and implementing the appropriate security measures, the integrity and security of public blockchains can be maintained. This chapter not only highlights the importance of a proactive approach to public blockchain security but also emphasizes the need for continuous learning and adaptation in the face of emerging threats. Studying real-world case studies offers valuable insights into the practical implications of security breaches and the lessons learned from them, ultimately contributing to the development of more secure and resilient public blockchain systems.

The next chapter focuses on the security challenges that private blockchains face, including internal issues such as insider attacks and external problems such as network breaches. It also talks about the security methods that can be used to prevent these threats.

As blockchain technology keeps developing, private blockchains have become a popular choice for businesses and organizations that want to use distributed ledger technology while maintaining control, privacy, and efficiency. This chapter looks at private blockchains, examining their traits, benefits, and possible use cases.

Further Readings

- "Security Challenges and Opportunities in Blockchain Technology" by D. Dhar and R. Luthra (2018).
- "Blockchain Security: Overview and Challenges" by A. Dorri, M. Steger, and S. Kanhere (2018).
- "Blockchain Security: Threats and Solutions" by S. Bhattacharya, P. Saha, and S. Sarkar (2020).
- "Blockchain Security: A Survey" by M. M. Alam, N. M. Khan, and A. Al-Fuqaha (2019).
- "Security and Privacy in Blockchain: A Survey" by K. Christidis and M. Devetsikiotis (2016).
- "Security and Privacy in Decentralized Energy Trading through Multi-signatures, Blockchain, and Smart Contracts" by A. Ameli, B. J. Lämmel, and J. R. C. van der Veen (2018).
- "Security Considerations for Blockchain Technology in the Internet of Things" by J. Xu, R. Li, and J. Zhou (2018).
- "A Survey on Security and Privacy Issues in Blockchain Technology" by M. Yasin and J. Kim (2018).
- "A Survey on Blockchain Security: Issues, Challenges, and Solutions" by S. Li, X. Chen, and H. Wang (2020).
- "An Overview of Blockchain Security Issues and Challenges" by S. K. Sahoo and S. P. Mohanty (2018).
- "Security Risks in Blockchain Technology: A Comprehensive Survey." IEEE Access, vol. 6, 2018, pp. 54033-54059. doi: 10.1109/access.2018.2871421.

- "Survey of attacks on Ethereum smart contracts." Journal of Information Security and Applications, vol. 46, 2019, pp. 1-11. doi: 10.1016/j.jisa.2019.03.006.
- "A Survey of Blockchain Security Issues and Challenges." Future Internet, vol. 11, no. 9, 2019, p. 197. doi: 10.3390/fi11090197.
- "A survey of security and privacy in decentralized applications." IEEE Communications Surveys & Tutorials, vol. 22, no. 1, 2019, pp. 810-836. doi: 10.1109/comst.2019.2934862.
- "Security threats to decentralized cryptocurrencies." Communications of the ACM, vol. 62, no. 11, 2019, pp. 98-107. doi: 10.1145/3342719.
- "A survey of blockchain security issues and challenges: current solutions and future research directions." Journal of Network and Computer Applications, vol. 126, 2019, pp. 50-70. doi: 10.1016/j.jnca.2018.11.008.
- "An Overview of Security Issues and Risks in Decentralized Applications." Proceedings of the 2018 International Conference on Computing, Networking and Communications (ICNC), 2018, pp. 862-867. doi: 10.1109/icnc.2018.8390344.
- "On Security Issues and Challenges in Blockchain Deployment." IEEE Security & Privacy, vol. 16, no. 4, 2018, pp. 54-63. doi: 10.1109/MSP.2018.2701179.
- "Blockchain security challenges: a survey." Journal of Internet Services and Applications, vol. 9, no. 1, 2018, p. 18. doi: 10.1186/s13174-018-0089-y.
- "Security analysis of blockchain consensus protocols." Future Generation Computer Systems, vol. 91, 2019, pp. 264-274. doi: 10.1016/j.future.2018.09.054.

Chapter 4
Security Challenges in Private Blockchains

Introduction

This chapter covers the security challenges faced by private blockchains, including internal threats such as insider attacks and external threats such as network attacks. The chapter also discusses the security measures that can be implemented to prevent these threats.

Structure

In this chapter, the following topics will be covered:

- Private Blockchain Security Overview
- Common Security Threats in Private Blockchains
- Security Measures for Private Blockchains
- Case Studies on Private Blockchain Security Breaches

Private Blockchain Security Overview

In the ever-evolving landscape of blockchain technology, private blockchains have emerged as a unique and compelling solution for businesses and organizations seeking to harness the power of distributed ledger technology while maintaining control, privacy, and efficiency. This section delves into the world of private blockchains, exploring their characteristics, benefits, and potential use cases.

Definition and Characteristics of Private Blockchains

A private blockchain, also known as a permissioned blockchain, is a type of blockchain network that limits access and participation to a select group of trusted entities. Unlike public blockchains, which are open to anyone interested in joining, private blockchains require an invitation and approval from either the network administrator or a group of organizations responsible for managing the network.

The characteristics of private blockchains are as follows:

- **Restricted access and participation**

In a private blockchain, access is limited to a predetermined group of trusted participants. These participants are typically pre-vetted by the network administrator or a governing consortium. This restricted access offers more control over the network, ensuring that only authorized parties can view and interact with the blockchain.

- **Faster transaction processing**

Due to the smaller number of participants in private blockchains, transaction processing tends to be more efficient. The consensus mechanisms employed by private blockchains are designed to be less resource-intensive than those used in public blockchains, which translates to faster transaction processing times.

- **Enhanced privacy**

Private blockchains offer a higher degree of privacy compared to public blockchains. Due to the controlled nature of the network, sensitive data is only accessible to authorized participants. This makes private blockchains ideal for use cases that require confidentiality and data protection.

- **Consensus mechanisms**

Private blockchains often employ different consensus mechanisms than public blockchains. In a public blockchain, the consensus mechanism is typically Proof of Work (PoW) or Proof of Stake (PoS), which require significant computational resources and can lead to slower transaction times. In contrast, private blockchains utilize consensus mechanisms like Practical Byzantine Fault Tolerance (PBFT) or Delegated Proof of Stake (DPoS), which are designed for efficiency and reduced resource consumption.

Benefits of Private Blockchains

The unique characteristics of private blockchains provide several advantages for businesses and organizations, including:

- **Scalability**

Private blockchains can handle a higher volume of transactions, thanks to their faster transaction processing capabilities. This makes them well-suited for large-scale enterprises and organizations with significant transaction throughput requirements.

- **Security**

By restricting access to a select group of trusted participants, private blockchains can offer enhanced security compared to public blockchains. Unauthorized access is minimized, and the risk of external attacks is reduced.

- **Customizability**

Private blockchains can be tailored to the specific needs of an organization. Businesses can customize the network's rules, permissions, and smart contracts to create a bespoke solution that aligns with their operational requirements and goals.

- **Cost-effectiveness**

The resource-efficient consensus mechanisms employed by private blockchains result in lower energy consumption and reduced operational costs compared to public blockchains that rely on PoW or PoS.

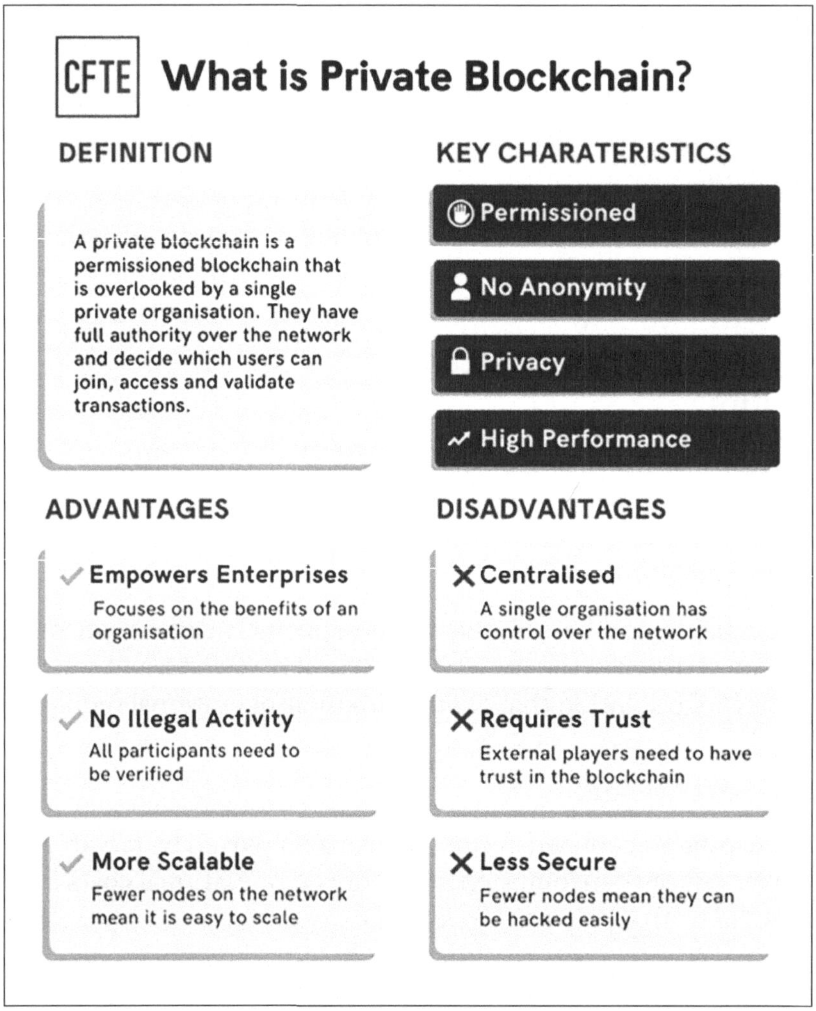

***Figure 4.1**: Private blockchain (source: https://blog.cfte.education/what-is-private-blockchain/)*

Use Cases for Private Blockchains

The unique advantages of private blockchains make them suitable for various applications across different industries, including:

- **Supply chain management**

Private blockchains can be used to create transparent and secure supply chain management solutions, allowing organizations to track and trace products from their origin to the point of consumption. With the ability to record and verify each step of the supply chain process, businesses can improve efficiency, reduce fraud, and ensure product quality.

- **Financial services**

Private blockchains can provide the foundation for secure and efficient financial services platforms. From streamlining cross-border payments to enabling real-time settlement of securities, private blockchains offer a range of benefits for financial institutions looking to reduce costs, enhance security, and improve customer experiences.

- **Healthcare**

In the healthcare industry, private blockchains can be used to securely store and share sensitive patient data among authorized healthcare providers. By providing a tamper-proof, distributed ledger for electronic health records (EHRs), private blockchains can improve data security, streamline information sharing, and enable better patient care.

- **Identity management**

Private blockchains can offer a decentralized and secure identity management solution. By storing and validating user identities on a permissioned blockchain, organizations can minimize the risk of identity theft and fraud while simplifying the authentication process for users.

- **Voting and governance**

Private blockchains can be leveraged to create secure and transparent voting systems for elections, corporate governance, and other decision-making processes. By providing a tamper-resistant ledger for recording and verifying votes, private blockchains can reduce the risk of fraud and improve trust in the voting process.

Real-world Examples of Private Blockchain Implementations

Private blockchains are decentralized networks that allow a selected group of participants to share data and transactions in a secure and efficient manner. Unlike public blockchains, which are open to anyone, private blockchains require permission to join and access the network. This gives the participants more control and privacy over their data and transactions, as well as the ability to customize the network rules and features to suit their specific needs and goals.

Several prominent organizations have successfully implemented private blockchains to address industry-specific challenges and improve their operations. Here are some notable examples:

- **IBM Food Trust**: IBM Food Trust is a private blockchain solution designed to enhance transparency and traceability in the food supply chain. It enables retailers, suppliers, and consumers to access information about the origin, safety, and quality of food products, improving trust and reducing foodborne illnesses. The platform also allows participants to share data and insights to optimize inventory management, reduce waste, and increase efficiency.
- **Corda**: Corda, developed by R3, is an open-source private blockchain platform specifically designed for use in the financial services industry. It enables institutions to streamline processes, reduce risk, and improve efficiency through secure, peer-to-peer transactions. The platform also supports smart contracts, which are self-executing agreements that can automate complex and multi-party transactions, such as trade, finance, syndicated loans, and derivatives.
- **Hyperledger Fabric**: Hyperledger Fabric, part of the Linux Foundation's Hyperledger project, is a permissioned blockchain infrastructure that allows organizations to build and deploy custom blockchain solutions. It is highly customizable, enabling businesses to tailor their blockchain network to their specific needs. The platform also supports modular and pluggable components, such as consensus mechanisms, membership services, and encryption algorithms, which can enhance the performance, security, and flexibility of the network.

While private blockchains offer numerous benefits, organizations must consider several factors before implementing this technology. The challenges and considerations for implementing private blockchains are as follows:

- **Interoperability:** Private blockchains may face challenges in communicating with other blockchains or legacy systems, limiting their scalability and compatibility. Organizations should ensure that their private blockchain solutions are interoperable with existing and potential partners, as well as with industry standards and regulations. For example, they may use common protocols, interfaces, or gateways to facilitate data exchange and collaboration across different platforms and networks.
- **Security:** Private blockchains rely on trusted validators to verify transactions and maintain consensus, which may expose them to malicious attacks or human errors. Organizations should implement robust security measures to protect their private blockchain networks from unauthorized access, data breaches, or tampering. For example, they may use encryption, authentication, authorization, or auditing mechanisms to safeguard the confidentiality, integrity, and availability of their data and transactions.

- **Governance:** Private blockchains require clear and effective governance mechanisms to define the roles, responsibilities, and rights of the participants, as well as the rules and policies for the network operation and maintenance. Organizations should establish transparent and fair governance structures that balance the interests and incentives of all stakeholders, and allow for flexibility and adaptability to changing needs and circumstances. For example, they may use voting, consensus, or arbitration mechanisms to resolve disputes, enforce compliance, or implement changes.
- **Network security**

While private blockchains offer improved security compared to public blockchains, they are not immune to cyber threats. Organizations must implement robust security measures to protect their network from potential attacks and vulnerabilities.

Private blockchains provide a unique and powerful solution for organizations seeking the benefits of distributed ledger technology without the drawbacks associated with public blockchains. With their ability to deliver enhanced control, privacy, and efficiency, private blockchains are well-suited for a wide range of industries and use cases. However, organizations must carefully consider the challenges and implications of implementing private blockchains to ensure a successful deployment that aligns with their strategic objectives.

Private Blockchains and Security Threats

Private blockchains, also known as permissioned blockchains, are gaining popularity among businesses and organizations due to their enhanced control, privacy, and efficiency. However, as with any technology, private blockchains must also address the critical issue of security to ensure the integrity and confidentiality of data stored on the blockchain. In this section, we will provide an overview of private blockchain security, discussing the unique security features of private blockchains, the potential threats they face, and the best practices for maintaining a secure private blockchain network.

Unique Security Features of Private Blockchains

Private blockchains offer several security features that set them apart from public blockchains. Some of these unique security features include:

- **Permissioned access**

Private blockchains restrict access to a select group of trusted participants, ensuring that only authorized users can view and interact with the blockchain.

This restricted access offers better control over the network and helps protect sensitive data from unauthorized access.

- **Consensus mechanisms**

Private blockchains employ different consensus mechanisms than public blockchains, often opting for more efficient and less resource-intensive algorithms. These consensus mechanisms, such as Practical Byzantine Fault Tolerance (PBFT) or the Raft algorithm, provide faster transaction processing and enhance network security by reducing the risk of attack.

Unlike public blockchains that rely on proof-of-work (PoW) or proof-of-stake (PoS) to reach consensus among a large and diverse set of participants, private blockchains use more centralized and deterministic algorithms that can achieve consensus with fewer nodes and less computational power. These algorithms, such as PBFT or the Raft algorithm, are based on the idea of quorum, which means that a minimum number of nodes must agree on the validity of a transaction before it is added to the blockchain. These algorithms can handle network failures and malicious nodes more efficiently than PoW or PoS, and can process transactions faster and with lower latency. However, they also sacrifice some degree of decentralization and trustlessness, as they depend on a predefined set of nodes that have the authority to validate transactions and update the blockchain state. Therefore, private blockchains use these consensus mechanisms to trade off some of the benefits of public blockchains for better performance and security.

- **Data privacy**

Private blockchains prioritize data privacy, offering a higher degree of confidentiality compared to public blockchains. Sensitive data is accessible only to authorized participants, making private blockchains an ideal solution for use cases that require strict data protection.

Potential Security Threats to Private Blockchains

Despite the unique security features of private blockchains, they still face several potential security threats, including:

- **Insider attacks**

Since private blockchains rely on a closed network of trusted participants, they are vulnerable to insider attacks. These attacks occur when an authorized participant misuses their access to the network, either intentionally or unintentionally, to compromise the system's security.

- **Sybil attacks**

In a Sybil attack, a malicious participant attempts to control multiple nodes in the network, undermining the consensus process and potentially compromising the integrity of the blockchain. While private blockchains are less susceptible to Sybil attacks than public blockchains due to their permissioned access, this type of attack remains a concern.

- **Data tampering**

One of the main benefits of blockchain technology is its ability to maintain the integrity of data through a distributed ledger. However, private blockchains are still susceptible to data tampering if attackers can gain unauthorized access or exploit vulnerabilities in the network.

- **External network attacks**

Private blockchains can also be targeted by external network attacks, such as Distributed Denial of Service (DDoS) attacks. These attacks aim to overwhelm the network with a flood of requests, causing it to become unresponsive and potentially compromising its security.

Best Practices for Private Blockchain Security

To maintain a secure private blockchain network, organizations should consider the following best practices:

- **Implement strong access control**

Implementing strong access control measures is crucial to ensure that only authorized users can access the private blockchain network. This includes using multi-factor authentication, role-based access control, and regularly reviewing user access privileges.

- **Employ robust consensus mechanisms**

Choosing an appropriate consensus mechanism is vital for maintaining the security and efficiency of a private blockchain. Organizations should opt for consensus algorithms that offer strong security guarantees while minimizing the risk of attack and resource consumption.

- **Regularly update and patch the network**

Keeping the private blockchain network up to date with the latest security patches and updates is essential to protect against newly discovered vulnerabilities and potential attacks. Organizations should have a robust patch management process in place to ensure timely updates.

- **Conduct security audits and assessments**

Performing regular security audits and assessments can help identify vulnerabilities and weaknesses in the private blockchain network. This process should include vulnerability assessments, penetration testing, and code reviews to ensure the network's integrity and security.

- **Educate participants on security best practices**

One of the most effective ways to ensure private blockchain security is by educating participants about security best practices. This includes training users on how to recognize and avoid potential threats, as well as providing guidelines for maintaining secure access to the network.

- **Develop and implement incident response plans**

Having a well-defined incident response plan in place is crucial for quickly identifying, containing, and resolving security breaches. This plan should outline the roles and responsibilities of the incident response team, as well as the steps to take in the event of a security breach.

- **Monitor and analyze network activity**

Continuous monitoring and analysis of network activity can help detect and prevent potential security threats. This includes monitoring network traffic, user access logs, and other relevant data to identify any unusual or suspicious activity.

- **Implement data encryption and secure storage**

Encrypting sensitive data both in transit and at rest is essential for maintaining data privacy in a private blockchain. Organizations should also ensure that data is securely stored, with regular backups and disaster recovery plans in place.

Security Measures for Protecting Private Blockchains

Here is the list of measures to protect private blockchains:

- **Access control and identity management:** Implement strict access control policies and node identity management to prevent unauthorized access to the network and its resources.
- **Smart contract audits:** Conduct regular audits and code reviews of smart contracts to identify and fix potential vulnerabilities.

- **Proper configuration:** Ensure correct configuration of endorsement policies, privacy settings, and consensus mechanisms to avoid potential security issues.
- **Monitoring and incident response:** Implement a robust monitoring and incident response system to detect and mitigate potential threats quickly.

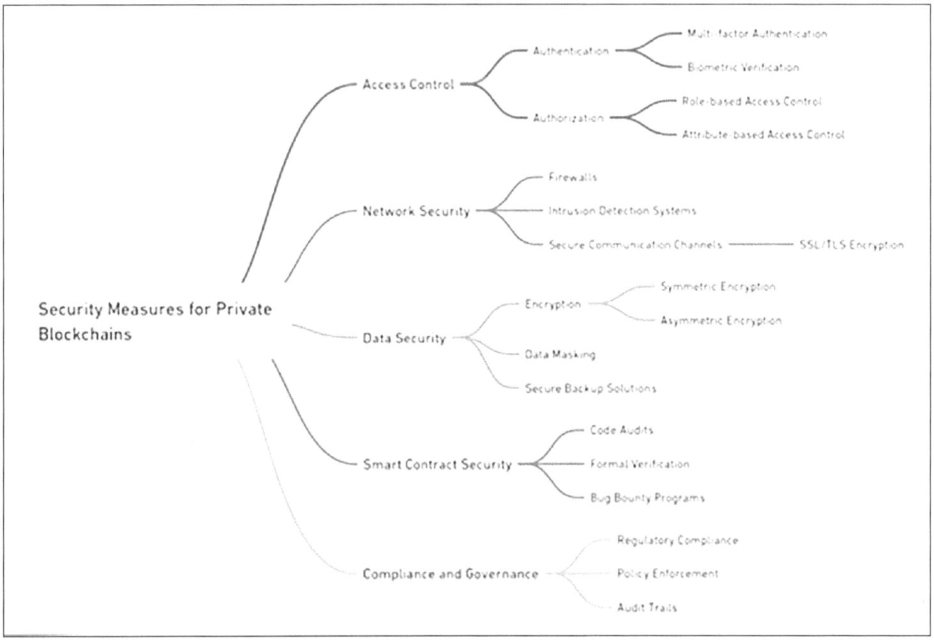

***Figure 4.2**: Security measures for private blockchain*

Best Practices for Maintaining Permissioned Blockchain Security

The following explains how to maintain permissioned blockchain security:

- **Choose a suitable consensus mechanism:** Select a consensus mechanism that best fits your private blockchain's requirements and minimizes the risk of potential attacks.
- **Encryption and data protection:** Use strong encryption algorithms to protect sensitive data and maintain the confidentiality of private transactions.
- **Regular software updates:** Keep your private blockchain software up-to-date to ensure you have the latest security patches and features.
- **Distributed architecture:** Maintain a decentralized network with a

distributed authority to reduce the risk of single points of failure and centralization.

- **Employee training and awareness:** Provide regular security training and awareness programs for your team members to help them identify potential security threats and follow best practices.
- **Third-party security assessments:** Periodically engage external security experts to perform audits and assessments of your private blockchain system, which can help identify potential vulnerabilities and weaknesses.

Learning from Private Blockchain Security Breaches: Key Takeaways

Understanding the risks associated with private blockchain security breaches and the lessons learned from previous incidents can help you better protect your permissioned blockchain network. Here are some key takeaways:

- **No system is immune to security breaches:** Even private blockchains with robust security features can fall victim to attacks. Continuous monitoring and proactive security measures are essential.
- **Human error plays a significant role:** Many security breaches are the result of human error, such as misconfiguration or improper access control. Implementing strict policies and procedures can help mitigate these risks.
- **Stay informed about the latest threats:** As the blockchain ecosystem evolves, new threats and vulnerabilities emerge. Stay informed about the latest security trends and developments to protect your private blockchain network effectively.

By implementing best practices and learning from past security incidents, you can significantly reduce the likelihood of security breaches in your private blockchain network. With a proactive approach to security and risk management, you can build a more resilient and secure permissioned blockchain system that meets the needs of your organization.

Common Security Threats in Private Blockchains

Private blockchains, while offering more control and privacy than public blockchains, are not immune to security threats. This section will discuss the most common security threats faced by private blockchains and the potential consequences of these threats. By understanding the risks and implementing effective security measures, organizations can protect their private blockchain networks from malicious attacks and vulnerabilities.

- **Insider attacks**

Insider attacks are one of the most significant security threats faced by private blockchains. These attacks occur when an authorized participant abuses their access privileges to compromise the network. Insider attacks can involve stealing confidential data, tampering with transactions, or sabotaging the network's infrastructure.

- **Collusion**

Collusion is another common security threat in private blockchains, where multiple participants conspire to undermine the network's integrity. This can involve manipulating transactions or the consensus process to gain unfair advantages, such as double-spending or prioritizing certain transactions over others.

- **Unauthorized access**

Unauthorized access to a private blockchain network can result from weak access control measures or successful phishing attacks. Attackers who gain unauthorized access can potentially steal sensitive data, tamper with transactions, or compromise the network's infrastructure.

- **Vulnerabilities in consensus mechanisms**

Private blockchains often use different consensus mechanisms than public blockchains, such as Practical Byzantine Fault Tolerance (PBFT) or Delegated Proof of Stake (DPoS). These mechanisms can be susceptible to various attacks, including Sybil attacks, where an attacker creates multiple fake nodes to manipulate the consensus process, or eclipse attacks, where an attacker controls a target node's network connections to manipulate its view of the blockchain.

- **Smart contract vulnerabilities**

Smart contracts, which are self-executing contracts with the terms of the agreement directly written into code, can be vulnerable to attacks if not properly designed and audited. Common smart contract vulnerabilities include reentrancy attacks, where an attacker repeatedly calls a contract function before its execution is complete, or integer overflow attacks, where an attacker manipulates the contract's arithmetic operations.

- **Data tampering**

Data tampering involves modifying the contents of a block or transaction without proper authorization. This can be achieved through various means, such as exploiting vulnerabilities in the network's architecture or leveraging compromised access credentials. Data tampering can have severe consequences, including financial losses or loss of trust in the blockchain system.

- **Denial of service (DoS) attacks**

DoS attacks involve overwhelming a network with excessive traffic or requests, rendering it unable to process legitimate transactions. In private blockchains, a DoS attack could target specific nodes or infrastructure components, causing significant disruptions to the network' s operations.

Some consequences of security threats in private blockchains are explained:

- **Financial losses**: One of the most immediate consequences of a security breach in a private blockchain is the potential for financial losses. Unauthorized transactions, double-spending, or data theft can result in substantial losses for businesses and organizations.
- **Loss of trust and reputation:** A security breach in a private blockchain can lead to a loss of trust in the network and its participants. This can negatively impact the organization's reputation and potentially result in a loss of clients or customers.
- **Legal and regulatory implications:** Security breaches in private blockchains can also have legal and regulatory implications. Depending on the nature of the breach, organizations may face fines, lawsuits, or increased regulatory scrutiny.

Although private blockchains offer enhanced control, privacy, and efficiency compared to public blockchains, they are still vulnerable to various security threats. Understanding these threats and implementing effective security measures can help organizations protect their private blockchain networks and maintain the integrity of their data.

Security Measures for Private Blockchains

Implementing robust security measures is crucial for maintaining the integrity and reliability of private blockchains. This section will discuss various security measures that can be applied to protect private blockchain networks from common threats and vulnerabilities. By proactively addressing potential risks, organizations can safeguard their blockchain systems and ensure the secure and efficient functioning of their networks.

Access Control and Authentication

In the realm of cybersecurity, safeguarding sensitive data and systems is paramount. Two pivotal mechanisms that stand at the forefront of this defense are Role-Based Access Control (RBAC) and Multi-Factor Authentication (MFA). These strategies play crucial roles in fortifying access control and authentication processes, ensuring that only authorized individuals can access critical resources and data.

- **Role-based access control (RBAC)**

Role-based access control involves assigning specific permissions to users based on their roles within the organization. RBAC ensures that users have access only to the resources necessary for their role, minimizing the potential for unauthorized access and data breaches.

- **Multi-factor authentication (MFA)**

Multi-factor authentication requires users to provide multiple forms of identification before gaining access to the blockchain network. This typically includes something the user knows (for example, a password), something the user has (for example, a hardware token), and something the user is (for example, a biometric identifier). MFA makes it more challenging for attackers to gain unauthorized access to the network.

Encryption and Data Security

In the digital age, ensuring the security and integrity of data as it is stored and transmitted has become a cornerstone of information technology practices. Central to this objective are three key strategies: the implementation of secure communication channels, the application of data encryption, and the adherence to secure key management. Each of these strategies plays a vital role in protecting data, particularly within blockchain networks, where the stakes for security are exceptionally high.

- **Secure communication channels**

Implementing secure communication channels, such as Transport Layer Security (TLS) or Secure Socket Layer (SSL), can protect the confidentiality and integrity of data transmitted between nodes within the blockchain network.

- **Data encryption**

Encrypting data stored on the blockchain ensures that sensitive information is protected from unauthorized access. This can be achieved using various encryption algorithms, such as Advanced Encryption Standard (AES) or RSA.

- **Secure key management**

Properly managing public and private keys is essential for maintaining the security of a private blockchain. Implementing a secure key management system, such as a hardware security module (HSM) or a secure key vault, can help protect cryptographic keys from theft or misuse.

Network and System Security

In the domain of network and system security, especially within blockchain technology, maintaining robust defenses against a myriad of cyber threats is crucial. This security is achieved through a combination of advanced strategies including, network segmentation, the use of firewalls and Intrusion Detection System (IDS) and the regular implementation of security audits and penetration testing. Each of these strategies plays a critical role in fortifying the security framework, ensuring the blockchain network remains resilient against unauthorized access and cyber-attacks.

- **Network segmentation**

Segmenting the blockchain network into separate zones with differing levels of access can help minimize the impact of a security breach. Network segmentation can also limit the potential damage caused by a compromised node or system.

- **Firewall and intrusion detection systems (IDS)**

Implementing firewalls and intrusion detection systems can help protect the private blockchain network from external threats. Firewalls restrict incoming and outgoing network traffic, while IDS monitor the network for malicious activities or policy violations.

- **Regular security audits and penetration testing**

Conducting regular security audits and penetration tests can help organizations identify vulnerabilities and potential attack vectors within their private blockchain networks. By addressing these vulnerabilities, organizations can proactively mitigate security risks. However, neglecting the security of various web2 components within a company can still lead to potential losses for users, even though blockchain technology is designed to ensure trust.

Here's how negligence of security in web2 components can impact users, despite the trust-enhancing features of blockchain:

- **User Data Breaches:** Companies often store sensitive user data on centralized servers, which are susceptible to data breaches if not properly secured. Even if a blockchain network is secure, if user data on web2 systems is compromised, it can lead to identity theft, fraud, or other forms of misuse, causing financial harm and reputational damage to users.
- **Phishing Attacks:** Neglecting security in web2 communication channels, such as email and social media can expose users to phishing attacks. Cybercriminals can impersonate legitimate entities, tricking users into revealing their private keys or other confidential information. Once compromised, blockchain's trust can be undermined as attackers gain unauthorized access to users' assets.
- **Smart Contract Vulnerabilities:** While blockchain technology itself may be secure, the smart contracts deployed on the blockchain can have vulnerabilities. If companies fail to conduct thorough code audits and security testing for these contracts, they may be exploited, resulting in financial losses for users who trust the contracts' execution.
- **Social Engineering Attacks:** Users may be targeted through social engineering attacks on web2 platforms. Attackers can manipulate users into taking actions on the blockchain network that compromise their assets or transactions, even if the blockchain itself remains secure.
- **Regulatory and Legal Risks:** Neglecting regulatory compliance and legal obligations on web2 platforms can lead to legal actions and fines against the company. Such incidents can affect the stability and reputation of the blockchain network, leading users to lose trust in the system.

Smart Contract Security

In the rapidly evolving world of blockchain technology, smart contracts have emerged as a revolutionary tool, automating transactions and agreements in a trustless environment. However, the security of these smart contracts is paramount, as vulnerabilities can lead to significant financial losses and damage to reputation. To mitigate these risks, three key strategies are employed: secure development practices, smart contract auditing, and formal verification. Each of these plays a critical role in ensuring the integrity and security of smart contracts.

- **Secure development practices**

Adopting secure development practices, such as code reviews and static code analysis, can help prevent vulnerabilities in smart contracts. Organizations should also provide security training for developers to ensure they understand common attack vectors and coding best practices.

- **Smart contract auditing**

Regularly auditing smart contracts for vulnerabilities and logic flaws is essential for maintaining the security of private blockchains. Third-party audits can provide an independent assessment of smart contract security and identify potential issues.

- **Formal verification**

Formal verification is a process that uses mathematical techniques to prove the correctness of a smart contract's code. Implementing formal verification can help ensure the security and reliability of smart contracts, reducing the likelihood of vulnerabilities and attacks.

Incident Response Planning

Developing a comprehensive incident response plan is vital for managing security breaches effectively. An incident response plan should include clear roles and responsibilities, communication protocols, and procedures for containing and mitigating security incidents. Regularly reviewing and updating the plan ensures that organizations are prepared to handle security breaches efficiently.

Education and Awareness

Educating employees and stakeholders about the importance of security and best practices can help reduce the likelihood of security breaches in private blockchains. Training should cover topics such as secure coding practices, access control, and incident response procedures. Regular security awareness training can help employees stay up-to-date with the latest threats and mitigation techniques.

Governance and Compliance

In the intricate landscape of private blockchain networks, the establishment of effective governance and adherence to compliance standards play pivotal roles in ensuring operational integrity and security. These aspects are critical not just for the smooth functioning of the blockchain but also for instilling trust among users and stakeholders. Two key strategies in this domain are establishing a governance framework and ensuring compliance with industry standards and regulations.

- **Establishing a governance framework**

Creating a robust governance framework is essential for managing and maintaining the security of a private blockchain network. This framework should define the roles and responsibilities of participants, the consensus mechanism, and the processes for updating and maintaining the network.

- **Compliance with industry standards and regulations**

Ensuring compliance with industry standards and regulations, such as the General Data Protection Regulation (GDPR) and the Payment Card Industry Data Security Standard (PCI DSS), can help organizations manage the security risks associated with private blockchains. Compliance with these standards can also demonstrate a commitment to security and privacy to clients and stakeholders.

Monitoring and Logging

In the ever-evolving landscape of private blockchain networks, ensuring the security and efficiency of these systems is of paramount importance. Two critical components in achieving this are continuous monitoring and logging and log analysis. These strategies are fundamental in detecting, responding to, and mitigating potential security threats, as well as in maintaining the overall health of the blockchain network.

- **Continuous monitoring**

Implementing continuous monitoring of the private blockchain network can help organizations identify and respond to potential security threats. Monitoring should include tracking network activity, node performance, and the status of smart contracts.

- **Logging and log analysis**

Maintaining detailed logs of network activity can help organizations identify potential security issues and investigate incidents. Implementing a centralized logging system can facilitate log analysis and enable organizations to detect patterns or anomalies indicative of security threats.

Disaster Recovery and Backup

In the intricate and dynamic world of private blockchain networks, preparing for the unexpected is not just prudent; it's essential. Two critical strategies that form the backbone of such preparedness are disaster recovery planning and data backup and storage. These measures are instrumental in ensuring the resilience, availability, and continuity of blockchain networks in the face of unforeseen adversities.

- **Disaster recovery planning**

Developing a disaster recovery plan is essential for ensuring the resilience and availability of a private blockchain network. The plan should outline procedures for recovering from various types of disasters, such as hardware failures, data breaches, or natural disasters.

- **Data backup and storage**

Regularly backing up data and securely storing backups offsite can help organizations protect their private blockchain networks from data loss. Implementing a robust data backup and storage strategy can minimize the impact of disasters and ensure the continuity of the network.

Case Studies on Private Blockchain Security

Private blockchain networks, such as Hyperledger Fabric and Quorum, have been praised for their security and privacy features, making them a popular choice for enterprises and organizations looking to implement decentralized solutions. However, as with any technology, private blockchains are not immune to security breaches. In this section, we will explore real-life case studies of private blockchain security breaches, discuss common vulnerabilities, and share best practices to help you mitigate risks and protect your private distributed ledger system.

Analyzing Real-Life Examples of Private Blockchain Attacks

Despite their inherent security features, private blockchains have suffered from various attacks and security incidents. Let's take a closer look at some notable examples of private blockchain security breaches and their consequences.

Permissioned Blockchain Security Incidents

Common vulnerabilities and exploits are explained as follows:

- **Hyperledger Fabric Configuration Vulnerability**

In 2018, researchers identified a vulnerability in Hyperledger Fabric's configuration process that could allow an attacker to bypass the endorsement policy and manipulate the chaincode.

Vulnerability: Misconfiguration of the endorsement policy and improper access control.

Lesson Learned: Ensure proper configuration of endorsement policies and access controls in private blockchains to prevent unauthorized access and manipulation.

- **Quorum Privacy Leak**

In 2020, it was reported that a vulnerability in Quorum's private transaction implementation could result in private transaction data being leaked to unauthorized parties.

Vulnerability: Flaws in private transaction implementation, leading to data leakage.

Lesson Learned: Robust privacy implementations and thorough testing are crucial for maintaining the confidentiality of private transactions in permissioned blockchains.

Consensus Algorithm Exploits: Threats to Decentralized Networks

- **Sybil Attack on Hyperledger Fabric**

In a Sybil attack, a single malicious entity creates multiple fake nodes in the network to gain control over the consensus process. Researchers have demonstrated that Hyperledger Fabric's consensus mechanism, Practical Byzantine Fault Tolerance (PBFT), is potentially vulnerable to Sybil attacks.

Vulnerability: Multiple fake nodes participating in the consensus process.

Lesson Learned: Implement strict node identity management and access control to minimize the risk of Sybil attacks in private blockchain networks.

- **51% Attack on Proof of Authority (PoA) Consensus**

Quorum, which uses a Proof of Authority (PoA) consensus mechanism, can be vulnerable to a 51% attack if a single entity controls the majority of validator nodes.

Vulnerability: Centralization of authority in PoA consensus.

Lesson Learned: Distribute authority across multiple trusted validator nodes to prevent centralization and reduce the risk of a 51% attack.

- **Enterprise Ethereum Case Study: Banco Santander's Bond Issuance**

In September 2019, Banco Santander, a Spanish multinational bank, successfully completed a pilot project to issue a $20 million bond on the Ethereum blockchain. The bank used Enterprise Ethereum to tokenize the bond securely and register it in a permissioned manner on the blockchain.

Vulnerability: Although the pilot project was successful, the bank had to ensure proper access control and data confidentiality in the Ethereum private network, as Ethereum was originally designed for public use.

Lesson Learned: Leveraging the benefits of Enterprise Ethereum requires implementing strict access control, identity management, and data confidentiality measures in the private network.

- **Hyperledger Fabric Case Study: IBM and Maersk's TradeLens Platform**

In 2018, IBM and Maersk, a global shipping company, launched TradeLens, a global supply chain platform based on Hyperledger Fabric. The platform aimed to streamline and secure international trade by digitizing and sharing shipment information among supply chain participants.

Vulnerability: Ensuring the scalability and resilience of the Hyperledger Fabric-based platform to handle a vast amount of data from different supply chain parties.

Lesson Learned: Implementing a modular and scalable architecture is crucial for handling large-scale, data-intensive applications on private blockchain platforms like Hyperledger Fabric.

- **Corda Case Study: Italian Banking Association's Spunta Project**

In 2020, the Italian Banking Association (ABI) launched the Spunta Project, a Corda-based platform for interbank reconciliation. The platform aimed to streamline the reconciliation process, reduce errors and discrepancies, and improve communication among banks.

Vulnerability: Ensuring that the platform's access control mechanisms and firewall features can effectively protect sensitive financial data and transactions.

Lesson Learned: The importance of robust access control and security measures in private blockchain platforms, especially in the financial sector, cannot be overstated.

- **Ripple Case Study: American Express and Santander's Cross-Border Payment Solution**

In 2017, American Express and Banco Santander partnered with Ripple to develop a cross-border payment solution using Ripple's blockchain technology. The solution aimed to offer faster, cheaper, and more transparent international payment services for their customers.

Vulnerability: Ensuring that the Ripple-based solution could handle high transaction volumes and maintain the necessary security and privacy levels.

Lesson Learned: Ripple's low transaction costs and fast processing speeds make it suitable for financial applications, but it's essential to ensure that the platform can handle the required transaction volume and maintain security.

- **Quorum Case Study: JP Morgan's Interbank Information Network (IIN)**

In 2018, JP Morgan launched the Interbank Information Network (IIN), a Quorum-based platform designed to minimize friction in the global payment process. The platform aimed to enable banks to exchange payment-related information in real-time, reducing delays and errors in cross-border transactions.

Vulnerability: Ensuring data privacy and security while maintaining the platform's high transaction speeds and low latency.

Lesson Learned: Quorum's focus on the financial sector, with its tailored privacy policies and consensus algorithms, makes it an excellent choice for applications requiring high security and transaction speeds. However, it's crucial to ensure that the platform meets the specific requirements of the financial application.

Conclusion

In this chapter, we learned how implementing comprehensive security measures is crucial for protecting private blockchains from various threats and vulnerabilities. By adopting robust access control, encryption, and network security measures, organizations can safeguard their blockchain networks and maintain the integrity of their data. Regular security audits, incident response planning, and ongoing education and awareness initiatives can further strengthen the security posture of private blockchain networks. We also understood that by proactively addressing potential risks, organizations can ensure the secure and efficient functioning of their private blockchain systems.

In the upcoming chapter, we will delve into the intricate world of *Security Challenges in Consortia Blockchains*. Consortia blockchains, which represent a collaborative approach involving multiple organizations, come with their unique set of security considerations. This chapter aims to shed light on the specific challenges faced in maintaining the integrity and security of these collaborative networks. We will explore how the shared governance models of consortia blockchains impact their vulnerability to security threats, the balancing act between transparency and privacy, and the complexities of managing consensus among diverse entities with potentially varying security protocols. This comprehensive examination will provide valuable insights into the nuanced security landscape of consortia blockchains, offering strategies and best practices for navigating these challenges effectively.

CHAPTER 5

Security Challenges in Consortia Blockchains

Introduction

Consortia blockchains have emerged as a compelling solution for businesses seeking to leverage the potential of distributed ledger technology while maintaining a controlled environment. By enabling a group of organizations to collaborate and share data in a transparent, tamper-proof, and efficient manner, consortia blockchains have found applications in various industries, including finance, supply chain management, and healthcare. However, as with any technology, ensuring the security of these systems is of paramount importance.

In this rapidly evolving digital landscape, consortia blockchains face a unique set of security challenges that stem from their hybrid nature. While they inherit some of the security properties of public blockchains, such as cryptographic protection and consensus mechanisms, they also need to address the risks associated with private, permissioned networks. These security challenges, if not effectively managed, can lead to significant consequences such as data breaches, financial losses, and reputational damage.

The aim of this chapter is to provide a comprehensive understanding of the security challenges faced by consortia blockchains and the various security measures that can be implemented to protect against these threats. The chapter is structured into five main sections:

- **Consortia Blockchain Security Overview:** This section presents the foundational concepts of blockchain technology and the unique features of consortia blockchains, setting the stage for understanding their security requirements and potential attack vectors.

- **Common Security Threats in Consortia Blockchains**: This section delves into the various security threats that consortia blockchains face, explaining each threat in detail and discussing its potential impact on the system.
- **Security Measures for Consortia Blockchains**: This section explores a range of security measures that can be implemented to protect consortia blockchains from security threats, including network-level, cryptographic, consensus-based, and application-level security measures.
- **Case Studies on Consortia Blockchain Security Breaches**: This section presents real-world case studies of security breaches in consortia blockchains, highlighting the lessons learned from each incident and emphasizing the importance of robust security measures.

By the end of this chapter, readers will have a thorough understanding of the security challenges faced by consortia blockchains and the various security measures that can be implemented to address them. This knowledge will be invaluable for consortia blockchain developers, architects, and decision-makers as they design and implement secure blockchain solutions.

Structure

In this chapter, the following topics will be covered:

- Principles of Blockchain Technology
- Consortia Blockchain Security Overview
- Common Security Threats in Consortia Blockchains
- Security Measures for Consortia Blockchains
- Case studies on Consortia Blockchain Security Breaches

Principles of Blockchain Technology

Blockchain technology is a decentralized, distributed ledger system that enables multiple parties to maintain a shared record of transactions. The core principles of blockchain technology are:

- **Decentralization:** Blockchain systems are distributed across a network of nodes, ensuring that no single entity has complete control over the system. This eliminates the need for a central authority and reduces the risk of a single point of failure.

- **Immutability:** Transactions recorded on the blockchain are cryptographically secured and cannot be altered once added to the ledger. This ensures the integrity and reliability of the data stored on the blockchain.
- **Consensus**: In a blockchain network, all participating nodes must agree on the validity of transactions before they are added to the ledger. This is achieved through consensus mechanisms, such as Proof of Work (PoW) or Proof of Stake (PoS), which prevent malicious actors from manipulating the data on the blockchain.
- **Transparency**: All transactions on the blockchain are publicly available and can be audited by any participant in the network, promoting trust and accountability among users.

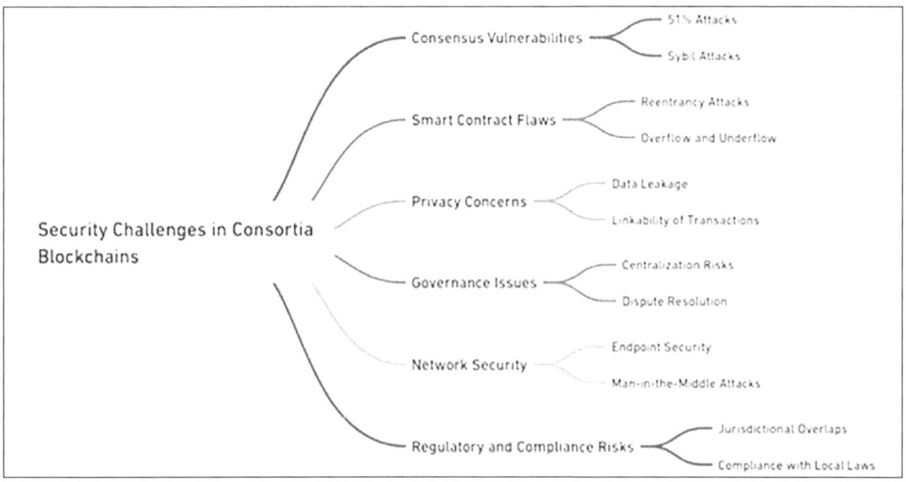

Figure 5.1*: Security Challenges in Consortia Blockchains*

Consortia Blockchain Security Overview

This section provides a comprehensive understanding of consortia blockchain security. It begins by explaining the fundamental principles of blockchain technology and the unique features of consortia blockchains. The section then discusses the key security requirements and potential attack vectors, providing the foundation for understanding the security challenges faced by consortia blockchains.

Features of Consortia Blockchains

Consortia blockchains, also known as permissioned blockchains, are a hybrid between public and private blockchains. They possess some unique features that differentiate them from their public and private counterparts. In this section, we will discuss the following key features in detail:

- Access Control
- Governance
- Scalability
- Privacy

Access Control

One of the main features of consortia blockchains is access control. Unlike public blockchains, which allow anyone to join and participate in the network, consortia blockchains restrict access to a predetermined group of participants. These participants must be authenticated and authorized to join the network and interact with the blockchain. Access control mechanisms in consortia blockchains serve several purposes:

- **Identity Verification**: Ensuring that only legitimate, known entities can join the network, helps to prevent malicious actors from infiltrating the system.
- **Role-Based Access**: Assigning roles to participants based on their function within the network, enabling fine-grained control over the resources and actions each participant can access.
- **Trust Management**: Establishing trust among participants, as they can be certain that other members of the network have also been authenticated and authorized.
- **Regulatory Compliance:** Ensuring that the network complies with relevant laws and regulations, such as data protection and privacy regulations, by controlling access to sensitive information.

Governance

Governance is another critical feature of consortia blockchains. Unlike public blockchains, which often have decentralized and community-driven governance structures, consortia blockchains have a defined governance structure that determines the rules and policies for network participation, consensus mechanisms, and data sharing. This allows for a more controlled and efficient decision-making process. Key aspects of governance in consortia blockchains include:

- **Decision-making**: Establishing a process for making decisions regarding the network's rules, policies, and updates, which may involve voting mechanisms or designated decision-making entities.

- **Consensus mechanisms**: Selecting and implementing appropriate consensus mechanisms tailored to the requirements of the consortia, such as Practical Byzantine fault tolerance (PBFT) or Raft-based consensus algorithms.
- **Network upgrades**: Coordinating upgrades and updates to the blockchain network, ensuring that all participants are aware of and prepared for any changes.
- **Dispute resolution**: Implementing mechanisms to resolve disputes or conflicts among network participants, promoting a stable and cooperative environment.

Scalability

Scalability is an essential feature of consortia blockchains, as it directly impacts the performance and efficiency of the network. Consortia blockchains can achieve higher transaction throughput and reduced latency compared to public blockchains, as they do not require the same level of resource-intensive consensus mechanisms. Scalability improvements in consortia blockchains can be achieved through several methods:

- **Optimized Consensus Mechanisms**: Implementing consensus algorithms that require less computational power and communication overhead, such as PBFT or Raft.
- **Off-Chain Transactions**: Processing certain transactions off the main blockchain, reducing the load on the network and allowing for faster transaction processing.
- **Sharding:** Dividing the network into smaller, parallel subnetworks (shards) that can process transactions independently, increasing overall throughput.
- **Layer 2 Solutions**: Utilizing additional layers built on top of the base blockchain protocol to handle specific functions, such as payment channels or smart contract execution, which can improve performance and scalability.

Privacy

While maintaining a certain level of transparency, consortia blockchains can implement privacy-preserving mechanisms that restrict the visibility of transaction data to authorized participants only, thereby protecting sensitive information. Privacy features in consortia blockchains can be achieved through various methods:

- **Permissioned Data Access**: Implementing access control mechanisms that grant visibility to transaction data based on predefined roles or permissions, ensuring that sensitive information is disclosed only to authorized participants.
- **Confidential Transactions**: Employing cryptographic techniques, such as zero-knowledge proofs or homomorphic encryption, that allow participants to validate transactions without revealing the actual transaction data, thereby preserving confidentiality.
- **Private Channels**: Creating private communication channels between specific participants within the network, allowing them to share data securely without exposing it to the entire network.
- **Data Masking and Anonymization**: Using data masking or anonymization techniques to obfuscate sensitive information in the transaction data, making it difficult for unauthorized parties to link the data to specific individuals or entities.

Consortia blockchains offer a range of unique features that differentiate them from public and private blockchains. These features, such as access control, governance, scalability, and privacy, are designed to cater to the specific needs of organizations collaborating within a consortium. Understanding these features and their implications is crucial for the successful implementation and management of consortia blockchain networks.

Security Requirements for Consortia Blockchains

Given the unique features and potential use cases of consortia blockchains, it is crucial to address a specific set of security requirements to ensure the integrity, confidentiality, and availability of the system. In this section, we will discuss the following key security requirements for consortia blockchains:

- Data confidentiality
- Data integrity
- Availability
- Authentication and authorization
- Non-repudiation
- Resilience

- **Data confidentiality**

Data confidentiality is a primary security requirement for consortia blockchains, as sensitive information must be accessible only to authorized participants. Several techniques can be employed to ensure data confidentiality:

- **Encryption:** Applying strong encryption algorithms to transaction data, ensuring that only participants with the appropriate cryptographic keys can access the information.
- **Private Channels**: Establishing secure communication channels between participants for sharing sensitive data without exposing it to the entire network.
- **Access Control Mechanisms**: Implementing role-based or attribute-based access control policies to restrict access to transaction data based on predefined roles or attributes of the participants.
- **Confidential Smart Contracts**: Designing smart contracts that process sensitive data in a confidential manner, using cryptographic techniques such as zero-knowledge proofs to ensure data privacy.

- **Data integrity**

Ensuring data integrity is vital for consortia blockchains, as the reliability and consistency of the data stored on the blockchain must be maintained. To guarantee data integrity, consortia blockchains should consider the following measures:

- **Cryptographic Hash Functions:** Employing secure hash functions to generate unique identifiers for each block in the blockchain, ensuring that any alteration to the data would result in a different hash and be easily detectable.
- **Consensus Mechanisms**: Utilizing consensus algorithms that require participants to agree on the validity of transactions before they are added to the blockchain, making it difficult for an attacker to manipulate the data.
- **Digital Signatures**: Using digital signatures to certify the authenticity and integrity of the data, ensuring that any unauthorized modification of the data can be detected and traced back to the responsible party.
- **Regular Audits**: Conducting periodic audits of the blockchain data to identify and rectify any discrepancies or inconsistencies in the data.

- **Availability**

Maintaining the continuous operation of the blockchain network is critical for consortia blockchains, as downtime or service disruptions can have significant consequences. To ensure availability, consortia blockchains should implement the following strategies:

- **Redundancy**: Distributing the blockchain data across multiple nodes in the network, ensuring that no single point of failure exists and that the system can continue to operate even if some nodes become unavailable.
- **Load Balancing**: Implementing load balancing techniques to distribute the workload evenly across the network nodes, preventing any single node from becoming a bottleneck and potentially causing service disruptions.
- **Fault Tolerance**: Designing the system to be resilient to failures, such as hardware malfunctions or network issues, and ensuring that the blockchain can continue to operate even in the presence of such failures.
- **Monitoring and Alerting**: Continuously monitoring the network's health and performance, and implementing alerting mechanisms to notify administrators of any potential issues or threats that could impact availability.

- **Authentication and authorization**

Verifying the identity of participants and controlling their access to resources within the network is crucial for consortia blockchains. To achieve robust authentication and authorization, consortia blockchains should consider:

- Digital certificates: Issuing digital certificates to participants, which serve as proof of their identity and can be used to authenticate them within the network.
- Multi-factor authentication: Implementing multi-factor authentication methods that require participants to provide multiple pieces of evidence to verify their identity, such as a combination of passwords, digital certificates, or biometric data.
- Role-based access control (RBAC): Defining roles within the consortium and assigning appropriate access permissions to each role, ensuring that participants can only access the resources and perform the actions allowed by their role.
- Attribute-based access control (ABAC): Controlling access to resources based on the attributes of the participants, such as their job function or organizational affiliation, allowing for more granular and dynamic access control.

- **Non-repudiation**

Non-repudiation is a critical security requirement for consortia blockchains, as it ensures that participants cannot deny their involvement in a transaction once it has been recorded on the blockchain. To achieve non-repudiation, consortia blockchains should employ the following techniques:

- **Digital signatures**: Requiring participants to sign their transactions with their private keys, ensuring that the transaction can be linked to the signer and that the signer cannot deny their involvement.
- **Timestamping:** Recording the time at which a transaction was added to the blockchain, providing a chronological record of events and making it difficult for participants to deny their involvement in past transactions.
- **Immutable records**: Leveraging the immutability of blockchain technology to ensure that once a transaction has been recorded on the blockchain, it cannot be altered or deleted, providing a permanent record of each participant's actions.
- **Audit trails**: Maintaining detailed audit trails of all transactions and events within the network, allowing for retrospective analysis and verification of each participant's actions.

- **Resilience**

Protecting the blockchain network against various attacks and ensuring its ability to recover from potential security breaches is essential for consortia blockchains. To achieve resilience, consortia blockchains should implement the following measures:

- **Intrusion detection and prevention systems (IDPS)**: Deploying IDPS solutions to monitor the network for signs of malicious activity, and taking appropriate action to block or mitigate such activity.
- **Regular security assessments**: Conducting periodic security assessments, such as penetration testing and vulnerability scanning, to identify and address potential weaknesses in the system.
- **Incident response planning**: Establishing a robust incident response plan that outlines the steps to be taken in the event of a security breach, ensuring that the consortium can quickly respond to and recover from any potential threats.
- **Security awareness training**: Providing regular security awareness training to consortium participants, ensuring that they are aware of potential threats and best practices for maintaining the security of the network.

Addressing these security requirements – data confidentiality, data integrity, availability, authentication and authorization, non-repudiation, and resilience – is crucial for the successful implementation and operation of consortia blockchains.

By understanding these requirements and implementing appropriate security measures, consortium members can work together in a secure, reliable, and efficient environment.

Before we delve into the specific attack vectors that consortia blockchains face, it is worth noting how they differ from traditional public blockchains in terms of security. Public blockchains, such as Bitcoin or Ethereum, rely on a large and decentralized network of nodes to validate transactions and maintain consensus. This makes them resilient to malicious attacks, as an attacker would need to control more than half of the network's computing power to compromise the system. However, public blockchains also face scalability and performance issues, as every node has to store and process the entire history of transactions.

Consortia blockchains, on the other hand, are designed to operate within a smaller and more trusted network of participants, who share a common goal and interest. This allows them to achieve higher throughput and lower latency, as well as customize the rules and governance of the network. However, consortia blockchains also face some unique security challenges, as they have to balance between the trust and privacy of the participants, as well as the integrity and availability of the data. Moreover, consortia blockchains may be more vulnerable to insider attacks, collusion, or corruption, as the number and diversity of nodes is limited. Therefore, consortia blockchains need to implement adequate security measures and mechanisms to prevent and mitigate potential security threats.

Attack Vectors in Consortia Blockchains

In this section, we will explore various security threats that consortia blockchains face, along with their potential impact on the system. Understanding these attack vectors and their implications is crucial for the successful implementation and management of consortia blockchain networks. The section is divided into the following sub-sections:

- **Sybil attacks**

In a Sybil attack, a malicious actor creates multiple fake identities or nodes within the network to subvert the consensus process, manipulate voting, or launch other attacks. Although consortia blockchains' access control mechanisms can mitigate this risk to a large extent, it is still essential to monitor for potential Sybil attacks. Examples of mitigation techniques include:

  - Robust identity verification during the onboarding process to prevent unauthorized entities from joining the network.

  - Implementing reputation systems that allow network participants to rate each other, making it more difficult for Sybil attackers to gain influence within the network.

- **Eclipse attacks**

Eclipse attacks occur when a malicious actor takes control of a victim's connections to the network, isolating them from the rest of the network and feeding them false information. In a consortium blockchain, this could lead to incorrect decision-making or fraudulent transactions. Mitigation strategies include:

  - Regularly monitoring and analyzing network connections to detect anomalies and signs of eclipse attacks.
  - Encouraging participants to establish diverse and redundant connections to other nodes in the network, reducing the likelihood of isolation.

- **Double spending attacks**

Double spending attacks involve a malicious actor attempting to spend the same cryptocurrency or digital asset twice, exploiting the decentralized nature of blockchain networks. While this is more prevalent in public blockchains, consortia blockchains can still be vulnerable if their consensus mechanisms are compromised. Mitigation approaches include:

  - Employing robust consensus algorithms that make it difficult for an attacker to control the decision-making process.
  - Implementing transaction validation mechanisms that prevent the same asset from being spent multiple times.

- **Consensus manipulation attacks**

In consensus manipulation attacks, an attacker gains control over a significant portion of the network nodes or resources to manipulate the consensus process, potentially leading to fraudulent transactions or network disruption. To mitigate consensus manipulation attacks, consortia blockchains can:

  - Use consensus algorithms that require a higher threshold of agreement among nodes, making it more difficult for an attacker to gain control.
  - Regularly monitor network nodes and resources to identify potential signs of consensus manipulation attacks.

- **Smart contract vulnerabilities**

Smart contracts are self-executing contracts with the terms of the agreement directly written into code. However, they may contain vulnerabilities or flaws that can be exploited by attackers. Examples of smart contract vulnerabilities in consortia blockchains include the following:

- **Reentrancy Attacks**: An attacker exploits a vulnerable smart contract to repeatedly call a function before the contract's state is updated, resulting in unintended consequences.
- **Integer Overflow and Underflow**: Errors in smart contract code that can lead to unexpected behavior and potential manipulation of contract variables.

To mitigate smart contract vulnerabilities, consortia blockchains can:

- Implement secure coding practices and conduct thorough code reviews before deploying smart contracts.
- Use formal verification techniques to validate the correctness and security of smart contract code.

- **Data tampering and forgery**

Data tampering and forgery involve unauthorized modification or creation of data within the blockchain. This could lead to incorrect decision-making, financial losses, or reputational damage for the consortium members. To mitigate data tampering and forgery risks, consortia blockchains can:

- Use cryptographic hashing and digital signatures to ensure data integrity and prevent unauthorized modifications.
- Implement access control mechanisms to restrict the ability to create or modify data to authorized participants only.

- **Denial of service (DoS) attacks**

DoS attacks aim to disrupt the normal operation of the blockchain network by overwhelming nodes or services with a flood of requests, resulting in decreased performance or service outages. In a consortium blockchain, this could lead to transaction delays or disruptions in the decision-making process. To mitigate DoS attacks, consortia blockchains can:

- Implement rate-limiting and throttling mechanisms to prevent individual nodes from consuming excessive network resources.
- Utilize load balancing and redundancy techniques to distribute the workload evenly across the network and maintain availability during an attack.

- **Insider threats**

Insider threats refer to security breaches that originate from within the consortium, such as employees or members with authorized access to the network. Insider threats can be particularly dangerous, as they often involve the misuse of legitimate access privileges. To mitigate insider threats in consortia blockchains, organizations can:

  - Implement the principle of least privilege, ensuring that participants have access only to the resources necessary for their role.
  - Conduct regular security audits and monitoring to detect potential signs of insider threats, such as unusual patterns of access or data transfers.

- **Phishing and social engineering attacks**

Phishing and social engineering attacks involve the manipulation of individuals within the consortium to gain unauthorized access or information. These attacks can lead to security breaches, data leaks, or financial losses. To mitigate phishing and social engineering attacks in consortia blockchains, organizations can:

  - Provide regular security awareness training for consortium members, focusing on the identification and prevention of phishing and social engineering attacks.
  - Implement strong authentication and authorization mechanisms to prevent unauthorized access, even if an attacker obtains valid credentials through phishing or social engineering.

- **Other security threats**

In addition to the specific threats outlined above, consortia blockchains can also face other security challenges, such as:

  - **Vulnerabilities in underlying infrastructure or software**: Ensuring that the infrastructure and software components used in the consortium blockchain are secure and up-to-date is critical for overall security.
  - **Legal and regulatory compliance**: Adhering to relevant data protection and privacy regulations, such as GDPR or HIPAA, is crucial for avoiding potential legal and financial penalties.

Understanding the various attack vectors that consortia blockchains face and implementing appropriate security measures to mitigate these risks is crucial for the successful operation of consortium networks. By proactively addressing these threats, consortium members can work together in a secure, reliable, and efficient environment.

Security Measures for Consortia Blockchains

This section explores various security measures that can be implemented to protect consortia blockchains from security threats. It covers a range of strategies and techniques, including network-level, cryptographic, consensus-based, and application-level security measures. Each subsection provides specific examples to help readers understand and apply these measures in their consortium blockchain networks.

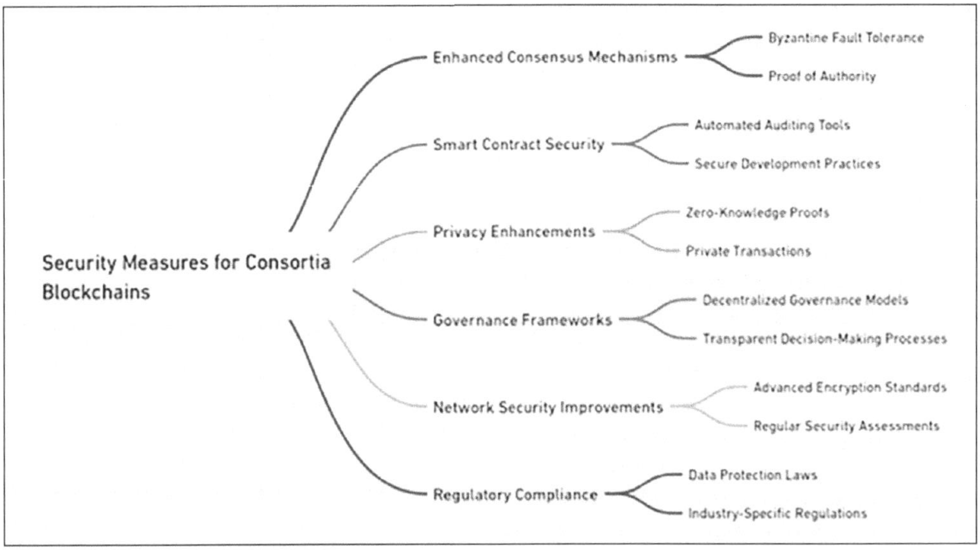

Figure 5.2: *Security Measures for Consortia Blockchains*

Network-level Security Measures

Network-level security measures focus on protecting the consortium blockchain network infrastructure from attacks and vulnerabilities. Some of the key network-level security measures include:

- **Firewall configuration**: Implementing properly configured firewalls to protect nodes and services from unauthorized access and potential attacks. For example, firewall rules can be set up to allow access only from known IP addresses of consortium members.
- **Intrusion detection and prevention systems (IDPS):** Deploying IDPS solutions to monitor the network for signs of malicious activity, such as unauthorized access or attempts to exploit vulnerabilities, and take appropriate action to block or mitigate the threats.

- **Virtual private networks (VPNs):** Establishing VPNs for secure communication between consortium members, ensuring that data transmitted between nodes is encrypted and protected from eavesdropping or man-in-the-middle attacks.
- **Network Segmentation:** Dividing the network into smaller, isolated segments to limit the potential impact of an attack or security breach, preventing attackers from gaining access to the entire network infrastructure.

Cryptographic Security Measures

Cryptography plays a vital role in securing consortium blockchain networks. Some of the key cryptographic security measures include:

- **Public key infrastructure (PKI):** Implementing a PKI to manage the secure distribution and validation of public keys, digital certificates, and digital signatures, ensuring secure communication and transactions within the consortium network.
- **Secure hashing algorithms:** Using secure and up-to-date hashing algorithms, such as SHA-256 or SHA-3, to ensure data integrity and verify the authenticity of transactions.
- **Encryption:** Employing encryption algorithms like AES or RSA to protect sensitive data stored on the blockchain, ensuring that only authorized participants can access and decrypt the data.

Consensus-based Security Measures

Consensus-based security measures focus on securing the consensus process to prevent attacks that target the decision-making process within the consortium network. Some of the key consensus-based security measures include:

- **Byzantine Fault Tolerance (BFT):** Implementing BFT-based consensus algorithms, such as Practical Byzantine Fault Tolerance (PBFT) or Tendermint, to ensure that the network can continue to operate correctly even in the presence of a certain number of malicious or faulty nodes.
- **Proof of Authority (PoA):** Using PoA consensus mechanisms, where a limited number of trusted and known nodes, called authorities or validators, are responsible for validating and confirming transactions, reducing the risk of consensus manipulation attacks.
- **Multi-Signature Transactions:** Requiring multiple signatures from different consortium members to approve a transaction, ensuring that no single member can unilaterally manipulate the network or execute fraudulent transactions.

Smart Contract Security Measures

Smart contract security measures focus on ensuring that the self-executing contracts deployed on consortium blockchains are secure and free from vulnerabilities. Key smart contract security measures include:

- **Secure Coding Practices:** Developing smart contracts using secure coding practices, such as following established coding standards and guidelines, to minimize the risk of vulnerabilities and exploits.
- **Code Review and Auditing:** Conducting thorough code reviews and audits to identify and address potential vulnerabilities in smart contracts before deployment.
- **Formal Verification:** Using formal verification techniques to validate the correctness and security of smart contract code, ensuring that the contract behaves as intended and is free from vulnerabilities.
- **Bug Bounty Programs:** Establishing bug bounty programs to encourage security researchers and developers to identify and report vulnerabilities in smart contracts, rewarding them for their efforts and helping to improve overall security.

Data Integrity Measures

Data integrity measures aim to ensure that the data stored on the consortium blockchain is accurate, consistent, and protected from unauthorized modifications. Some of the key data integrity measures include:

- **Cryptographic hashing:** Utilizing cryptographic hashing functions to create a unique and secure representation of the data, ensuring that even minor changes to the data result in a completely different hash value, making tampering easily detectable.
- **Merkle trees:** Employing Merkle trees to organize and validate large sets of data efficiently, allowing consortium members to quickly verify the integrity of data without needing to download the entire dataset.
- **Immutable storage:** Storing data in a manner that prevents unauthorized modifications or deletions, ensuring the long-term integrity and reliability of the data stored on the consortium blockchain.

Access Control and Authentication Measures

Access control and authentication measures are crucial for restricting access to consortium blockchain networks and resources to authorized participants only. Key access control and authentication measures include:

- **Identity and Access Management (IAM):** Implementing IAM systems to manage the lifecycle of digital identities, ensuring that consortium members can be authenticated and authorized to access the network and its resources according to their roles and permissions.
- **Multi-Factor Authentication (MFA):** Employing MFA mechanisms, such as hardware tokens, biometrics, or one-time passwords, to provide an additional layer of security for user authentication, reducing the risk of unauthorized access due to compromised credentials.
- **Role-Based Access Control (RBAC):** Using RBAC models to assign permissions to users based on their roles within the consortium, ensuring that they have access only to the resources necessary for their roles and limiting the potential impact of insider threats.

Security Audits and Best Practices

Regular security audits and adherence to best practices are essential for maintaining the overall security of consortium blockchain networks. Key security audit and best practice measures include:

- **Penetration Testing:** Conducting regular penetration tests to identify potential vulnerabilities and weaknesses in the consortium network's infrastructure, software, and configurations, allowing for proactive remediation of any issues discovered.
- **Security Monitoring and Incident Response**: Implementing continuous security monitoring and establishing an incident response plan to ensure the timely detection, containment, and remediation of security incidents and breaches.
- **Compliance and Regulatory Adherence:** Ensuring that consortium blockchain networks comply with relevant data protection and privacy regulations, such as GDPR, HIPAA, or CCPA, to avoid potential legal and financial penalties.

Implementing a combination of network-level, cryptographic, consensus-based, and application-level security measures is critical for protecting consortium blockchains from security threats. Regular security audits and adherence to best practices further enhance the security posture of these networks, enabling consortium members to collaborate securely and efficiently.

Case Studies on Consortia Blockchain Security Breaches

This section presents real-world case studies of security breaches in consortia blockchains. It highlights the lessons learned from each incident, providing readers with valuable insights into the consequences of security failures and the importance of implementing robust security measures.

Case Study 1: Quorum Consortium Blockchain Security Breach

In 2018, a vulnerability was discovered in Quorum, a permissioned blockchain platform based on Ethereum, used by several financial institutions and enterprises for conducting transactions and sharing information. The vulnerability allowed an attacker to crash any Quorum node by sending a specially crafted packet to it.

- **Lessons learned:**
    - Regular security audits and vulnerability assessments are crucial for identifying and addressing potential weaknesses in consortium blockchain platforms.
    - Implementing robust network security measures, such as firewalls and intrusion detection systems, can help mitigate the risk of similar attacks.
    - Promptly applying patches and updates to consortium blockchain platforms is essential to maintain security and protect against known vulnerabilities.

Case Study 2: R3 Corda Consortium Blockchain Security Breach

In 2019, a security researcher discovered a vulnerability in R3's Corda, a popular consortium blockchain platform used by banks and other financial institutions for secure transactions and data sharing. The vulnerability allowed an attacker to gain unauthorized access to sensitive data by exploiting a flaw in the platform's access control mechanism.

- **Lessons learned:**
    - Ensuring proper implementation of access control mechanisms is crucial for protecting sensitive data in consortium blockchain networks.

- Regularly reviewing and updating access control policies to keep up with the evolving threat landscape is essential.
- Investing in security awareness training for consortium members can help prevent human errors that may lead to security breaches.

Case Study 3: Hyperledger Fabric Consortium Blockchain Security Breach

In 2020, a security breach occurred in a supply chain consortium that utilized Hyperledger Fabric as its underlying blockchain platform. The breach was attributed to a smart contract vulnerability that allowed an attacker to manipulate the supply chain data, causing financial losses and reputational damage for the consortium members.

- **Lessons learned:**
  - Implementing secure coding practices and thorough code reviews are essential for developing secure smart contracts.
  - Utilizing formal verification and bug bounty programs can help identify and address potential vulnerabilities in smart contracts before deployment.
  - Monitoring and auditing smart contract execution can help detect and mitigate the impact of security breaches.

Case Study 4: B3i Consortium Blockchain Security Breach

In 2021, a security breach occurred in the B3i consortium, which focuses on developing blockchain solutions for the insurance industry. The breach was due to an insider threat, where a rogue employee misused their access privileges to manipulate data and commit fraud.

- **Lessons learned:**
  - Implementing the principle of least privilege and role-based access control is crucial for mitigating the risk of insider threats.
  - Regular security audits and monitoring of user activity can help detect potential signs of insider threats.
  - Establishing a robust incident response plan can help contain and remediate the impact of security breaches.

Case Study 5: Energy Web Chain Consortium Blockchain Security Breach

In 2020, a consortium focused on building blockchain solutions for the energy sector using the Energy Web Chain platform suffered a security breach. The attackers used a phishing attack to gain access to sensitive data and disrupt the operations of the consortium members.

- **Lessons learned:**
  - Providing regular security awareness training to consortium members can help prevent phishing and social engineering attacks.
  - Implementing strong authentication and authorization mechanisms can reduce the risk of unauthorized access due to compromised credentials.
  - Ensuring compliance with data protection and privacy regulations can help minimize the potential legal and financial repercussions of security breaches.

These case studies highlight the importance of implementing robust security measures in consortia blockchain networks. Consortium members should learn from these incidents and invest in proactive security practices, such as regular audits, vulnerability assessments, and security training. Adopting a comprehensive security strategy can help protect consortium blockchains from various threats, ensuring the secure and efficient operation of the network.

Conclusion

In this chapter, we explored the various security challenges faced by consortia blockchains and the measures that can be implemented to protect against these threats. Consortia blockchains, as a hybrid between public and private blockchains, possess unique features, such as access control, governance, scalability, and privacy. These characteristics give rise to specific security requirements and potential attack vectors that need to be addressed to ensure the secure operation of the consortium network.

To conclude, consortium members must recognize and address the security challenges inherent in their blockchain networks. By implementing a combination of network-level, cryptographic, consensus-based, and application-level security measures, consortia blockchains can be safeguarded against various threats. Regular security audits and adherence to best practices further enhance the security posture of these networks, enabling consortium members to collaborate securely and efficiently. Learning from real-world case studies of security breaches in consortia blockchains can provide valuable insights into the consequences of security failures and the importance of maintaining a robust security infrastructure. Ultimately, a proactive approach to security is essential for the long-term success of consortia blockchain networks. In the next chapter, we will learn the security challenges faced by decentralized finance (DeFi) applications, including smart contract vulnerabilities and attacks on decentralized exchanges.

CHAPTER 6

Security Challenges in Decentralized Finance

Introduction

Decentralized Finance (DeFi) has been one of the most transformative developments in the financial industry in recent years. Its exponential growth is a testament to the sector's potential in democratizing access to financial services and enhancing financial inclusion. However, while DeFi offers a host of opportunities, it also comes with its own set of unique security challenges. This chapter aims to provide an overview of DeFi's security landscape and the measures being taken to address its vulnerabilities.

DeFi is a financial ecosystem built on blockchain technologies, particularly Ethereum, that aims to recreate traditional financial systems such as lending, borrowing, trading, and earning interest, but in a decentralized manner. Rather than relying on intermediaries like banks or brokers, DeFi applications use smart contracts to automate financial transactions. As of 2023, the total value locked (TVL) in DeFi applications has exceeded $100 billion, up from less than $1 billion in early 2020, underscoring the significant growth and potential of this sector.

DeFi brings numerous benefits, but security remains a significant challenge. The immutable nature of blockchain leaves smart contracts vulnerable to exploitation, as bugs and vulnerabilities cannot be easily rectified. Complex smart contracts have been targets of attacks, such as the DAO hack in 2016. Decentralized Exchanges (DEXs) face threats like front-running and flash loan attacks. Moreover, phishing and social engineering attacks target DeFi users. To address these challenges, DeFi platforms focus on rigorous testing, third-party audits, security measures like batch auctions, and traditional cybersecurity practices such as multi-factor authentication and bug bounty programs. By prioritizing security, DeFi can realize its potential and gain broader user trust.

Structure

In this chapter, we will discuss the following topics:

- Decentralized Finance Security Overview
- Common Security Threats in Decentralized Finance
- Security Measures for Decentralized Finance
    - Case Studies on Decentralized Finance Security Breaches

Decentralized Finance Security Overview

Decentralized finance (DeFi) is a rapidly evolving ecosystem that aims to revolutionize traditional financial systems by leveraging blockchain technology and smart contracts. While DeFi offers exciting opportunities, it also introduces unique security challenges. The main security concerns in DeFi include smart contract vulnerabilities, hacking attacks, governance risks, and user errors. Smart contract audits, code reviews, and bug bounties are crucial measures to mitigate risks. Additionally, robust identity verification, secure key management, and ongoing security monitoring are essential for protecting user funds and maintaining trust in the DeFi ecosystem. Continuous research, innovation, and collaboration between developers, auditors, and the community are vital to ensure the long-term security and growth of DeFi.

Introducing DeFi and its Growing Importance

Decentralized Finance, more commonly known as DeFi, has emerged as a potent disruptor in the finance world, challenging the very core of traditional financial systems. The central idea behind DeFi is to utilize blockchain technologies, primarily Ethereum, to recreate and redefine financial systems and services such as lending, borrowing, insurance, asset trading, and interest earning. However, unlike traditional systems, DeFi aims to operate in a decentralized, transparent, and permissionless manner, eliminating the need for intermediaries.

Through the use of DeFi applications (dApps), financial services are no longer confined to the hands of banking institutions and other centralized bodies. Instead, power is put back into the hands of individuals. The advantages are manifold - with DeFi, financial transactions can occur round the clock without the need for a central authority's approval. They also offer borderless access, enabling individuals worldwide, including those in unbanked or underbanked regions, to participate in the financial ecosystem.

However, it is not just the ideology of DeFi that's making waves, but the magnitude of its growth. According to data from DeFi Pulse, the total value locked (TVL) in DeFi protocols has seen a meteoric rise from less than $1 billion in early 2020 to over $100 billion by 2023. The TVL, which refers to the amount of assets committed to a DeFi protocol, is a common metric used to measure the growth and popularity of DeFi. This staggering increase in TVL signifies not only the exponential adoption and growth of DeFi applications but also underscores its increasing importance in the financial landscape.

However, it's essential to understand that this rapid growth comes with its own set of challenges, particularly on the security front. As DeFi continues to gain prominence, it's crucial to address these challenges to ensure a robust and secure DeFi ecosystem.

In the following sections, we will delve deeper into the architecture of DeFi, how it differs from traditional finance, and the key security challenges faced by the sector.

DeFi Architecture versus Traditional Finance

Decentralized Finance (DeFi) represents a shift from the centralized structures of traditional finance towards a system that is decentralized, open, and transparent. The architecture of DeFi is significantly different from its traditional counterpart, leveraging public blockchains and smart contracts to automate and facilitate financial transactions. This design offers several advantages, including transparency, trustless interactions, censorship resistance, and enhanced accessibility.

At the heart of DeFi applications, also known as dApps, lies the blockchain - a distributed, immutable ledger of transactions. While multiple blockchains support DeFi, Ethereum has emerged as the most popular choice, owing to its flexibility and its smart contract capabilities. These smart contracts are self-executing contracts where the terms of the agreement are directly written into lines of code. Smart contracts automate the execution of a transaction once predetermined conditions are met, eliminating the need for an intermediary and thereby reducing the likelihood of errors and fraud.

Protocols are a key component of the DeFi architecture. They serve as the building blocks of the DeFi ecosystem, each protocol serving a specific financial function such as lending, borrowing, or asset swapping. Protocols can be layered and composed together, leading to an ecosystem where each protocol interacts with others, an attribute often referred to as 'composability' or 'money legos'. This composability allows for the creation of complex financial products and services that can be built and customized according to individual needs.

Decentralized exchanges (DEXs), lending and borrowing platforms, yield farming platforms, and stablecoins are some of the popular applications within the DeFi ecosystem, each contributing to a vibrant and growing marketplace.

In stark contrast, traditional financial systems rely heavily on intermediaries such as banks, brokers, insurance companies, and other financial institutions to facilitate transactions. These intermediaries play a crucial role in maintaining trust in the system, verifying transactions, and enforcing contracts. However, this centrality comes with its own set of challenges. It often leads to increased costs (in the form of fees and commissions), slower processes (due to manual verification and operational hours), and central points of failure. Furthermore, these intermediaries often maintain strict control over who can access their services, leading to the financial exclusion of a large segment of the global population.

The DeFi architecture presents a radical departure from this centralized model. It opens up financial systems to anyone with an internet connection, reduces costs by removing intermediaries, operates around the clock, and promotes financial inclusion. However, it's crucial to understand that while DeFi holds significant advantages, it also brings with it new challenges and risks, particularly in terms of security. As we delve deeper into the DeFi world, understanding and addressing these security challenges will be vital to the growth and sustainability of this disruptive financial landscape.

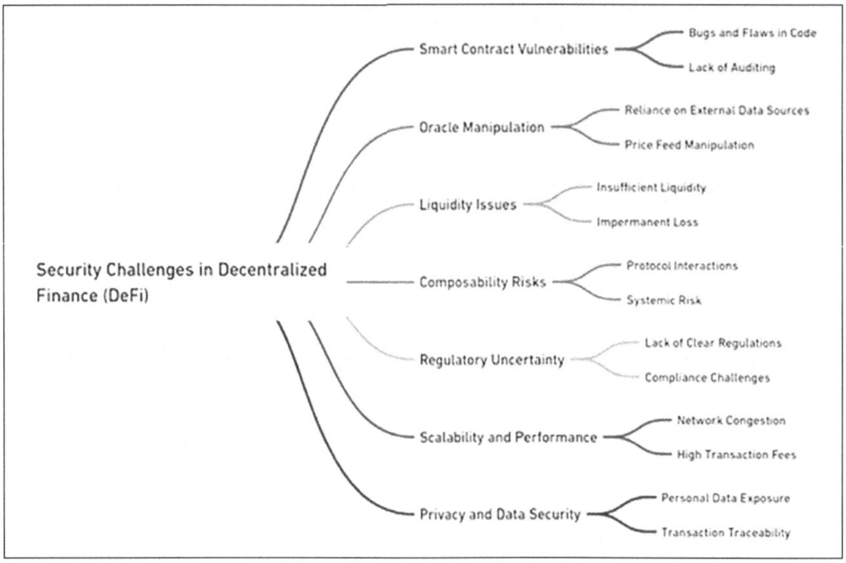

Figure 6.1: *Security challenges in Decentralized Finance (DeFI)*

Key Security Challenges in DeFi and their Implications

The unique and disruptive architecture of DeFi has paved the way for financial democratization, but it has also unveiled a host of new security challenges. These challenges pose significant risks to users and the broader financial ecosystem, highlighting the need for effective security measures.

Smart Contract Vulnerabilities

At the core of DeFi applications are smart contracts. These digital contracts automatically execute transactions on the blockchain when their coded conditions are met. This self-executing and immutable nature is a double-edged sword – while it ensures trustless and tamper-proof transactions, it also means any coding mistakes or security oversights made during their creation can be ruthlessly exploited by malicious actors.

Reentrancy Attacks

One prevalent type of smart contract vulnerability is the reentrancy attack, which came to prominence after the infamous DAO hack in 2016. In a reentrancy attack, an attacker can repeatedly call a function in the smart contract within a single transaction, before the first function call has had a chance to finish. This can lead to unintended behavior, allowing the attacker to drain funds from the contract.

Malleability Attacks

Another class of vulnerabilities arises from the malleability of transaction inputs. Here, an attacker can change the transaction details after the user signs it but before it gets confirmed on the blockchain. This can be used to manipulate contract interactions in a way that benefits the attacker.

Lack of Upgradeability

Although blockchains are immutable, we can bypass this by using the concept of proxy contracts. Next, place a smart contract pointing to the actual logic. If a bug is there in the logic, just change the pointing contracts to a brand-new contract.

Front-Running

Front-running is an attack where the perpetrator gains prior knowledge of pending transactions and exploits this information for profit. Owing to the transparency of the blockchain, an attacker can see a pending transaction and place their own transaction with a higher gas fee, ensuring their transaction is processed first. This is especially damaging in DeFi, where it can lead to significant financial losses for the original transactor.

Flash Loan Attacks

Flash loans are unique to DeFi, allowing users to borrow assets without collateral, provided the loan is returned within the same transaction block. While innovative, this feature has been exploited in several attacks. In a flash loan attack, an attacker borrows assets, manipulates the market, and then pays back the loan within a single transaction, all while making a profit at the expense of other market participants.

Common Security Threats in DeFi

Smart contracts are at the very heart of DeFi platforms. These automated, self-executing contracts carry the terms of an agreement directly within their code, which streamlines and enhances the efficiency of transactions. However, they also present unique security vulnerabilities, particularly if not executed or deployed correctly. Some common security threats in DeFi include:

- **Gas Limit Issues**: In Ethereum, every operation requires a certain amount of gas. If a smart contract function consumes more gas than provided by a transaction or block, it may lead to an "out of gas" exception. This abruptly halts the contract's execution and reverts all state changes, but the consumed gas is not refunded, causing a loss to the user. Accurate estimation of gas is a complex task, and underestimation can lead to financial loss and transaction failures.

- **Timestamp Dependence**: Some smart contracts use the timestamp of the latest block for critical functions like calculating time durations or generating random numbers. However, block miners have slight control over the timestamp, which can be manipulated to a certain degree. An attacker miner could manipulate the timestamp to influence contract behaviors for their gain, posing a significant threat to such timestamp-dependent contracts.
- **Coding Errors**: Even the smallest of coding errors can trigger catastrophic outcomes in the DeFi space, particularly considering the value often held within these contracts. The 2017 Parity wallet incident serves as a poignant reminder where a coding bug enabled an unknown user to take ownership of the library contract, leading to the freezing of over $150 million worth of Ether. The variety of potential coding errors is vast; each carries the potential to expose smart contracts to exploits and attacks. Therefore, meticulous code reviews, adherence to best coding practices, comprehensive testing before deployment, and third-party audits are critical to avoid such pitfalls.
- **Reentrancy Attacks**: In a reentrancy attack, attackers exploit the ability to call a function within a smart contract repeatedly within a single transaction to deplete funds. The infamous DAO hack in 2016 saw around $60 million worth of Ether stolen through the exploitation of a reentrancy vulnerability. The potential for these attacks stems from the nature of function calls in Ethereum smart contracts. This issue underscores the importance of thorough code audits and the implementation of mitigating strategies like using modifier checks or the Checks-Effects-Interactions pattern.
- **Other Common Vulnerabilities**: Apart from coding errors and reentrancy attacks, other common vulnerabilities include overflow and underflow bugs (when a variable exceeds or falls below its maximum or minimum limit) and front-running (when a malicious actor gets prior knowledge of a transaction and uses this information for personal gain before the transaction is confirmed). Each of these vulnerabilities poses significant risks and underlines the need for secure coding practices, rigorous testing, and third-party audits.
- **Attacks on DEXs Decentralized exchanges (DEXs)**: It operate without a central authority, a feature that, while ensuring privacy and control for users, also opens the door to unique security threats.

- **Sandwich Attacks**: Another type of attack specific to DEXs is the sandwich attack. Here, an attacker spots a lucrative transaction in the mempool and places a transaction both before and after it. The initial transaction raises the price, the targeted transaction is then executed at this inflated price, and finally, the following transaction sells the asset, driving the price down. This manipulation allows the attacker to make a profit at the expense of the victim.
- **Impersonation Attacks:** In the context of DEXs, impersonation attacks often involve an attacker creating a pool for a fake or fraudulent token that imitates a legitimate one. Users, failing to recognize the fake, trade their genuine assets for worthless tokens.
- **Front-Running**: Front-running is a specific type of attack where a malicious actor gains prior knowledge of a pending transaction and acts on this information, often by setting a higher gas price, before the original transaction gets confirmed. This can significantly impact scenarios like token sales, where those who transact earlier may have a substantial advantage.
- **Flash Loan Attacks:** Flash loans, a DeFi innovation, allow users to borrow an asset without collateral, provided the loan is paid back within the same transaction. However, flash loans can be used for manipulative market practices. In a flash loan attack, an attacker borrows a large number of assets, manipulates the market to their advantage, and then pays back the loan within the same transaction, thereby making a profit. A clear illustration of this was the bZx attacks in 2020.
- **Other Common Security Threats Phishing**: Phishing attacks are quite common, where attackers trick users into revealing sensitive information, like private keys or wallet passwords, usually through a fake website resembling a legitimate DeFi platform.
- **Social Engineering**: Social engineering involves manipulating users into breaching standard security procedures. An attacker might pose as a support staff member from a DeFi platform to persuade a user to reveal sensitive information.
- **Fake Tokens**: Attackers often create tokens that imitate popular DeFi tokens. Unwary users may end up buying these counterfeit tokens under the impression that they are legitimate assets.
- **DNS Hijacking**: In a DNS hijacking attack, the attacker reroutes the domain name request to a different IP address - often a fake website controlled by them. The website could resemble a popular DeFi platform, and users entering their credentials unknowingly provide the attacker access to their funds.

- **Sybil Attacks**: In a Sybil attack, a single adversary controls multiple nodes in a network to overwhelm the system or gain control. While blockchain networks are typically resistant to Sybil attacks due to proof-of-work or proof-of-stake mechanisms, some aspects of DeFi applications, like governance votes, can still be manipulated if an attacker accumulates enough tokens.
- **Pump and Dump Schemes**: These schemes involve artificially inflating ("pumping") the price of a token through coordinated buying or misleading promotional practices. Once the price has been pumped, organizers "dump" their tokens at the inflated prices to unwitting participants, causing the price to crash and resulting in losses for those who bought at the inflated prices.

A "rug pull" is a deceptive and malicious act that occurs in the world of cryptocurrency and decentralized finance (DeFi). It typically involves a person or a group of individuals creating a cryptocurrency token through a smart contract, where the smart contract includes a hidden or malicious logic that allows the creator (deployer) of the contract to transfer funds or assets from the token to themselves, often at the expense of unsuspecting investors or users.

Here's how rug pulls typically work:

1. **Token Creation:** The individual or group creates a new cryptocurrency token, often with the promise of high returns, a unique use case, or some other attractive feature that lures investors.

2. **Smart Contract Deployment:** The token is deployed on a blockchain platform, such as Ethereum, using a smart contract. The smart contract contains code that defines the token's functionality, including how it can be bought, sold, and transferred.

3. **Hidden Malicious Logic:** Within the smart contract, the creator includes hidden or malicious logic that gives them special privileges or control over the token. This can be in the form of a function or condition that allows the creator to manipulate the token's behavior in their favor.

4. **Initial Hype and Investment:** The creator promotes the token through various means, often using social media, online forums, and other marketing tactics to attract investors. As more people invest in the token, its price and market capitalization increase, creating a sense of FOMO (Fear of Missing Out) among potential investors.

5. **Rug Pull:** Once a substantial amount of funds has been invested in the token, the creator triggers the hidden logic in the smart contract. This logic typically allows them to do one or more of the following:
   - Drain the liquidity pool: The creator withdraws the liquidity provided by users, causing the token's price to plummet.
   - Disable transfers: The creator may freeze transfers or sales of the token, preventing investors from selling or withdrawing their funds.
   - Mint new tokens: The creator may create additional tokens for themselves, diluting the value of existing tokens held by investors.
6. **Exit Scam:** After executing the rug pull, the creator often disappears from the project, social media, and communication channels, making it difficult for investors to seek recourse or trace the responsible party.

Rug pulls are fraudulent activities designed to deceive and defraud investors. They exploit the trust and enthusiasm of the cryptocurrency community, leading to significant financial losses for unsuspecting investors. To protect themselves from rug pulls, investors should exercise caution, conduct thorough research, and avoid investing in projects that lack transparency or have anonymous developers. It's crucial to verify the legitimacy of projects, read smart contract code if available, and be skeptical of promises that seem too good to be true. Additionally, participating in well-established and reputable DeFi platforms can reduce the risk of falling victim to rug pulls

The evolution of DeFi continues at a rapid pace, with the industry's potential only matched by the ingenuity of those seeking to exploit it. As such, understanding these threats and planning for their eventuality is crucial for any DeFi project, not only to protect the users and their funds but also to ensure the longevity and credibility of the project. Regular audits, rigorous testing, and user education are among the strategies that can help mitigate these risks.

Security Measures for DeFi

Securing DeFi platforms is crucial to their growth and continued success. This section will explore the security measures and best practices that can help mitigate the prevalent risks in DeFi. We'll delve into secure smart contract development and auditing, measures to secure DEXs, and additional security measures like multi-factor authentication, encryption, and bug bounty programs.

Best Practices for Secure Smart Contract Development and Auditing

Given the crucial role that smart contracts play in DeFi platforms, secure development and thorough auditing are essential to maintaining their integrity and user trust.

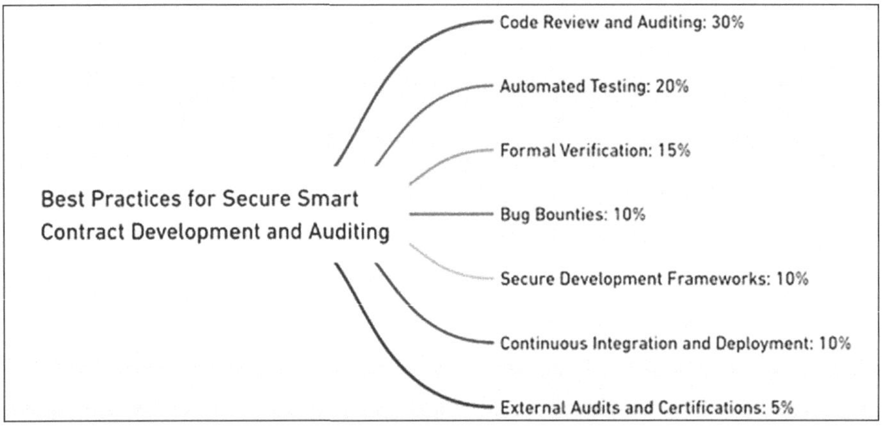

Figure 6.2: *Best practices*

Secure Development Practices

The Decentralized Finance (DeFi) space, though groundbreaking, has proven vulnerable to a variety of security threats. As these risks primarily stem from the software's inherent technical intricacies, secure development practices become paramount. By adhering to these practices, developers can reduce the risk of attacks, ensuring the safety of user funds and the integrity of their platforms.

Use of Established Languages and Frameworks

Cryptocurrency ecosystems typically have recommended languages and frameworks for writing smart contracts. For example, Solidity is the language of choice for Ethereum-based applications, while the Polkadot ecosystem often employs Rust. These languages have undergone extensive testing, have robust documentation, and are continually updated to enhance security and performance.

Similarly, leveraging established frameworks simplifies the development process and minimizes the risk of errors. Truffle and Hardhat, for instance, are popular choices for Ethereum-based projects. They provide a suite of tools that aid in smart contract development, testing, and deployment, which can improve code quality and efficiency.

Implement Modularity

Modularity in coding refers to breaking down the smart contract into smaller, simpler modules. Each module should focus on executing a single function, making the code easier to understand, maintain, and test. A well-structured, modular codebase is more readable and promotes easier bug identification and isolation.

Moreover, modularity allows for more straightforward upgrades and iterations. Instead of modifying an entire smart contract–which could inadvertently introduce new vulnerabilities–developers can adjust individual modules as needed.

Avoid Complexity

The KISS (Keep It Simple, Stupid) principle is essential in the realm of smart contract development. Unnecessary complexity can obfuscate the contract's workings, making it harder to spot potential vulnerabilities. Developers should aim to keep their smart contracts as simple and straightforward as possible.

The benefits of simplicity extend beyond security. Simple, efficient smart contracts use less gas when executing on the Ethereum network, which can lead to significant cost savings for users.

Use Reputable Libraries

Libraries are collections of pre-written code that developers can use to perform common functions, saving them the time and effort of coding these functions from scratch. However, using a poorly written or untested library can introduce vulnerabilities into the smart contract.

Thus, it's advisable to use reputable and widely-used libraries, such as OpenZeppelin for Ethereum, which offers secure, community-vetted, standard implementations of key components. They are continuously updated and audited by the community, providing a level of trust and reliability.

Peer Review and Auditing

After the development process, a thorough review of the codebase is crucial. Peer reviews can catch potential issues, logical errors, and security vulnerabilities that the original developers might have missed. After peer review, the code should undergo a comprehensive security audit by a reputable third-party firm. These audits add another layer of security and increase users' confidence in the platform.

Test Coverage

A well-tested contract is crucial in the DeFi space, where bugs can lead to substantial financial losses. Developers should aim for comprehensive test coverage, ensuring that every part of the contract—including edge cases—is tested under a variety of conditions. Automated testing tools can help execute tests quickly and repeatedly, ensuring that the code works as expected even after numerous iterations.

Security practices are crucial to creating a successful DeFi application. By using established languages and frameworks, implementing modularity, avoiding unnecessary complexity, using reputable libraries, and thoroughly testing and auditing, developers can reduce the potential risks and create secure, reliable DeFi platforms.

Smart Contract Auditing

In the realm of Decentralized Finance (DeFi), where substantial financial transactions occur, the security and reliability of smart contracts are paramount. Given that smart contracts automatically execute transactions without intermediary supervision, any loophole or vulnerability in their code can lead to significant losses. This underscores the importance of smart contract auditing, a thorough evaluation of the smart contract's code to identify and rectify any potential security issues.

A Comprehensive Approach to Auditing

A thorough smart contract audit leverages both manual and automated strategies. Manual code review involves seasoned developers meticulously scrutinizing the smart contract line by line. These experts look for logic flaws, vulnerabilities, and compliance with established coding standards and best practices. They also verify that the contract behaves as intended under a variety of conditions, including edge cases.

On the other hand, automated analysis involves using tools designed to scan the smart contract's code for known vulnerabilities, such as reentrancy attacks, integer overflows, and out-of-gas errors. Tools like Mythril, Securify, and Slither, among others, can detect common vulnerabilities. However, they are not infallible and often can't detect complex attack vectors or logic flaws in the contract. Therefore, automated analysis should complement, not replace, manual code reviews.

The Role of Third-Party Audit Firms

While internal reviews and automated testing are essential, employing an external, third-party audit firm brings an additional layer of scrutiny and objectivity to the process. These firms specialize in analyzing smart contracts for potential security vulnerabilities. Their expertise, coupled with their detachment from the development process, allows them to evaluate the contract from a fresh perspective, often catching issues that internal teams may have missed.

Audit firms like Certik, OpenZeppelin, Trail of Bits, and Quantstamp are renowned for their comprehensive auditing services. An audit report from a reputable firm not only uncovers potential security issues but also significantly enhances user trust in a DeFi platform. It serves as a public testament to the platform's commitment to security and transparency, critical factors in gaining user confidence.

The Audit Report: What it Contains

An audit report typically starts with an executive summary, outlining the audit's scope, methods employed, and key findings. This is followed by an in-depth analysis of the smart contract's functionality and any identified vulnerabilities, classified according to severity: critical, high, medium, or low.

Critical and high severity vulnerabilities typically involve issues that could lead to significant financial loss or other devastating consequences if exploited. Medium and low severity issues may not directly lead to financial losses but could still pose risks or inefficiencies that need addressing.

For each vulnerability identified, the report provides detailed information, including a description of the issue, the contract's sections whcrc it was found, and recommendations for fixing it. It is essential to understand that the responsibility of the auditors typically ends with providing these recommendations–it is up to the development team to implement the fixes and potentially arrange a re-audit to ensure the vulnerabilities have been adequately addressed.

Regular Audits and Continuous Monitoring

It's important to note that smart contract auditing isn't a one-time event but rather a continuous process. As the DeFi platform evolves, smart contracts are often updated or new ones are added. Each change introduces potential new vulnerabilities, necessitating regular audits. Furthermore, new attack vectors constantly emerge as hackers become more sophisticated. Therefore, continuous monitoring and periodic audits are vital in maintaining the security and integrity of DeFi platforms.

In summary, smart contract auditing plays an integral role in the DeFi landscape. By adopting a comprehensive auditing approach, leveraging both manual and automated strategies, and employing third-party audit firms, DeFi platforms can safeguard against potential security vulnerabilities, boosting user confidence and ensuring the smooth operation of their services.

Approaches to Securing DEXs

As Decentralized Exchanges (DEXs) continue to flourish within the blockchain ecosystem, they have become attractive targets for malicious actors. The unique security challenges they face necessitate innovative and proactive solutions. This section delves into several approaches to bolstering DEX security, including order book protection, limiting access to privileged functions, and rate limiting.

Order Book Protection

Front-running remains a prevalent issue on DEXs. This occurs when malicious actors gain prior knowledge of a transaction and act on that information before the transaction is confirmed, usually by offering a higher gas price to prioritize their transaction.

One way to combat front-running is by implementing measures that batch orders into blocks and randomly select one for execution. This process, often referred to as 'commit-reveal' mechanism, reduces the predictability of transaction ordering, making it difficult for front-runners to ascertain which transactions will be processed first.

Another technique involves cryptographic concealment of order information until execution. Known as Zero-Knowledge Proofs (ZKPs), this method allows transaction validation without revealing the transaction's details. Thus, even if a malicious actor sees a transaction, they cannot determine its specifics, reducing the effectiveness of front-running attempts.

Limiting Access to Privileged Functions

Smart contracts govern the functionality of DEXs, and some of these functions have elevated privileges. These privileged functions can modify key parameters or even pause the contract, so their misuse can lead to significant damage. As such, access to these functions should be strictly controlled.

By adopting a principle of least privilege, DEXs can limit user access only to functionalities required for their operations. Privileged functions, such as those for upgrading contracts or changing parameters, should be restricted to specific addresses, typically the contract's owner or a multi-signature wallet.

Implementing multi-signature (multisig) wallets further enhances security. These wallets require multiple signatories to approve a transaction, reducing the likelihood of unauthorized access or changes. By distributing control among multiple parties, the risk associated with a single point of failure is significantly mitigated.

Rate Limiting

Flash loan attacks are another security concern for DEXs. Here, an attacker borrows a large amount of assets without collateral, manipulates the market to their advantage, and pays back the loan within the same transaction. This maneuver can lead to substantial losses for the DEX and its users.

Implementing rate limiting can help counteract flash loan attacks. This approach caps the number of transactions a user can make within a specified time. By restricting the volume of transactions, the potential for market manipulation decreases. Rate limiting can also prevent denial-of-service attacks, where a malicious actor overwhelms the system with a flood of transactions, rendering it unusable for other users.

While these methods significantly improve DEX security, they are not a panacea. Security is an ongoing endeavor, requiring constant vigilance, timely updates, and proactive measures to counteract emerging threats. With continued advancements in blockchain technology and cybersecurity, DEXs can fortify their platforms and provide their users with a secure and trustworthy trading environment.

Other Security Measures

Beyond secure development and exchange-specific measures, other security measures can help protect users and platforms, which are listed as follows:

Multi-Factor Authentication (MFA)

Multi-Factor Authentication, commonly known as MFA, is a security measure that requires users to provide two or more pieces of evidence when logging in. This typically involves something the user knows (like a password), something they have (like a mobile device), or something they are (like a biometric characteristic such as a fingerprint).

MFA is vital in DeFi due to the pseudonymous nature of blockchain transactions, which makes stolen funds virtually irrecoverable. By implementing MFA, DeFi platforms can significantly decrease the risk of unauthorized account access, as the likelihood of an attacker obtaining all required authentication factors is much lower. It's important to note, though, that MFA should be implemented with user privacy in mind to avoid creating new security vulnerabilities.

Encryption

Encryption is a method of encoding information so that only authorized parties can access it. It's a fundamental security measure used throughout the digital world, and it's particularly crucial in the realm of DeFi, where sensitive data, such as private keys, needs to be protected.

Public key encryption, a form of asymmetric encryption, is widely used in blockchain technology. It involves two keys - a public key that can be freely shared and a private key that must be kept secret. Any data encrypted with the public key can only be decrypted with the corresponding private key, thus ensuring secure communication.

Furthermore, secure encryption algorithms, such as AES (Advanced Encryption Standard), should be used to secure stored data. Robust encryption practices not only protect sensitive user data but also enhance user trust in DeFi platforms.

Bug Bounty Programs

Bug bounty programs incentivize independent security researchers and ethical hackers to find and report vulnerabilities in a DeFi platform's software in exchange for a reward or "bounty". These programs can take various forms, from public competitions to private programs involving specially invited researchers.

Bug bounty programs provide several benefits. They harness the collective intelligence and skills of the cybersecurity community, often uncovering vulnerabilities that internal audits might miss. They also promote transparency and help build trust with users, demonstrating the platform's commitment to security.

However, for a bug bounty program to be successful, it must be well managed. Clear guidelines should be established, including how to report a bug, what constitutes a valid vulnerability, and how rewards are determined. There should also be a swift and efficient process for validating reports and deploying patches for the discovered vulnerabilities.

Securing DeFi platforms is indeed a complex task. It involves not only secure development practices and bespoke measures for particular components like DEXs but also a suite of additional security measures like MFA, encryption, and bug bounty programs. By implementing these measures, DeFi platforms can effectively mitigate risks, protect their users, and foster an environment of trust - a critical factor for the continued growth and success of DeFi.

Case Studies

Some use cases are listed as follows:

"**The DAO Hack (2016)**- Impacting Trust and Governance"

Title: The DAO Hack and Smart Contract Vulnerabilities

Elaboration: This case study explores the infamous DAO hack, which resulted in the theft of millions of dollars' worth of Ether. We examine the vulnerability in the DAO's smart contract code that allowed an attacker to exploit the system. The impact on user trust and the subsequent Ethereum hard fork are discussed in detail.

Lessons Learned: The DAO hack highlighted the critical importance of thorough smart contract audits, code reviews, and the need for effective governance mechanisms to prevent and mitigate vulnerabilities in DeFi projects.

"**The Parity Multi-Sig Wallet Breach (2017)** - Lessons in Secure Key Management"

Title: The Parity Multi-Sig Wallet Breach and Key Management Risks

Elaboration: This case study delves into the Parity multi-signature wallet breach, where a vulnerability in the smart contract code resulted in the loss of a significant amount of Ether. We analyze the impact on affected users, the challenges in recovering the funds, and the importance of robust key management practices, including multi-factor authentication and secure storage solutions.

Lessons Learned: The Parity incident emphasizes the criticality of secure key management practices to protect user funds. It underscores the need for implementing multi-factor authentication, thorough security audits, and ongoing monitoring of key management systems.

"**The BZX Protocol Exploits (2020)** - Smart Contract Vulnerabilities

Title: The BZX Protocol Exploits and Smart Contract Weaknesses

Elaboration: This case study investigates the security breaches that occurred in the BZX protocol, leading to flash loan attacks and price manipulation. We examine the vulnerabilities in the smart contract code that were exploited by attackers and the impact on affected users and the protocol's reputation. The steps taken to enhance security and auditing processes in DeFi projects are also discussed.

Lessons Learned: The BZX protocol exploits highlight the importance of comprehensive smart contract audits, rigorous testing, and continuous monitoring to identify and address vulnerabilities. They underscore the need for robust risk management strategies to detect and prevent flash loan attacks.

"**The Alpha Homora Attack (2021)** - Understanding Flash Loan Attacks:

Title: The Alpha Homora Attack and Flash Loan Vulnerabilities

Elaboration: This case study explores the Alpha Homora attack, where an attacker leveraged flash loans to manipulate the borrowing and lending mechanisms within the protocol. We analyze the impact on affected users and the security implications of flash loan attacks. The challenges in detecting and preventing such attacks are discussed, along with the importance of enhanced risk management strategies.

Lessons Learned: The Alpha Homora attack emphasizes the need for DeFi platforms to implement robust risk management measures to detect and mitigate flash loan attacks. It underscores the significance of real-time monitoring and anomaly detection to maintain the integrity of DeFi protocols.

"**The Yearn Finance Exploit (2020)** - Cross-Protocol Risks

Title: The Yearn Finance Exploit and Cross-Protocol Vulnerabilities

Elaboration: This case study examines the Yearn Finance exploit, where an attacker exploited vulnerabilities across multiple DeFi protocols to drain funds from Yearn Finance's vaults. We analyze the interplay between different protocols and the implications of cross-protocol risks. The impact on users, as well as the subsequent security enhancements and protocol upgrades, are discussed.

Lessons Learned: The Yearn Finance exploit highlights the importance of considering and addressing cross-protocol risks in the DeFi ecosystem. It underscores the need for increased collaboration between protocols, thorough security audits, and ongoing vulnerability assessments to mitigate such vulnerabilities.

"**The PancakeSwap Flash Loan Attack (2021)** - Decentralized Exchange Vulnerabilities":

Title: The PancakeSwap Flash Loan Attack and DEX Security Risks

Elaboration: This case study focuses on the PancakeSwap flash loan attack, where an attacker exploited a vulnerability in the decentralized exchange's smart contract to manipulate token prices and profit from arbitrage opportunities. We examine the impact on affected users, the vulnerabilities in the DEX's design, and the subsequent security enhancements implemented by PancakeSwap.

Lessons Learned: The PancakeSwap flash loan attack emphasizes the need for robust security measures in decentralized exchanges. It underscores the importance of rigorous testing, secure code development, and ongoing vulnerability assessments to safeguard user assets and maintain the integrity of the DEX ecosystem.

"**The Uranium Finance Exploit (2021)** - Vulnerabilities in Token Contracts

Title: The Uranium Finance Exploit and Token Contract Weaknesses

Elaboration: This case study explores the Uranium Finance exploit, where an attacker exploited vulnerabilities in the token contract, resulting in the loss of user funds. We analyze the specific weaknesses in the token contract design and implementation, the impact on affected users, and the subsequent security improvements implemented by Uranium Finance.

Lessons Learned: The Uranium Finance exploit highlights the critical importance of robust token contract design and thorough auditing. It emphasizes the need for secure token standards, comprehensive testing, and continuous monitoring to protect user funds and maintain the integrity of token-based DeFi projects.

"**The Cream Finance Flash Loan Attack (2021)** - Liquidity Pool Exploitation

Title: The Cream Finance Flash Loan Attack and Liquidity Pool Risks

Elaboration: This case study focuses on the Cream Finance flash loan attack, where an attacker manipulated liquidity pools to exploit vulnerabilities in the protocol and drain funds. We examine the impact on affected users, the vulnerabilities in liquidity pool mechanisms, and the measures taken by Cream Financc to enhance security and prevent similar attacks.

Lessons Learned: The Cream Finance flash loan attack emphasizes the need for robust security measures in liquidity pools. It underscores the importance of advanced risk management strategies, rigorous auditing of pool mechanisms, and enhanced monitoring to detect and prevent exploitative behaviors.

"**The Cover Protocol Exploit (2020)** - Oracle Manipulation Risks

Title: The Cover Protocol Exploit and Oracle Manipulation Vulnerabilities

Elaboration: This case study investigates the Cover Protocol exploit, where an attacker manipulated price oracles to exploit vulnerabilities and drain funds from the protocol. We analyze the impact on users, the risks associated with oracle manipulation, and the steps taken to strengthen oracle security and data integrity within decentralized finance.

Lessons Learned: The Cover Protocol exploit highlights the critical role of secure and reliable oracles in DeFi. It underscores the need for decentralized oracle solutions, robust data verification mechanisms, and ongoing collaboration between projects and oracle providers to mitigate oracle manipulation risks.

"**The Harvest Finance Exploit (2020)** - Economic Attack on Yield Farming

Title: The Harvest Finance Exploit and Yield Farming Economic Attacks

Elaboration: This case study examines the Harvest Finance exploit, where an attacker executed an economic attack by manipulating yield farming strategies to drain funds. We analyze the impact on affected users, the vulnerabilities in yield farming mechanisms, and the measures taken to enhance security, including improved strategy diversification and implementation of circuit breakers.

Lessons Learned: The Harvest Finance exploit underscores the need for robust risk management in yield farming protocols. It emphasizes the importance of diversified strategies, rigorous auditing of farming mechanisms, and the implementation of protective mechanisms to mitigate economic attacks and safeguard user funds.

"**The Alchemix Finance Exploit (2021)** - Leveraged Stablecoin Risks

Title: The Alchemix Finance Exploit and Risks of Leveraged Stablecoin Models

Elaboration: This case study explores the Alchemix Finance exploit, where an attacker exploited vulnerabilities in the leveraged stablecoin model, resulting in the loss of funds. We analyze the impact on affected users, the risks associated with leveraged stablecoin protocols, and the steps taken to enhance security, including changes to the protocol's collateralization mechanism.

Lessons Learned: The Alchemix Finance exploit highlights the need for careful risk assessment and management in leveraged stablecoin models. It emphasizes the importance of robust collateralization mechanisms, stress testing, and community-driven security audits to identify and mitigate potential vulnerabilities.

Conclusion

The security of DeFi remains a critical consideration as it continues to disrupt traditional financial services. DeFi's security landscape is characterized by unique challenges that stem from its foundational components, such as smart contracts and DEXs. However, the presence of these challenges should not deter us from realizing the enormous potential that DeFi presents. Instead, they should inform our strategies for developing robust security measures to guard against potential threats.

Effective security in DeFi involves more than just safe coding practices or platform-specific security measures. It requires a holistic approach that includes measures like multi-factor authentication, encryption, and bug bounty programs. By taking this approach, we can protect user funds, preserve the integrity of DeFi platforms, and bolster the trustworthiness of this burgeoning financial ecosystem.

In the upcoming chapter, we will delve into the realm of supply chain management, exploring how blockchain is transforming it, the security threats that this transformation faces, and the measures that can be put in place to secure the blockchain-based supply chain. The chapter will also highlight some real-life case studies where supply chain security breaches have occurred and lessons learned from these incidents.

The journey towards a more secure and robust blockchain-based ecosystem continues, and understanding these security challenges and solutions in DeFi and SCM will contribute significantly to that journey.

Further Readings

- Investigating Security Risks in Decentralized Finance: A Case Study - Journal of Cryptology
- Smart Contract Auditing in Decentralized Finance: Challenges and Best Practices - IEEE Security and Privacy
- A Comprehensive Review of Security Measures in Decentralized Finance - ACM Transactions on Information and System Security (TISSEC)
- Security Assessment Framework for Decentralized Finance Platforms - International Journal of Information Security
- Mitigating Cyber Threats in Decentralized Finance Ecosystems - Journal of Computer Security
- Decentralized Finance and Fraud Prevention: A Case Study Analysis - Computers and Security
- Secure Smart Contract Development for Decentralized Finance Applications - IEEE Transactions on Dependable and Secure Computing
- A Study on Financial Crime in Decentralized Finance - Journal of Financial Crime
- Security Challenges and Solutions in Decentralized Exchanges for Decentralized Finance - Journal of Cybersecurity

Chapter 7

Security Challenges in Supply Chain Management

Supply Chain Management (SCM) is an intricate and critical component of modern business operations, facilitating the efficient flow of goods and services from raw material suppliers to manufacturers, distributors, and consumers. As SCM processes become increasingly reliant on technology, blockchain technology has emerged as a potent tool for enhancing transparency, traceability, and efficiency. However, the adoption of blockchain-based SCM systems also introduces new security challenges that organizations must address comprehensively to safeguard their operations and data.

Structure

In this comprehensive exploration, we will delve into the fundamental principles of supply chain management security within the context of blockchain technology. Throughout this chapter, we will dissect these topics in detail:

- Introduction to Supply Chain Management
- Role of Blockchain in SCM
- Security Challenges in SCM
- Common Security Threats in Blockchain-Based SCM
- Security Measures and Best Practices
- Case Studies of SCM Security Breaches
- Preventing Security Threats in SCM

Through this in-depth analysis, we aim to provide organizations and professionals with a robust understanding of the security intricacies and potential vulnerabilities within blockchain-based supply chain management.

Introduction to Supply Chain Management

Supply chain management is the lifeblood of any business, orchestrating the movement of products, services, information, and finances across a network of interconnected entities. Its core objective is to optimize processes, minimize costs, reduce inefficiencies, and enhance overall productivity. A well-managed supply chain enables businesses to respond swiftly to market demands, maintain competitive advantages, and satisfy customer expectations.

The key elements of supply chain management encompass:

- **Planning**: Forecasting demand, managing inventory, and strategizing production schedules are essential components of SCM planning. Effective planning ensures that resources are allocated efficiently to meet demand while minimizing wastage.
- **Sourcing**: This phase involves identifying suppliers, establishing relationships, and negotiating contracts. Choosing reliable and ethical suppliers is critical to maintaining the integrity of the supply chain.
- **Production**: Managing production processes efficiently, adhering to quality standards, and minimizing defects are paramount to ensuring that products meet customer expectations.
- **Logistics**: Transportation, warehousing, and distribution are pivotal in ensuring timely and cost-effective delivery to customers. These logistics processes require careful coordination.
- **Delivery and Returns**: Managing the last mile of delivery and handling returns effectively can significantly impact customer satisfaction and overall supply chain performance.
- **Information Flow**: Timely and accurate information sharing among supply chain partners is crucial for real-time decision-making, demand forecasting, and risk management.
- **Financial Management**: Managing financial transactions, invoices, and payments within the supply chain is essential for maintaining trust and financial stability.

- **Sustainability:** Sustainable practices, including responsible sourcing and reducing environmental impact, have become integral to modern supply chain management, aligning with societal and environmental concerns.

Role of Blockchain in SCM

Blockchain technology, originally designed as the underlying infrastructure for cryptocurrencies like Bitcoin, has transcended its origins and found applications across various industries. In supply chain management, blockchain serves as a decentralized, immutable ledger that records transactions and data securely and transparently. Its introduction into SCM brings several advantages:

- **Transparency**: Blockchain's distributed ledger provides real-time visibility into transactions and activities at every stage of the supply chain. This transparency enhances trust among supply chain participants and allows for more accurate tracking and traceability.
- **Security:** The cryptographic nature of blockchain ensures data integrity and security. Once data is recorded on the blockchain, it is nearly impossible to alter or delete, reducing the risk of data tampering and fraud.
- **Efficiency:** Smart contracts, self-executing agreements with predefined rules, automate various supply chain processes, such as payments and compliance checks. This automation streamlines operations and reduces the need for intermediaries.
- **Traceability**: Blockchain enables end-to-end traceability of products and components, crucial for industries like food and pharmaceuticals. Consumers can verify the authenticity and origin of products, reducing the risk of counterfeit goods.
- **Reduced Fraud:** By eliminating intermediaries and providing tamper-proof records, blockchain reduces the opportunities for fraud and corruption within the supply chain.
- **Streamlined Auditing**: Auditors can access a secure and immutable record of transactions, simplifying the auditing process and reducing the chances of discrepancies.

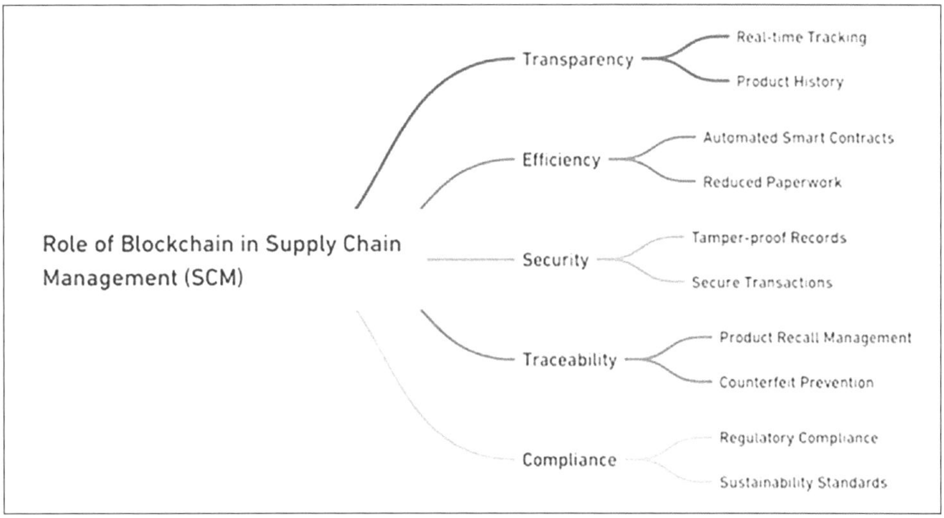

Figure 7.1: *Role of blockchain in SCM*

Blockchain's integration into supply chain management has the potential to revolutionize the industry by addressing long-standing challenges, such as counterfeiting, inefficiencies, and data silos. However, as blockchain adoption grows, so do the security challenges.

Improved Efficiency and Cost Savings: Blockchain enables faster and more accurate transactions, eliminating the need for paper-based documentation and reducing human errors. Blockchain also lowers operational costs by removing intermediaries and facilitating peer-to-peer transactions.

These advantages make blockchain a superior alternative to traditional SCM systems, which often suffer from a lack of trust, coordination, and visibility among supply chain actors. However, blockchain adoption is not without challenges. Some of the potential barriers include:

- **Technological Complexity**: Blockchain requires a high level of technical expertise and infrastructure to implement and maintain. It also poses compatibility issues with existing SCM systems and standards.
- **Initial Costs**: Blockchain involves significant upfront investments in hardware, software, and training. The return on investment may not be immediate or clear, especially for small and medium-sized enterprises.
- **Regulatory Uncertainty**: Blockchain operates in a largely unregulated environment, where legal frameworks and standards are still evolving. This creates risks and uncertainties for businesses that want to use blockchain for cross-border transactions or compliance purposes.

The Transformative Role of Blockchain in Supply Chain Management

Blockchain technology, initially conceived as the foundation for cryptocurrencies like Bitcoin, has evolved far beyond its origins. It has found applications in a multitude of industries, with one of its most promising domains being supply chain management (SCM). The incorporation of blockchain into SCM introduces an array of substantial benefits, fundamentally altering the way businesses orchestrate their supply chains.

Enhanced Transparency and Real-time Visibility

At the core of blockchain's impact on SCM is its ability to provide unparalleled transparency and real-time visibility into the flow of goods, information, and transactions. Unlike traditional supply chain systems, which are often plagued by data silos and a lack of interoperability, blockchain creates a shared and decentralized ledger that all authorized participants can access and trust. Each transaction, be it the movement of raw materials, production milestones, or final product delivery, is recorded as an immutable block on the blockchain. This transparency eliminates the opacity and information asymmetry that can hinder decision-making and lead to inefficiencies.

In practical terms, this means that stakeholders across the supply chain—from suppliers to manufacturers, logistics providers, regulators, and consumers—can track products' progress and status in real-time. For instance, in the food industry, consumers can use their smartphones to scan QR codes on product packaging to access a wealth of information about the product's journey, including its origin, processing, and safety certifications. This heightened transparency instills trust in the supply chain, reduces the potential for disputes, and enhances overall accountability.

Unwavering Data Integrity and Security

Another fundamental advantage of blockchain is its cryptographic underpinning, which ensures data integrity and security. In the world of SCM, where sensitive data, such as pricing agreements, quality certifications, and shipment records, is exchanged between parties, safeguarding the veracity and confidentiality of this information is paramount.

Blockchain achieves this by making data tampering virtually impossible. Once data is recorded on the blockchain, it is cryptographically sealed and added to a chain of blocks. Changing any information in a previous block necessitates altering all subsequent blocks in the chain, which, in a decentralized and widely distributed network, is a highly arduous task, if not impossible. This immutability significantly mitigates the risk of fraudulent activities, such as unauthorized changes to records or counterfeit product introductions.

Additionally, blockchain networks employ consensus mechanisms that ensure all participants agree on the validity of transactions. This consensus-based approach prevents malicious actors from manipulating the ledger's content, further fortifying data security.

Efficiency Through Smart Contracts

Blockchain's impact on SCM extends beyond data management; it also revolutionizes the execution of contracts and agreements within the supply chain. Smart contracts, self-executing pieces of code that automatically enforce predefined rules when specific conditions are met, are at the heart of this transformation.

In traditional supply chain operations, numerous intermediaries, including banks, brokers, and legal entities, are involved in contract execution. This multiplicity of intermediaries leads to delays, added costs, and a heightened risk of disputes. Smart contracts eliminate the need for intermediaries by autonomously executing contract terms when predetermined conditions are met. For example, upon the successful delivery of goods, a smart contract can automatically release payment to the supplier. This not only streamlines operations but also reduces the likelihood of errors and disputes.

Moreover, smart contracts have the potential to revolutionize other aspects of SCM, such as compliance checks, quality control, and regulatory reporting. By encoding complex business logic into smart contracts, supply chain processes can become more efficient and less reliant on human intervention.

End-to-End Traceability

The advent of blockchain has ushered in a new era of traceability in SCM—an era where stakeholders can track the journey of products from their inception to their final destination with unparalleled precision. This level of traceability has profound implications for industries with stringent quality and safety requirements, such as pharmaceuticals, automotive, and food.

By recording each step of a product's journey on the blockchain, including its manufacturing, quality testing, shipping, and handling, organizations can ensure end-to-end traceability. In the event of a product recall or quality issue, pinpointing the affected products becomes a matter of minutes rather than days or weeks. This rapid response capability can save lives, protect brand reputation, and minimize financial losses.

Combatting Fraud and Corruption

The supply chain ecosystem is not immune to fraudulent activities and corruption, which can have severe consequences for businesses and consumers alike. Blockchain's ability to create tamper-proof records and enforce transparent, predefined rules through smart contracts represents a formidable deterrent to fraudulent practices.

For example, in the diamond industry, where the origin and authenticity of precious gems are of utmost importance, blockchain technology can be used to create a digital certificate of authenticity for each diamond. These certificates, once recorded on the blockchain, serve as irrefutable proof of a diamond's provenance and characteristics, reducing the risk of trading in conflict diamonds or counterfeit gems.

Furthermore, by eliminating the opacity that can facilitate corrupt practices, such as bribery or unauthorized alterations to contracts, blockchain promotes ethical conduct throughout the supply chain.

Streamlined Auditing and Compliance

Traditional auditing processes in SCM can be time-consuming, costly, and prone to errors. Blockchain simplifies and accelerates auditing by providing auditors with access to an immutable and comprehensive ledger of all transactions and activities.

Auditors can efficiently verify the accuracy of records and compliance with regulations by inspecting the blockchain. The trustworthiness of the data reduces the need for extensive data reconciliation, which is often a cumbersome and error-prone task in traditional auditing.

This streamlined auditing process not only reduces costs but also enhances the accuracy and reliability of audit results, fostering greater confidence among stakeholders.

In conclusion, the role of blockchain in supply chain management is nothing short of transformative. Its ability to enhance transparency, ensure data integrity, automate processes through smart contracts, enable end-to-end traceability, combat fraud and corruption, and streamline auditing sets the stage for a more efficient, accountable, and secure supply chain ecosystem. As blockchain adoption in SCM continues to expand, businesses and organizations that embrace this technology stand to gain a competitive edge and contribute to the evolution of a more trustworthy and resilient global supply chain.

The current state and challenges of Supply Chain Management (SCM) in 2024 are multifaceted and influenced by various global and technological factors, including:

- **Global Shipping and Geopolitical Issues:** One of the major challenges affecting SCM is the impact of geopolitical issues on global shipping routes. For instance, disruptions in the Red Sea have led to significant rerouting of shipping, adding to transit times and costs. This situation is compounded by factors like drought conditions affecting the Panama Canal, which has implications for global trade and the North American industrial market. These disruptions result in increased maritime transit times and costs, affecting the supply chain's efficiency and profitability.
- **Operational and Financial Challenges in Shipping:** The shipping industry faces a complex situation characterized by rising fuel costs, falling freight rates, and increases in container capacity. This dynamic poses challenges, especially for shipping companies, as they deal with rising operational expenses and market pressures for reduced freight rates. The situation leads to diminishing revenues and profits for these companies. Additionally, the trucking sector has faced severe challenges due to high interest rates, inflated insurance costs, and expensive new trucks, leading to reduced profit margins.
- **Technological Advancements and Data Management:** The rise of technologies such as AI and IoT is reshaping SCM, offering solutions to manage existing challenges and improve operational efficiency. However, one of the core challenges remains managing the vast amount of data generated across the supply chain. The proliferation of digital technologies has led to data silos, and managing data availability, quality, and consistency is crucial for informed decision-making and operational optimization. The industry is moving towards a 'Total Trade' approach, leveraging technology to facilitate smoother cross-border trade and compliance with regulatory requirements.
- **Focus on Sustainability and Cyber Resilience:** Amidst these challenges, sustainability remains a key focus. Companies are increasingly adopting sustainable practices to minimize environmental impacts, such as optimizing transportation routes and integrating sustainable packaging solutions. Additionally, given the critical role of technology in SCM, cyber resilience has become essential to protect against potential vulnerabilities.
- **Labor Shortages and Inflation:** Labor shortages and rising inflation continue to be significant risks in SCM. Labor shortages, particularly in manufacturing, have ripple effects across the supply chain, leading to slower production, disrupted distribution, and delayed deliveries. Managing these risks effectively is crucial for maintaining a resilient supply chain.

In summary, SCM in 2024 is navigating a complex landscape shaped by geopolitical disruptions, operational and financial challenges in shipping, technological advancements, a focus on sustainability, and labor and inflation challenges. The use of advanced technologies and data management strategies is key to addressing these challenges and improving the efficiency and resilience of supply chains.

Security Challenges in SCM

The implementation of blockchain technology in supply chain management brings both benefits and security challenges. As organizations embrace blockchain-based SCM solutions, they must be acutely aware of potential vulnerabilities and develop strategies to mitigate them. Key security challenges in blockchain-based SCM include:

- **Smart Contract Vulnerabilities**: Smart contracts are susceptible to coding errors and vulnerabilities. Flawed smart contracts can lead to financial losses or unauthorized access.
- **Private Key Management**: The security of private keys is paramount in blockchain. If private keys are compromised, malicious actors can gain unauthorized access to the blockchain and manipulate data.
- **Network Security**: Blockchain networks are not immune to distributed denial-of-service (DDoS) attacks, which can disrupt supply chain operations.
- **Identity Management:** Verifying the digital identity of participants is crucial for security. Weak identity management can result in unauthorized access or data breaches.
- **Data Privacy:** While blockchain offers transparency, it can also expose sensitive information to all participants. Striking a balance between transparency and data privacy is a challenge.
- **Interoperability:** Integrating blockchain with existing systems and ensuring data consistency can be complex, potentially introducing security vulnerabilities.

Common Security Threats in Blockchain-Based SCM

Understanding the security threats that can impact blockchain-based supply chain management is pivotal to developing effective countermeasures. Let's delve deeper into these threats:

- **Counterfeit Products and Components**: The transparency of blockchain can be exploited by counterfeiters who may attempt to introduce fake products or components into the supply chain. These counterfeit items can compromise product quality and consumer safety.
- **Data Tampering and Privacy Breaches:** Blockchain's immutability is one of its strengths, but it can also be a weakness. If unauthorized parties gain access to the blockchain, they may tamper with data or compromise sensitive information, leading to privacy breaches.
- **Distributed Denial of Service (DDoS) Attacks**: DDoS attacks can disrupt the availability of blockchain-based supply chain systems, causing delays and financial losses.

Common Security Threats in Blockchain-Based Supply Chain Management: A Comprehensive Examination

Blockchain technology has ushered in a new era of transparency and security in supply chain management (SCM). However, as organizations increasingly rely on blockchain-based SCM systems, it is essential to recognize and mitigate the security threats that could potentially compromise the integrity and functionality of these systems. In this comprehensive exploration, we will delve into the common security threats that can impact blockchain-based SCM and propose strategies to counter them effectively.

Counterfeit Products and Components

One of the most prevalent security threats in blockchain-based SCM is the risk of counterfeit products and components infiltrating the supply chain. Blockchain's transparency, while a boon for traceability, can inadvertently provide counterfeiters with a means to exploit the system. Here's how this threat manifests and potential countermeasures:

Threat Description

Counterfeiters may attempt to introduce fake products or components into the supply chain by creating fraudulent entries on the blockchain. These counterfeit items pose serious risks, compromising product quality, consumer safety, and brand reputation.

Countermeasures

Enhanced Verification Protocols: Implement robust verification protocols at each stage of the supply chain to confirm the authenticity of products and components. These protocols can include physical inspections, digital signatures, and QR code verification.

Digital Certificates: Issue digital certificates for products or components that are recorded on the blockchain. These certificates can serve as trusted proof of authenticity and can be verified by consumers and supply chain participants.

Tamper-evident Packaging: Employ tamper-evident packaging for products to ensure that any interference with the packaging is immediately visible. The status of the packaging can be recorded on the blockchain for added transparency.

Data Tampering and Privacy Breaches

Blockchain's immutability, a hallmark feature, can be both a strength and a potential weakness. Unauthorized parties gaining access to the blockchain can exploit this immutability to tamper with data or compromise sensitive information. Let's delve into this threat and strategies to combat it:

Threat Description

If malicious actors gain unauthorized access to the blockchain, they may tamper with data records, insert false information, or compromise sensitive data, leading to significant privacy breaches and undermining the integrity of the supply chain.

Countermeasures

- **Secure Access Controls**: Implement rigorous access controls to restrict who can read, write, and modify data on the blockchain. Multi-factor authentication and strong password policies are essential components of access control.
- **Encryption:** Encrypt sensitive data both in transit and at rest. Employ robust encryption algorithms to protect data from eavesdropping and unauthorized access.
- **Blockchain Auditing**: Regularly audit the blockchain for any irregularities or unauthorized changes. Blockchain forensics tools can help identify suspicious activities and unauthorized access attempts.
- **Zero-Knowledge Proofs:** Utilize zero-knowledge proofs, a cryptographic technique that allows one party to prove knowledge of specific information without revealing the information itself. This can enhance data privacy on the blockchain.

Distributed Denial of Service (DDoS) Attacks

Despite blockchain's inherent security features, the infrastructure on which it operates can still be vulnerable to Distributed Denial of Service (DDoS) attacks. These attacks can disrupt the availability of blockchain-based SCM systems, causing delays and financial losses:

Threat Description

DDoS attacks involve overwhelming a network or system with a flood of traffic, rendering it inaccessible to legitimate users. In the context of blockchain-based SCM, DDoS attacks can disrupt operations and lead to financial losses due to downtime.

Countermeasures

DDoS Mitigation Services: Employ DDoS mitigation services and solutions to detect and mitigate DDoS attacks in real-time. These services can filter out malicious traffic and ensure uninterrupted blockchain operation.

Redundancy and Failover: Design the blockchain infrastructure with redundancy and failover mechanisms to ensure continued operation even in the face of a DDoS attack on specific nodes or components.

Rate Limiting: Implement rate-limiting measures to restrict the number of requests that can be made to the blockchain, preventing it from becoming overwhelmed by excessive traffic.

Insider Threats and Collusion

Insider threats, including collusion between malicious actors within an organization or its supply chain partners, pose a unique challenge in blockchain-based SCM:

Threat Description

Malicious insiders, whether within an organization or among its supply chain partners, may collude to manipulate data, steal valuable information, or engage in fraudulent activities. These threats can be challenging to detect and prevent, as the actors often have legitimate access to the blockchain.

Countermeasures

- **Role-Based Access Control:** Implement role-based access control to restrict users' permissions based on their roles within the supply chain. Limiting access reduces the potential for unauthorized changes or malicious activities.
- **Transaction Monitoring**: Continuously monitor blockchain transactions for anomalies and suspicious patterns. Advanced analytics and machine learning can help identify potentially malicious behavior.
- **Blockchain Auditing and Forensics**: Employ blockchain auditing and forensics tools to trace the source of security breaches and malicious activities. This can deter insiders from engaging in fraudulent actions.

- **Whistleblower Mechanisms**: Establish anonymous reporting mechanisms for employees and supply chain partners to report suspicious activities without fear of retaliation.

Supply Chain Complexity

As supply chains become more intricate, involving multiple parties, geographical locations, and diverse technologies, the attack surface increases.

Threat Description

Complex supply chain ecosystems offer multiple entry points for malicious actors to exploit vulnerabilities. The interconnected nature of modern supply chains can make it challenging to manage security effectively across the entire ecosystem.

Countermeasures

- **Supply Chain Assessments**: Conduct comprehensive security assessments of all supply chain participants to identify vulnerabilities and weaknesses.
- **Standardization**: Promote the use of standardized security practices and protocols across the supply chain ecosystem to ensure consistency and alignment with best practices.
- **Collaboration**: Foster collaboration and information sharing among supply chain partners to collectively address security threats and vulnerabilities.
- **Continuous Monitoring**: Employ continuous monitoring solutions to detect and respond to security incidents in real-time, reducing the impact of potential breaches.

In conclusion, understanding and proactively addressing these common security threats is essential to harnessing the full potential of blockchain-based supply chain management. While blockchain technology offers transformative benefits, organizations must remain vigilant and implement robust security measures to safeguard their supply chain operations and protect the integrity, confidentiality, and availability of their data. The evolving threat landscape requires continuous adaptation and a commitment to maintaining the highest standards of security within the blockchain-based SCM ecosystem.

Security Measures and Best Practices

To fortify the security of blockchain-based supply chain management, organizations must implement a multi-faceted approach encompassing various security measures and best practices:

- **Digital Identity and Authentication**: Robust identity management and authentication mechanisms are critical. Every participant in the supply chain should have a verified digital identity, and access to the blockchain should be restricted to authorized users only.
- **Encrypted Communication Channels**: Secure communication channels must be established to protect data in transit. End-to-end encryption should be used for sensitive information exchanges between supply chain participants.
- **Consensus Mechanisms and Smart Contracts**: Employing consensus mechanisms, such as Proof of Work (PoW) or Proof of Stake (PoS), ensures the integrity of the blockchain. Smart contracts can automate and enforce agreements, reducing the risk of fraudulent activities.
- **Blockchain Forensics**: Implement blockchain forensics tools and techniques to monitor and investigate suspicious activities on the blockchain. These tools can help in identifying and tracing the source of security breaches.
- **Access Control and Permissioning**: Utilize role-based access control to restrict users' permissions based on their roles within the supply chain. Limiting access reduces the attack surface and prevents unauthorized changes.
- **Regular Audits and Penetration Testing**: Conduct regular security audits and penetration testing to identify vulnerabilities and weaknesses in the system. This proactive approach helps in addressing potential threats before they are exploited.
- **Supply Chain Transparency**: Maintain a transparent ledger that allows all stakeholders to track the movement of goods at every stage. This transparency discourages fraudulent activities and counterfeit products.
- **Incident Response Plan**: Develop a comprehensive incident response plan to address security breaches swiftly and effectively. This plan should include steps for containment, recovery, and communication with affected parties.
- **Security Tokens**: Implement security tokens as a means of enhancing identity verification and access control within the supply chain ecosystem.
- **Legal Compliance**: Ensure compliance with relevant data protection and cybersecurity laws to mitigate legal risks.

These measures, when implemented holistically, create a robust security framework that significantly reduces the risk of security breaches within blockchain-based supply chain management.

Case Studies of SCM Security Breaches

To illustrate the real-world impact of security challenges in supply chain management, we will explore three notable case studies:

Case Study 1: Maersk and the NotPetya Ransomware Attack

In June 2017, Maersk, one of the world's largest shipping companies, experienced a devastating cyberattack that originated from the NotPetya ransomware. The attack quickly spread through Maersk's computer systems, crippling its operations worldwide. Here's a detailed analysis of the incident:

Attack Details:

- The NotPetya ransomware attack encrypted critical data and demanded a ransom in Bitcoin for decryption.
- Maersk's IT infrastructure, including email, booking systems, and operational controls, was severely affected.
- The attack disrupted port operations, container tracking, and delivery schedules, causing massive delays and financial losses.
- Maersk decided not to pay the ransom, opting instead to rebuild its systems from scratch.

Impact on Supply Chain:

- Maersk's supply chain was severely disrupted, affecting not only the company but also its customers and partners.
- Delays in cargo deliveries led to additional costs and supply chain bottlenecks.
- The incident highlighted the need for enhanced cybersecurity measures in the shipping and logistics industry.

Case Study 2: The DAO Hack and its Impact on Supply Chain Transparency

Introduction:

The Decentralized Autonomous Organization (DAO) was a groundbreaking blockchain-based venture capital fund that aimed to revolutionize the world of decentralized finance and investment. In 2016, the DAO suffered a catastrophic security breach that led to the theft of a significant amount of cryptocurrency, ultimately challenging the perceived security and transparency of blockchain-based systems. This incident had a profound impact on investor confidence, especially in projects related to supply chain transparency.

Background:

The DAO was launched in May 2016 on the Ethereum blockchain, and it operated as a smart contract that collected and managed investments from participants. The primary objective of the DAO was to fund various decentralized projects and startups in the cryptocurrency space. The DAO was unique in that it was governed by its token holders, allowing them to vote on investment decisions.

The DAO Hack:

In June 2016, just a month after its launch, the DAO experienced a critical security breach. The attack exploited a vulnerability in the DAO's smart contract code, enabling the hacker to drain a substantial amount of cryptocurrency from the fund. This theft amounted to approximately $50 million worth of Ether (ETH) at the time.

The immediate aftermath of the hack was chaotic, as it exposed a glaring weakness in the smart contract's security. The decentralized nature of the blockchain meant that there was no centralized authority to reverse or rectify the theft, leading to contentious debates within the Ethereum community on how to proceed.

Impact on Supply Chain Transparency:

While the DAO hack was primarily a financial incident, it had far-reaching implications for the broader blockchain and cryptocurrency ecosystem. One area profoundly affected was the development of blockchain solutions for supply chain transparency and accountability.

Doubts About Smart Contract Security: The DAO hack raised doubts about the security of smart contracts, which are fundamental to many blockchain-based supply chain solutions. Investors and enterprises began questioning whether blockchain technology could truly provide the security and transparency promised.

Regulatory Scrutiny: The hack brought increased regulatory scrutiny to the blockchain and cryptocurrency industry. Governments and regulatory bodies sought to understand how such incidents could impact consumer protection and financial stability, especially when applied to supply chain processes.

Investor Caution: The loss of investor funds in the DAO hack made potential investors more cautious about participating in blockchain-based projects. This caution extended to supply chain solutions, where investors questioned the viability and security of blockchain implementations.

Revisions in Smart Contract Development: The DAO hack prompted developers to reevaluate their smart contract coding practices. Security audits and best practices became more critical, particularly in the context of supply chain applications where data integrity is paramount.

Lessons Learned:

The DAO hack serves as a pivotal moment in the history of blockchain technology, especially concerning its impact on supply chain transparency. It highlighted the importance of thorough security audits, community consensus, and regulatory compliance in the blockchain space.

Security First: Security should be a top priority when developing blockchain solutions, especially in areas like supply chain transparency. Rigorous testing and auditing of smart contracts are essential to prevent vulnerabilities.

Community Governance: Governance structures in decentralized systems should be carefully designed to handle unforeseen events like security breaches. Community consensus mechanisms should be robust and responsive.

Regulatory Compliance: Projects aiming to disrupt traditional industries, including supply chains, must navigate the complex regulatory landscape to gain trust and legitimacy.

Transparency and Communication: Open and transparent communication with stakeholders is vital, especially when security incidents occur. Addressing issues promptly and honestly can help mitigate the long-term impact.

In conclusion, the DAO hack of 2016 had a profound impact on the blockchain industry, including supply chain transparency initiatives. While it initially shook confidence in blockchain technology, it also led to valuable lessons and improvements in security practices, ultimately contributing to the continued evolution of blockchain-based solutions in supply chain management.

Case Study 3: The 2018 Vertcoin Attack and its Impact on Supply Chain Integrity

While not directly related to supply chain management, the 2018 Vertcoin attack showcased the vulnerability of smaller blockchain networks to 51% attacks. This has implications for supply chain integrity on blockchain:

Attack Details (Vertcoin Attack):

- Attackers gained majority control of the Vertcoin blockchain's mining power, enabling them to manipulate transactions.

- Double-spending attacks were executed, undermining the integrity of the Vertcoin network.

Impact on Supply Chain Integrity:

- Although Vertcoin was not a supply chain system, the attack raised concerns about blockchain security.
- It demonstrated the potential for malicious actors to compromise the integrity of a blockchain network, which could have severe implications for supply chain data.

These case studies underscore the critical importance of security in supply chain management and blockchain technology. In the following sections, we will delve into each case study in detail, analyzing the security breaches and their consequences.

Lessons Learned - Case Study 1: Maersk and the NotPetya Ransomware Attack

- The Maersk incident emphasized the importance of regular system updates and patch management to protect against known vulnerabilities.
- Robust backup and disaster recovery plans are crucial for business continuity.
- Collaboration and communication with affected stakeholders are essential during a crisis.

This case study underscores the devastating consequences of a supply chain security breach and serves as a cautionary tale for organizations relying on blockchain-based supply chain systems.

Lessons Learned - Case Study 2: The DAO Hack and its Impact on Supply Chain Transparency

- Smart contract development and auditing are critical to preventing vulnerabilities that can be exploited.
- The incident highlighted the importance of clear governance structures in decentralized systems.
- Transparency in blockchain projects is essential to maintain trust among stakeholders.

The DAO hack serves as a reminder of the potential risks associated with blockchain technology, even in applications beyond cryptocurrency.

Lessons Learned - Case Study 3: The 2018 Vertcoin Attack and its Impact on Supply Chain Integrity

- Smaller blockchain networks are more vulnerable to 51% of attacks, highlighting the need for robust security measures.
- Blockchain security is not solely about encryption but also about maintaining the integrity of the network.
- Supply chain systems relying on blockchain technology must consider potential attacks on the underlying blockchain infrastructure.

Preventing Security Threats in SCM

In light of the security challenges and case studies discussed, it's evident that proactive measures are essential to prevent security threats in supply chain management. Here are some key strategies:

- **Continuous Monitoring**: Employ real-time monitoring of blockchain transactions and network activity to detect anomalies and potential threats promptly.
- **Education and Training:** Ensure that all supply chain participants are educated about cybersecurity best practices and are trained to recognize and report suspicious activities.
- **Third-Party Audits:** Engage third-party cybersecurity experts to conduct regular audits and assessments of the supply chain system's security.
- **Multi-Factor Authentication**: Implement multi-factor authentication (MFA) for all users to add an extra layer of security to user accounts.
- **Regular Updates**: Keep blockchain software and related systems up-to-date with the latest security patches and improvements.
- **Collaboration**: Foster collaboration and information sharing among supply chain partners to collectively address security threats.
- **Security Tokens:** Utilize security tokens to enhance identity verification and access control within the supply chain ecosystem.
- **Blockchain Governance**: Establish clear governance structures and mechanisms for dispute resolution within blockchain-based supply chain networks.
- **Legal Frameworks**: Ensure compliance with relevant data protection and cybersecurity laws to mitigate legal risks.
- **Supply Chain Resilience**: Develop contingency plans and redundancy measures to maintain supply chain operations during security incidents.

By implementing these strategies, organizations can bolster the security of their blockchain-based supply chain management systems and minimize the risk of security breaches. Let's delve further into these strategies:

- **Security Tokens (Continued):** Implementing security tokens adds an additional layer of security by requiring users to possess a physical or digital token, such as a smart card or mobile app, for authentication. This two-factor authentication method enhances identity verification and access control within the supply chain ecosystem.
- **Blockchain Governance (Continued):** Establishing clear governance structures within blockchain-based supply chain networks is essential. These governance mechanisms should outline roles, responsibilities, decision-making processes, and dispute-resolution procedures. Transparent governance fosters trust among participants and ensures that security concerns are addressed promptly.
- **Legal Frameworks (Continued):** Compliance with data protection and cybersecurity laws is critical to mitigating legal risks. Organizations must stay informed about evolving regulations in the jurisdictions in which they operate. Legal experts specializing in blockchain and supply chain management can provide guidance on compliance.
- **Supply Chain Resilience (Continued):** Developing contingency plans and redundancy measures is crucial for maintaining supply chain operations during security incidents. Organizations should identify critical processes, establish backup systems, and ensure that data and resources can be quickly restored in the event of an attack.

Additionally, organizations should consider the following:

- **Blockchain Consortiums**: Collaborate with industry-specific blockchain consortiums to share best practices and stay updated on emerging threats and solutions. Consortiums often provide a platform for collective defense against security challenges.
- **Incident Response Team:** Establish a dedicated incident response team with clear roles and responsibilities. This team should be well-trained and prepared to respond swiftly to security incidents, ensuring minimal disruption to the supply chain.
- **Supply Chain Ecosystem Assessments**: Regularly assess the security posture of all participants in the supply chain ecosystem. Identify vulnerabilities and work collectively to address them.
- **Security Awareness Training**: Continuously educate employees, partners, and stakeholders about security best practices. Human error

is a common factor in security breaches, and awareness training can mitigate this risk.

- **Red Team Exercises:** Conduct red team exercises, where ethical hackers simulate attacks to uncover vulnerabilities. These exercises help organizations proactively identify and address weaknesses in their security measures.

Conclusion

In this expanded exploration of supply chain management security within the context of blockchain technology, we have covered a wide range of topics. From the foundational principles of supply chain management to the role of blockchain, security challenges, common threats, and comprehensive security measures, we've provided a thorough understanding of the complex landscape of blockchain-based SCM security.

The case studies of security breaches, including the Maersk NotPetya ransomware attack, the DAO hack, and the Vertcoin attack, underscore the critical importance of proactive security measures in supply chain management. These real-world incidents serve as valuable lessons for organizations aiming to secure their blockchain-based SCM systems.

As organizations continue to leverage blockchain technology for supply chain management, they must remain vigilant, adaptable, and informed about evolving security threats. The strategies and best practices outlined in this chapter provide a solid foundation for safeguarding the integrity, confidentiality, and availability of data within blockchain-based supply chain management systems.

In the ever-evolving landscape of technology and cybersecurity, proactive measures and a commitment to continuous improvement are paramount. By addressing security challenges head-on, organizations can harness the transformative power of blockchain while ensuring the security and resilience of their supply chain operations.

The next chapter provides an in-depth exploration of security challenges in identity management, particularly focusing on the implications and applications of blockchain technology. It delves into the evolution of identity management systems, contrasting traditional centralized approaches with the emerging decentralized methods powered by blockchain. Additionally, the chapter addresses critical concerns such as privacy issues in centralized systems, the role of trust in both centralized and decentralized contexts, and the unique advantages of blockchain in mitigating identity theft and fraud. Through this comprehensive analysis, the chapter sheds light on how blockchain technology is revolutionizing identity management, offering robust solutions to the challenges that have long plagued conventional systems.

Key Terms

- **Supply Chain Management**: The management of the flow of goods and services, involving the movement and storage of raw materials, work-in-process inventory, and finished goods from point of origin to point of consumption.
- **Blockchain:** A decentralized, distributed ledger technology that records the provenance of a digital asset.
- **Transparency**: The quality of being easily seen through, understood, or detected. In SCM, it refers to the clear visibility of all processes and transactions to the involved parties.
- **Traceability:** The capability to trace the history, application, or location of an entity by means of recorded identifications.
- **Security:** Measures taken to guard against espionage or sabotage, crime, attack, or escape. In the context of SCM and blockchain, it involves protecting data and transactions from unauthorized access or alterations.
- **Efficiency:** The ability to accomplish something with the least waste of time and effort; competency in performance.
- **Data:** Facts and statistics collected together for reference or analysis. In SCM, data is crucial for decision-making, forecasting, and optimizing processes.
- **Technology**: The application of scientific knowledge for practical purposes, especially in industry. In SCM, technology like blockchain is used to enhance operations.
- **Operations:** The activities involved in managing and organizing the work or activities of a business or organization, especially regarding production and delivery.
- **Innovation**: A new method, idea, product, and more. In SCM, innovation can lead to improved efficiency, reduced costs, and enhanced competitiveness.

Chapter 8
Security Challenges in Identity Management

Introduction

In an increasingly digitized world, the management and protection of personal identities have become paramount. Traditional identity management systems, often centralized and reliant on third-party intermediaries, have proven vulnerable to data breaches, identity theft, and privacy violations. In response to these challenges, blockchain technology has emerged as a disruptive force in identity management.

Structure

In this chapter, we will cover the following topics:

- Introduction to Blockchain-based Identity Management
- Comparison with Traditional Identity Management Systems
- Security Challenges in Blockchain-based Identity Management
- Security Measures for Blockchain-based Identity Management
- Privacy-Preserving Techniques
- Blockchain Governance and Standards
- Case Studies on Identity Management Security Challenges
- Future Trends and Emerging Technologies

Evolution of Identity Management

Historically, identity management revolved around physical credentials such as passports, driver's licenses, and social security cards. As society transitioned into the digital age, the need for secure, verifiable digital identities became apparent. Centralized databases and identity providers became the norm, granting organizations significant control over users' personal information.

However, centralized systems are susceptible to single points of failure and data breaches, as exemplified by numerous high-profile security incidents. The need for a more secure and user-centric identity management approach led to the exploration of blockchain technology.

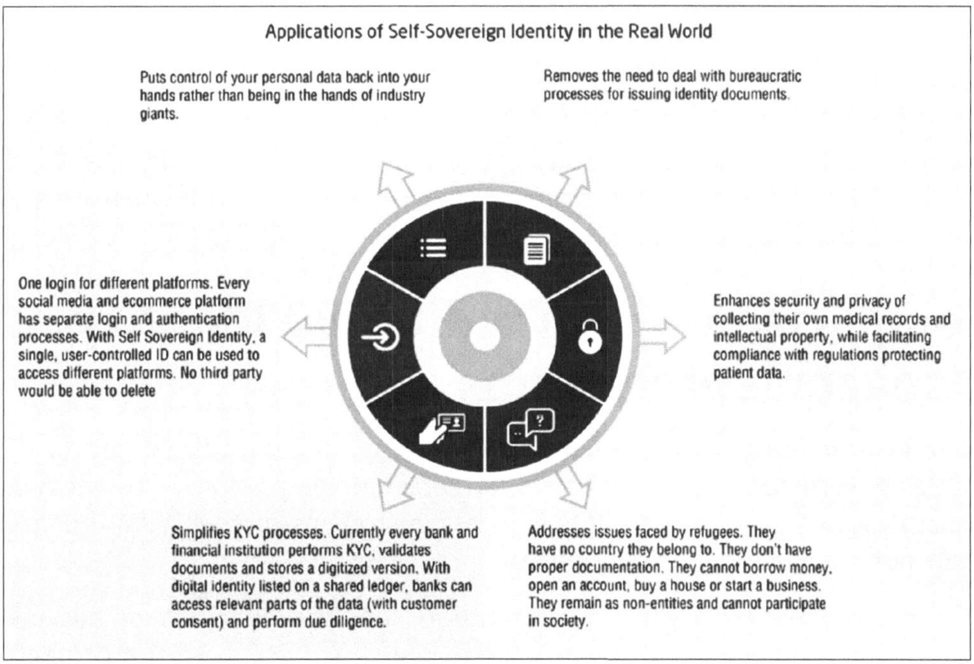

Figure 8.1: *Blockchain-based Identity Management (source - https://www.nec.com/en/global/solutions/blockchain/blockchain-for-digital-identity.html)*

Role of Blockchain in Identity Management

Blockchain, the technology underpinning cryptocurrencies like Bitcoin, introduces decentralized and trustless identity management systems. It offers a secure and immutable ledger where user identities and associated credentials can be stored and verified without the need for intermediaries. This self-sovereign identity (SSI) model empowers individuals with control over their personal data.

Advantages of Blockchain-based Identity Management

Blockchain-based identity management brings several advantages:

- Security: Blockchain's immutability and cryptographic security measures reduce the risk of data breaches and unauthorized access.
- Privacy: Users can selectively disclose information without revealing their entire identity, enhancing privacy protection.
- Interoperability: Blockchain facilitates cross-platform identity verification, improving trust and reducing reliance on central authorities.

In this chapter, we will delve into the security challenges faced by blockchain-based identity management systems and explore the security measures and privacy-preserving techniques that can be employed to mitigate these challenges.

Comparison with Traditional Identity Management Systems

Traditional identity management systems rely on centralized authorities, such as government agencies, banks, or social media platforms, to verify and authenticate users. These entities serve as custodians of user data, creating a single point of failure and vulnerability.

In an era defined by digital transformation, identity management has taken center stage in ensuring secure access to online services and the protection of sensitive personal data. Over time, two distinct approaches have evolved for managing identities: the conventional centralized systems and the more recent decentralized systems underpinned by blockchain technology. In this comprehensive exploration, we will delve into the fundamental distinctions between these two paradigms, unraveling the unique challenges and advantages they present.

In our progressively digitalized world, the significance of robust identity management cannot be overstated. Individuals and organizations alike rely on secure and efficient methods to verify identities and safeguard confidential information. In this section, we will embark on a journey through the following central themes:

- Centralized Identity Management
- Decentralized Identity Management
- Trust and Interoperability

Centralized Identity Management

Centralized Identity Authorities:

Centralized identity management systems predominantly rely on trusted authorities, encompassing government agencies, financial institutions, and social media platforms. These entities play a pivotal role in the verification and maintenance of user identities.

Key aspects to consider include:

- Verification and Authentication: In centralized systems, identity verification and authentication primarily hinge on the validation of documents such as passports and driver's licenses by central authorities.
- Single Point of Failure: The Achilles' heel of centralized systems is their susceptibility to single points of failure. A breach or compromise of the central authority can result in catastrophic security lapses.
- Data Custodianship and Privacy Concerns: The control wielded by central entities over extensive volumes of user data raises concerns about data custodianship and the potential for privacy violations.
- Authentication and Trust: Centralized systems establish trust in user identities through the reputation and authority of central entities. The mechanisms for authentication are usually centralized and may require significant trust in these entities.

Decentralized Identity Management

Empowering Self-Sovereign Identity (SSI):

Blockchain technology is a transformative force in identity management, enabling the concept of self-sovereign identity (SSI). Within the realm of decentralized identity management:

- **Decentralization and User Control**: Blockchain empowers individuals with complete control over their digital identities. Users become the ultimate custodians of their identity data, reducing reliance on third-party entities.

- **Trust in Cryptography and Consensus**: Trust in decentralized systems is forged through cryptographic methods and consensus mechanisms. These robust security measures replace centralized trust with mathematical certainty.
- **Transparency and Immutability**: Blockchain's inherent transparency and immutability elevate the integrity of identity data. Transactions related to identity are recorded in a tamper-resistant ledger.
- **Privacy and Data Minimization**: Decentralized systems prioritize privacy by enabling users to share only necessary information. Data minimization practices mitigate the exposure of sensitive data.

Trust and Interoperability

Trust in Centralized Systems:

Centralized identity systems foster trust primarily through the reputation and authority of central authorities. This trust is pivotal in establishing secure identities and engendering user confidence.

- **Decentralized Trust Mechanisms**: Decentralized systems introduce unique trust mechanisms, notably blockchain's immutable ledger and cryptographic security. These mechanisms reduce dependence on centralized trust entities.
- **Interoperability Challenges**: Interoperability has become a paramount concern in decentralized systems. Different blockchain networks may adhere to varying standards and protocols, potentially hindering seamless cross-platform identity verification.
- **Bridging the Trust Gap**: Efforts to bridge the trust gap between centralized and decentralized identity management systems are ongoing. Innovations aim to enhance interoperability and address trust-related concerns to create a unified identity ecosystem.

As we navigate an ever-evolving digital landscape, identity management emerges as a critical focal point. The coexistence of centralized and decentralized identity management systems offers a diverse array of options. Each approach possesses its unique strengths and weaknesses, demanding a nuanced understanding. Striking the right balance between security, trust, privacy, and interoperability will remain at the forefront of identity management considerations as technology continues to advance.

Security Challenges in Blockchain-based Identity Management

In the digital age, where personal data is increasingly valuable and vulnerable, the security of identity management systems is of utmost concern. Blockchain-based identity management presents a promising solution, but it comes with its own set of unique security challenges. In this comprehensive examination, we will delve into the critical security challenges inherent in blockchain-based identity management:

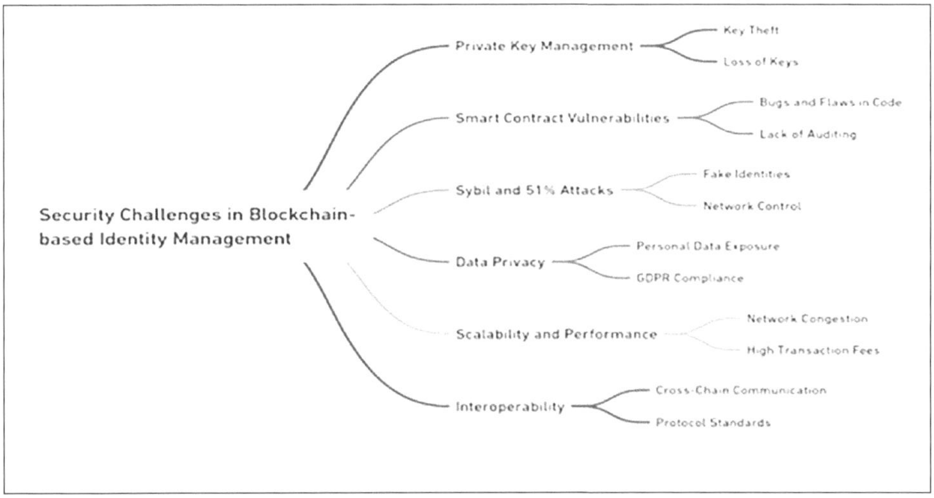

Figure 8.2: *Security challenges*

Privacy and Confidentiality Concerns

- **Transparency versus Privacy**: Blockchain's fundamental principle of transparency can pose a dilemma when it comes to privacy. While transparency enhances accountability, it also exposes potentially sensitive identity data to anyone with access to the blockchain. Balancing this transparency with privacy rights is a delicate challenge.
- **GDPR Compliance**: The European Union's General Data Protection Regulation (GDPR) establishes strict guidelines for data protection and privacy. Adhering to GDPR while operating a blockchain-based identity system can be challenging due to the irreversible nature of blockchain transactions.
- **Data Retention Policies**: Blockchain's immutability implies that once data is recorded, it cannot be erased. Developing effective data retention policies that comply with legal requirements and user consent while ensuring data minimization is a complex task.

Unauthorized Access to Personal Data

- **Insider Threats**: While blockchain is designed to be secure, insider threats within the network can compromise the security of identity data. Malicious actors within the organization or network may misuse their privileges to access sensitive information.
- **Smart Contract Vulnerabilities**: Many blockchain-based identity systems use smart contracts to automate identity verification processes. Vulnerabilities in smart contracts can lead to unauthorized access or manipulation of identity data, potentially exposing users to harm.
- **Identity Theft through Breaches**: If a blockchain network's security is breached, malicious actors could gain access to a trove of identity data, which may be used for identity theft or fraudulent activities.

Risks of Identity Theft and Fraud

- **Identity Forgery**: Blockchain-based identity systems are not immune to identity forgery. Determined attackers may falsify identity credentials, exploiting vulnerabilities in the system's verification processes.
- **Phishing Attacks**: Phishing attacks are a constant threat, where attackers trick users into revealing sensitive identity information or private keys, compromising their digital identities.
- **Social Engineering**: Cleverly orchestrated social engineering attacks can manipulate individuals into divulging identity-related information or performing actions that compromise their identity security.

Sybil Attacks and Identity Proliferation

- **Sybil Attack Overview**: Sybil attacks involve creating multiple fake identities or nodes within a blockchain network to manipulate or disrupt it. In the context of identity management, Sybil attacks can undermine the trust and integrity of the system.
- **Preventing Sybil Attacks**: Implementing robust mechanisms to detect and prevent Sybil attacks is a security challenge. Solutions may include identity verification processes, reputation systems, or consensus algorithms that make Sybil attacks economically unviable.
- **Identity Proliferation's Impact**: A successful Sybil attack can lead to identity proliferation, where the network becomes inundated with fraudulent or duplicate identities, diluting the trustworthiness of the system.

In navigating the security challenges of blockchain-based identity management, it is imperative to develop and implement comprehensive security measures, prioritize user education on identity protection, and continually adapt to emerging threats. As the digital landscape evolves, so too must our strategies for securing our digital identities.

Security Measures for Blockchain-based Identity Management

Blockchain-based identity management offers enhanced security and user control, but it also requires robust security measures to protect sensitive identity data. In this comprehensive examination, we will delve into the essential security measures employed in blockchain-based identity management:

Encryption and Secure Storage of Identity Data

- **Cryptographic Algorithms**: Utilizing state-of-the-art cryptographic algorithms, blockchain-based identity management systems encrypt and secure identity data. Public key cryptography, hashing, and encryption techniques ensure the confidentiality and integrity of the data.
- **Cold and Hot Storage:** Identity data can be stored in both cold (offline) and hot (online) storage. Cold storage minimizes the exposure of sensitive data to potential breaches, while hot storage facilitates immediate access when required.
- **Data Integrity:** Ensuring data integrity through cryptographic hashing and checksums is crucial. Any tampering with identity data stored on the blockchain is immediately detectablc, maintaining the integrity of the system.

Access Controls and Permissions

- **Role-Based Access Control:** Implementing role-based access control (RBAC) allows organizations to define access levels and permissions based on roles. This restricts unauthorized access to identity data and ensures that only authorized personnel can perform certain actions.
- **Smart Contract Permission Models**: Many blockchain-based identity systems leverage smart contracts to manage access and permissions. These contracts can specify who can access specific identity data and under what conditions, adding granularity to access control.
- **Identity Revocation:** In cases of compromised identities or changing circumstances, the ability to revoke access to identity data is vital. Blockchain-based systems often include mechanisms to revoke access or credentials when necessary.

Multifactor Authentication and Biometric Verification

- **Biometric Data Security:** Biometric verification methods, such as fingerprint or facial recognition, enhance identity security. Secure storage and encryption of biometric data are essential to prevent unauthorized access or breaches.
- **Mobile Authentication Apps**: Many blockchain-based identity systems use mobile apps to provide multifactor authentication. These apps generate one-time passwords (OTPs) or cryptographic keys, adding an extra layer of security.
- **Hardware Tokens:** Hardware tokens, like USB security keys, provide physical security for identity verification. These tokens are difficult to compromise remotely, enhancing the security of identity access.

Self-sovereign Identity (SSI) Models

- **User-Centric Identity:** SSI models prioritize user-centric identity control. Users have complete authority over their identity data, determining how and when it is shared, reducing reliance on third parties.
- **Decentralized Identifiers (DIDs):** Decentralized Identifiers (DIDs) are a fundamental component of SSI models. They enable users to create unique, persistent, and cryptographically secure identifiers on the blockchain, enhancing security and control.
- **Verifiable Credentials**: Verifiable credentials issued by trusted entities provide a mechanism for users to prove their identity without revealing unnecessary personal information. This selective disclosure enhances privacy and security.

Identity Verification and Credential Issuance

- **Trusted Issuers:** Establishing a network of trusted issuers is crucial for blockchain-based identity systems. These entities issue verifiable credentials, enhancing the trustworthiness of identities and credentials.
- **Zero-Knowledge Proofs for Verification**: Zero-knowledge proofs allow users to prove specific information about their identity without disclosing the underlying data. This privacy-preserving technique ensures that only necessary information is shared during verification.
- **Revocation Mechanisms**: Credential revocation mechanisms enable the removal of compromised or outdated credentials from the blockchain. This prevents the misuse of expired or invalidated identity data.

In summary, security measures for blockchain-based identity management encompass encryption, access controls, multifactor authentication, user-centric models, and identity verification mechanisms. These measures collectively enhance the security and privacy of digital identities, providing a robust foundation for the evolving landscape of identity management.

Privacy-Preserving Techniques in Blockchain-based Identity Management

Blockchain-based identity management not only enhances security but also prioritizes privacy. To achieve this, a range of privacy-preserving techniques are employed. In this comprehensive examination, we will delve into the essential privacy-preserving techniques utilized in blockchain-based identity management:

Zero-Knowledge Proofs

Zero-knowledge proofs are cryptographic techniques that allow one party (the prover) to prove to another party (the verifier) that a statement is true without revealing any information about the statement itself. In the context of identity management:

- **Privacy in Authentication**: Zero-knowledge proofs enable users to prove their identity without disclosing specific details. For example, a user can prove they are of a certain age without revealing their birthdate.
- **Selective Disclosure:** Users can selectively disclose only the necessary information, enhancing privacy. Zero-knowledge proofs ensure that extraneous data remains confidential.
- **Reduced Data Exposure**: By using zero-knowledge proofs, identity-related information remains private, reducing the risk of data breaches or identity theft.

Differential Privacy

Differential privacy is a privacy-preserving technique that focuses on minimizing the impact of an individual's data when included in a dataset. The key aspects of differential privacy include:

- **Statistical Noise Addition:** When aggregating data, a small amount of statistical noise is added to individual data points. This obscures specific details while still providing meaningful insights.
- **Data Anonymization**: Personal data is anonymized and generalized, making it challenging to identify specific individuals within the dataset.
- **Privacy-Preserving Data Sharing**: Differential privacy ensures that sharing data for analysis or research purposes does not compromise individual privacy.

Homomorphic Encryption

Homomorphic encryption is a cryptographic technique that allows computation on encrypted data without revealing the underlying information. The common aspects of homomorphic encryption include:

- **Secure Computations:** Identity data can be encrypted and processed without being decrypted. This enables secure identity verification and data analysis while preserving privacy.
- **Protecting Identity Data**: Even when data is processed or used in computations, it remains confidential and secure, reducing the risk of data exposure.
- **Secure Outsourcing**: Homomorphic encryption allows third parties to perform computations on encrypted data without access to the plaintext, enhancing privacy in identity-related transactions.

Data Minimization

Data minimization is a fundamental privacy principle that involves collecting and retaining only the minimum amount of data necessary for a specific purpose. In blockchain-based identity management, some common aspects are:

- **Reducing Data Exposure**: By collecting and retaining only essential identity data, the risk of data breaches or unauthorized access is significantly reduced.
- **Enhancing Privacy**: Users have greater control over their data, knowing that only essential information is collected and stored.
- **Regulatory Compliance**: Data minimization aligns with data protection regulations like GDPR, ensuring that personal data is not used excessively.

In summary, privacy-preserving techniques in blockchain-based identity management encompass zero-knowledge proofs, differential privacy, homomorphic encryption, and data minimization. These techniques collectively safeguard user privacy while allowing for secure identity verification and data processing. In an era where data privacy is paramount, these techniques play a vital role in enhancing user trust and protecting sensitive information.

Blockchain Governance and Standards in Identity Management

Blockchain technology has introduced innovative approaches to identity management, but ensuring effective governance and adherence to standards is critical. In this comprehensive examination, we will delve into the vital aspects of blockchain governance and standards in the context of identity management.

Establishing Governance Frameworks

Overview of Governance Frameworks:

Governance in blockchain-based identity management involves creating structures, processes, and rules to ensure the system's integrity, security, and effectiveness. Key aspects include:

- **Governance Models:** Different blockchain identity projects adopt varying governance models, including on-chain governance (decision-making through blockchain-based voting) and off-chain governance (decision-making by external entities or consortiums).
- **Consensus Mechanisms**: Governance frameworks define the consensus mechanisms that determine how decisions are made within the identity network. Common mechanisms include proof of stake (PoS) and delegated proof of stake (DPoS).
- **Decentralized Decision-Making**: Governance frameworks should emphasize decentralized decision-making, reducing the influence of single entities and promoting community involvement.

Industry Standards and Consortiums

Role of Industry Standards:

Industry standards play a pivotal role in ensuring interoperability, security, and compliance within blockchain-based identity management. Key aspects include:

- **Interoperability Standards**: Standards such as the W3C Verifiable Credentials Data Model and Decentralized Identifier (DID) specification promote interoperability between different blockchain identity systems.
- **Data Protection Standards:** Compliance with data protection regulations like GDPR is essential. Industry standards guide identity projects in implementing privacy-preserving measures and user consent mechanisms.

- **Credential Issuance Standards:** Establishing standards for the issuance and revocation of credentials ensures trust in the identity system. Verifiable Credential standards are critical in this regard.

Consortiums and Collaborations:

Consortiums and collaborative efforts within the industry foster cooperation and the development of common standards. Key aspects include:

- **Cross-Industry Collaborations**: Identity management often involves collaboration between industries, including finance, healthcare, and technology, to create universally applicable standards.
- **Ecosystem Development**: Consortiums bring together stakeholders, including identity providers, service providers, and regulatory bodies, to work on common standards, share best practices, and develop governance structures.
- **Regulatory Engagement**: Collaborations with regulatory bodies and government agencies help align blockchain-based identity systems with legal and compliance requirements.

In summary, blockchain governance and standards in identity management encompass establishing governance frameworks to ensure effective decision-making and adherence to industry standards and consortium-based collaboration. These elements are crucial for fostering trust, interoperability, and compliance within the evolving landscape of blockchain-based identity management.

As of 2024, several startups are developing innovative solutions in the field of blockchain-based identity management. Here's an overview of some notable companies in this space:

- **SoluLab**: Specializing in blockchain-based identity management, SoluLab offers secure and decentralized solutions, leveraging blockchain's immutability and transparency.
- **Hu-manity.co**: This company focuses on creating software that manages data-related contracts using artificial intelligence, aiming to restore trust and transparency in digital technologies.
- **Evernym**: Evernym develops software to build trusted digital relationships worldwide, focusing on protecting personal data on the blockchain.
- **Edge**: Edge is known for its mobile app that supports leading cryptocurrencies, emphasizing users' control over their online data.
- **Fractal**: An open-source protocol, Fractal aims to exchange user information fairly and openly, automating processes like KYC and AML using blockchain technology.

- **Metadium Technology**: Focusing on creating a decentralized identity ecosystem, Metadium introduces the concept of Self-Sovereign Identity on the blockchain.
- **Civic Technologies**: Civic provides identity management tools for Web3, offering on-chain representation of reusable identities.
- **Validated ID**: This startup helps businesses send and sign documents online efficiently and securely, integrating electronic signatures with blockchain technology.
- **TheKey**: TheKey offers blockchain-powered identity verification, incorporating dynamic multidimensional identification (BDMI) for authentication.
- **uPort**: Developed by the ConsensSys team, uPort uses the Ethereum blockchain for digital identity management, allowing users to recover their details via smart contracts.
- **ShoCard**: Focusing on mobile and security, ShoCard encrypts identities and stores them on the blockchain, with users controlling access to their information.
- **Netki**: Netki provides both user and wallet ID services, enabling financial service providers to meet compliance requirements on blockchains.
- **HYPR**: HYPR takes biometric security to a new level, offering decentralized authentication over the Bitcoin blockchain.
- **BlockVerify**: Focused on anti-counterfeit measures, BlockVerify's blockchain technology is applicable to a range of products, tracking diverted goods and fraudulent transactions.
- **Bitnation**: Known for providing government-like services decentralized on the blockchain, Bitnation offers blockchain-based passport and marriage certificate solutions.

These companies are at the forefront of leveraging blockchain technology to revolutionize the way identity management is handled, each bringing unique solutions

Case Studies on Identity Management Security Challenges

Understanding the security challenges faced by identity management systems is essential in fortifying our digital infrastructure. Examining real-world case studies provides valuable insights into the vulnerabilities and consequences of security lapses. In this comprehensive exploration, we will delve into three prominent case studies that shed light on the security challenges and their far-reaching consequences.

The Equifax Data Breach

Overview of the Equifax Data Breach:

The Equifax data breach, which occurred in 2017, stands as a monumental example of a centralized identity management system's vulnerability. This breach compromised the personal information of approximately 147 million individuals in the United States.

The key security challenges and consequences were:

- **Centralized Vulnerability:** Equifax's identity management system was centralized, meaning that it relied heavily on a single, massive database to store sensitive personal information. This centralized architecture presented an attractive target for cybercriminals, as a breach would yield an extensive trove of valuable data.
- **Data Protection Failures**: The breach was the result of inadequate security measures and a delayed response to known vulnerabilities in Equifax's systems. The incident highlighted the critical importance of proactive security measures, timely patching of vulnerabilities, and robust intrusion detection systems.
- **Identity Theft and Fraud**: Following the breach, millions of individuals became victims of identity theft and fraud. Cybercriminals leveraged the stolen data to open fraudulent accounts, take out loans, and engage in various forms of financial fraud. This case underscored the far-reaching consequences of identity management security failures on individuals and organizations alike.

The Cambridge Analytica Scandal

Overview of the Cambridge Analytica Scandal:

The Cambridge Analytica scandal, which unfolded in 2018, was not a traditional identity management breach but had significant implications for user privacy and consent. This incident involved the unauthorized harvesting of data from millions of Facebook users for political and advertising purposes.

The key challenges and consequences were:

- **User Consent and Data Control:** The scandal raised fundamental questions about user consent and control over personal data. Users were largely unaware of how their data was being used, highlighting the importance of transparent data practices and informed consent.

- **Privacy Violations**: The incident resulted in massive privacy violations, as users' personal data was used without their knowledge or explicit permission. It demonstrated that privacy breaches can occur on a vast scale, even in contexts not primarily focused on identity management.
- **Regulatory Scrutiny**: In the wake of the scandal, regulatory bodies around the world, including the European Union, took a more proactive stance on data privacy and protection. The implementation of regulations like the General Data Protection Regulation (GDPR) signaled a shift towards stricter oversight and enforcement of data privacy regulations.

Blockchain-based Identity Projects

Overview of Blockchain-based Identity Projects:

Several blockchain-based identity projects have emerged to address the security and privacy challenges inherent in traditional identity management systems. These projects aim to provide self-sovereign identity (SSI) solutions, offering individuals greater control over their identity data. The key features and challenges of these projects include:

- **Security Advancements**: Blockchain-based identity projects leverage cryptographic techniques, decentralization, and user-centric models to enhance security. By shifting control from centralized data custodians to individual users, they mitigate the risks associated with centralized data repositories.
- **Privacy-Preserving Technologies:** These projects incorporate cutting-edge privacy-preserving technologies like zero-knowledge proofs and selective disclosure. These techniques allow users to share only necessary information while safeguarding their privacy, a crucial step towards addressing the privacy challenges in identity management.
- **Interoperability Challenges**: While blockchain identity projects hold great promise, they face challenges related to interoperability and industry standards. Achieving seamless cross-platform identity verification remains a complex task, requiring collaboration and the development of common standards.

In conclusion, these case studies serve as cautionary tales, emphasizing the critical importance of security, privacy, and user control in identity management. The Equifax data breach and the Cambridge Analytica scandal underscore the need for robust security measures, transparent data practices, and regulatory compliance. In contrast, blockchain-based identity projects represent a promising avenue for addressing these challenges by empowering individuals with self-sovereign identity and enhanced security and privacy controls. As technology continues to advance, the lessons learned from these case studies will remain instrumental in shaping the future of identity management.

Future Trends and Emerging Technologies in Identity Management

The future of identity management is undergoing a paradigm shift, driven by emerging technologies and evolving user expectations. In this comprehensive exploration, we will delve into three pivotal future trends and emerging technologies that are poised to revolutionize the field of identity management.

Decentralized Identifiers (DIDs)

Decentralized Identifiers are a fundamental building block of the emerging self-sovereign identity (SSI) paradigm. They represent a transformative shift in how digital identities are created, managed, and verified.

Key aspects include:

- **Unique and Secure Identifiers**: DIDs are cryptographically secure identifiers that are not dependent on any central authority. They are often rooted in blockchain technology, providing immutability and trustworthiness. Each individual can possess their unique DID, reducing the risk of identity fraud and central points of failure.
- **User-Centric Control**: One of the core principles of DIDs is user-centricity. Individuals gain unprecedented control over their digital identities. They can create, modify, and revoke DIDs as needed, eliminating the need for reliance on centralized identity providers.
- **Interoperability:** DIDs are designed with interoperability in mind. They enable seamless identity verification across different platforms, services, and even blockchain networks. This interoperability is essential for the widespread adoption of decentralized identity solutions.
- **Privacy and Selective Disclosure**: DIDs allow users to exercise fine-grained control over what identity attributes they share with others. Through selective disclosure, individuals can prove specific attributes (for example, age or qualifications) without revealing unnecessary personal information, thus enhancing privacy protection.

Verifiable Credentials

Verifiable Credentials are digital attestations issued by trusted entities, serving as a cornerstone of the emerging decentralized identity ecosystem. These credentials are designed to be secure, tamper-evident, and verifiable without the need for intermediaries.

Key aspects include:

- **Credential Issuance**: Verifiable credentials represent a digital transformation of traditional documents and certificates. They are issued digitally and are securely stored in a tamper-resistant format. Entities such as universities, employers, or government agencies can issue verifiable credentials, covering a wide range of personal qualifications and attributes.
- **Selective Disclosure and Privacy:** Verifiable credentials enable individuals to exercise granular control over the information they disclose. Users can selectively share specific credentials with third parties, providing proof of qualifications or attributes without exposing unnecessary personal data. This selective disclosure empowers users to protect their privacy.
- **Trust and Interoperability**: Trust in verifiable credentials is established through cryptographic signatures and the reputation of the issuing entities. These credentials can be verified across different identity systems, platforms, and industries, enhancing interoperability and reducing redundancy in identity verification processes.

Role of Artificial Intelligence

Artificial Intelligence plays a pivotal role in shaping the future of identity management, offering innovative solutions to enhance security and streamline identity-related processes.

Key aspects include:

- **Biometric Verification**: AI-powered biometric recognition systems, such as facial recognition and fingerprint scanning, provide robust and convenient identity verification mechanisms. These technologies analyze unique physical or behavioral traits to confirm a user's identity.
- **Behavioral Biometrics**: AI is increasingly utilized for behavioral biometrics, which analyzes user behavior patterns. This includes typing speed, mouse movements, and touchscreen interactions. These unique behavioral profiles enhance identity verification and fraud detection, as anomalies can trigger alerts.
- **Risk-Based Authentication**: AI-driven risk assessment models continuously analyze user behavior, transaction data, and contextual information to detect anomalies and assess the risk level of a particular activity or login attempt. This adaptive approach strengthens security while minimizing user friction by requiring additional authentication only when necessary.

- **Identity Verification Automation**: AI automates identity verification processes, reducing manual intervention and improving efficiency. Document verification, facial recognition, data validation, and even liveness detection are areas where AI excels. These technologies enhance the speed and accuracy of identity verification, making them crucial in various industries, from financial services to e-commerce.

In summary, the future of identity management is undergoing a profound transformation driven by Decentralized Identifiers (DIDs) and Verifiable Credentials, which empower individuals with greater control, privacy, and interoperability. Artificial Intelligence (AI) plays a central role in enhancing security, introducing innovative biometric verification methods, behavioral biometrics, risk-based authentication, and automation of identity verification processes. As these technologies continue to mature and integrate, the identity management landscape will evolve to meet the demands of an increasingly digital and interconnected world, where user control, privacy, and security are paramount.

The Evolving Landscape of Identity Management

The landscape of identity management is in a state of dynamic transformation, driven by technological advancements, changing user expectations, and a growing awareness of the critical role identity plays in our digital lives. In this concluding segment, we will reflect on the evolving nature of identity management and the fundamental imperative of security in this context.

Identity management has come a long way from its origins in physical credentials like passports and driver's licenses. In our increasingly digital and interconnected world, where individuals interact with countless online services and platforms, the need for robust, user-centric, and privacy-preserving identity solutions has become paramount.

Key Trends and Shifts:

- **Decentralization and Self-Sovereign Identity (SSI):** Decentralized Identifiers (DIDs) and Verifiable Credentials are at the forefront of this transformation, empowering individuals with control over their digital identities. Users are no longer mere subjects of identity providers but active participants in identity management.
- **Privacy and Selective Disclosure:** The demand for privacy and data protection has given rise to privacy-preserving techniques like zero-knowledge proofs, differential privacy, and homomorphic

encryption. Users can now share identity attributes with precision, safeguarding their personal information.

- **Interoperability and Standards:** Industry standards and consortiums have emerged to ensure interoperability between different identity systems and promote best practices. These standards facilitate trust and cooperation among diverse stakeholders.
- **Artificial Intelligence and Automation:** Artificial Intelligence plays a pivotal role in enhancing security and streamlining identity processes. Biometric verification, behavioral biometrics, risk-based authentication, and automation have transformed identity verification methods.

Zero-Knowledge Proofs and Identity Management

One of the most promising privacy-preserving techniques in identity management is zero-knowledge proofs (ZKPs). ZKPs allow users to prove that they possess certain attributes or credentials without revealing any other information. For example, a user can prove that they are over 18 years old without disclosing their date of birth or name. ZKPs enable selective disclosure and granular consent, enhancing user privacy and control.

However, not every identity protocol or system is actively using ZKPs, and there are still challenges and limitations to overcome. ZKPs are computationally intensive and require complex cryptographic protocols, which may affect scalability and performance. Moreover, the landscape of ZKPs is constantly evolving, with new variants and applications emerging. Therefore, it is essential to keep up with the latest developments and innovations in ZKPs and assess their suitability and feasibility for different identity scenarios.

The Imperative of Security in Identity Management

Security lies at the heart of identity management, and its importance cannot be overstated. The Equifax data breach and the Cambridge Analytica scandal serve as stark reminders of the devastating consequences of security lapses. Security in identity management encompasses not only data protection but also user authentication, access control, and fraud prevention.

Key Security Imperatives:

- **Decentralization to Mitigate Risk**: Decentralized identity solutions like DIDs reduce the risk of centralized data breaches. By dispersing identity data and control, the impact of a single security failure is minimized.

- **Privacy-Preserving Technologies**: Privacy-preserving techniques, including zero-knowledge proofs and homomorphic encryption, protect personal information and ensure selective disclosure. These techniques strike a balance between security and user privacy.
- **Biometrics and AI:** Biometric verification methods and AI-driven risk assessment enhance identity security. They offer both convenience and robust authentication, while risk-based models adapt to evolving threats.
- **Compliance and Regulation**: Adherence to data protection regulations like GDPR is paramount. Compliance ensures that individuals' rights are respected, and their data is handled responsibly.

Conclusion

The evolving landscape of identity management is marked by decentralization, privacy preservation, interoperability, and the integration of advanced technologies like Artificial Intelligence. In this chapter, we learned that security remains a cornerstone of this transformation, and the lessons learned from past security breaches underscore its critical importance. As identity management continues to evolve, striking the right balance between user empowerment, privacy protection, and robust security will be essential in building a trusted and resilient digital identity ecosystem for the future.

In the next chapter, we will learn about the best practices for ensuring robust security in blockchain systems which involve a multi-faceted approach, prioritizing both technical and organizational measures. Technologically, it's crucial to implement strong cryptographic techniques, including advanced encryption standards and secure hashing algorithms, to safeguard data integrity and confidentiality. Regular security audits and vulnerability assessments are essential to identify and mitigate potential security threats. In terms of network security, maintaining a decentralized consensus mechanism, such as proof of work or proof of stake, helps prevent attacks like the 51% attack. Organizational best practices include establishing clear governance models and standard operating procedures for blockchain operations, ensuring transparency and accountability. User education and awareness are also important as informed users are less likely to fall prey to phishing attacks and other security breaches. Furthermore, implementing multi-factor authentication and rigorous access controls for network participants enhances security. Adherence to these best practices ensures a robust, resilient blockchain ecosystem, capable of resisting a wide array of cyber threats.

Key Terms

- **Security:** Defined as the reduction of risk of data breaches and unauthorized access through blockchain's immutability and cryptographic security measures.
- **Privacy:** Refers to verifiable credentials enabling individuals to control the information they disclose, enhancing privacy.
- **Interoperability:** Defined as the establishment of trust in verifiable credentials through cryptographic signatures and the reputation of issuing entities.
- **Authentication:** Described as the use of zero-knowledge proofs to prove identity without disclosing specific details.
- **Failure:** Refers to the susceptibility of centralized systems to single points of failure, termed as their Achilles' heel.
- **Privacy Concerns:** Concerns about data custodianship and potential privacy violations due to the control central entities have over extensive user data.
- **Trust:** In centralized systems, trust in user identities is established through the reputation and authority of central entities.
- **User Control:** Blockchain technology empowers individuals with complete control over their digital identities.
- **Consensus:** Trust in decentralized systems is established through cryptographic methods and consensus mechanisms.
- **Immutability:** Blockchain's transparency and immutability enhance the integrity of identity data.

CHAPTER 9
Best Practices for Blockchain Security

Introduction

Blockchain technology has emerged as a transformative force across various industries, offering unparalleled transparency, security, and trust in digital transactions. However, as blockchain adoption continues to expand, so do the threats and challenges to its security. In this chapter, we delve into the realm of blockchain security, providing you with a comprehensive guide to best practices that will help safeguard your blockchain networks and applications.

Structure

In our exploration of blockchain security best practices, we have structured this chapter into four distinct sections, each focusing on essential aspects of securing your blockchain ecosystem:

- Key Principles of Blockchain Security
    - Cryptography Basics
    - Consensus Algorithms
    - Immutable Ledger
    - Permissioning

- Best Practices for Blockchain Development
  - Threat Modeling
  - Secure Coding Practices
  - Smart Contract Security
  - Open-source and Community Involvement
- Best Practices for Blockchain Deployment and Operations
  - Access Control
  - Network and System Hardening
  - Data Protection
  - Incident Response
- Continuous Monitoring and Improvement of Blockchain Security
  - Threat Intelligence
  - Regular Security Assessments
  - Security Awareness Training
  - Iterative Security Improvement

Key Principles of Blockchain Security

Blockchain technology has ushered in a new era of trust and security in the digital world. It relies on a set of foundational principles that ensure the integrity, confidentiality, and availability of data within a decentralized network. In this section, we will delve into the key principles of blockchain security, highlighting the role of cryptography, consensus algorithms, immutability, and permissioning.

Cryptography Basics

Cryptography is at the heart of blockchain security, providing the tools and techniques needed to secure data and transactions. Here, we explore the fundamental cryptographic principles:

Hash Functions

Hash functions are mathematical algorithms that take an input (or 'message') and produce a fixed-size string of characters, typically a hexadecimal number. The role of hash functions in blockchain security is paramount:

- **Data Integrity**: Hash functions generate unique hash values for data. Even a minor change in the input data results in a significantly different hash value. This property ensures the integrity of data on the blockchain, as any tampering with a transaction or block becomes readily apparent.

- **Efficient Data Retrieval**: Hashes serve as identifiers for data on the blockchain. They enable quick retrieval and verification of data, facilitating efficient blockchain operations.
- **Mining in Proof of Work (PoW):** In PoW-based blockchains like Bitcoin, miners compete to find a nonce (a random number) that, when hashed with the block's data, produces a hash value with specific properties. This computational puzzle adds security to the network.

Digital Signatures

Digital signatures are cryptographic techniques that provide proof of the authenticity and integrity of a digital message or document. In blockchain, digital signatures play a pivotal role:

- **Authentication:** Digital signatures ensure that transactions on the blockchain are authentic and have not been tampered with. They are created using the sender's private key and can be verified using the sender's public key.
- **Non-Repudiation:** A digital signature provides strong evidence that a transaction or message was indeed created by the claimed sender, preventing them from denying their involvement.
- **Security of Funds:** In cryptocurrencies, digital signatures are used to authorize transactions, ensuring that only the legitimate owner of a private key can spend their funds.

Public and Private Keys

Public and private key pairs are the cornerstone of blockchain security. They form the basis of identity verification, data encryption, and transaction authorization:

- **Public Keys:** These are shared openly and serve as addresses on the blockchain. They are used for encrypting data or verifying digital signatures. Anyone can use a public key to verify the authenticity of a message or transaction.
- **Private Keys**: Kept secret by their owners, private keys are used for decrypting data, creating digital signatures, and authorizing transactions. The security of private keys is of utmost importance, as compromising them could lead to unauthorized access and loss of assets.
- **Key Pair Relationship:** The pairing of public and private keys ensures secure communication and transaction authorization. Data encrypted

with a public key can only be decrypted with the corresponding private key, and vice versa.

Consensus Algorithms

Consensus mechanisms are the protocols that ensure all participants in a blockchain network agree on the state of the blockchain. Different consensus mechanisms provide security in various ways, including:

Proof of Work (PoW)

- **Overview:** PoW requires participants, known as miners, to solve complex mathematical puzzles to add new blocks to the blockchain. This process consumes significant computational resources.
- **Role in Security**: PoW ensures that adding blocks to the blockchain requires substantial computational effort. Changing a block's content or history becomes computationally infeasible, making the blockchain resistant to tampering.
- **Energy Consumption:** PoW's energy-intensive nature is a trade-off for its security. It necessitates miners to invest in hardware and electricity, deterring malicious actors.

Proof of Stake (PoS)

- **Overview:** PoS selects validators to create new blocks based on the amount of cryptocurrency they 'stakc' as collateral. Validators are chosen proportionally to their stake in the network.
- **Role in Security**: PoS reduces energy consumption compared to PoW and enhances security by aligning the interests of validators with the network's security. Malicious actions would risk the loss of their staked assets.

Practical Byzantine Fault Tolerance (PBFT)

- **Overview:** PBFT is a consensus algorithm that tolerates a certain number of malicious nodes or Byzantine faults. It requires a two-thirds majority of nodes to agree on the state of the blockchain.
- **Role in Security**: PBFT ensures that the majority of nodes in the network must agree on the state of the blockchain. It is resilient to malicious actors who control a minority of nodes.

Immutable Ledger

Immutability is a core principle of blockchain security. It guarantees that once data is added to the blockchain, it cannot be altered or deleted:

- **Data Integrity:** Immutability ensures that data stored on the blockchain remains unchanged over time. Each block contains a reference to the previous block, creating a linked chain of blocks that cannot be altered without changing the entire chain's history.
- **Transparency:** Immutability contributes to transparency by allowing anyone to audit the entire history of transactions. This transparency builds trust among participants and stakeholders.
- **Security Against Tampering**: Immutability provides security against unauthorized changes to data. Even if a single entity attempts to tamper with a block, the entire network will reject the change, making tampering extremely difficult.

Permissioning

Permissioning refers to the control of access to a blockchain network. It defines who can participate, interact, and perform actions within the network. Key aspects of permissioning include:

- **Public versus Private Blockchains**: Public blockchains, like Bitcoin and Ethereum, are open to anyone, while private blockchains restrict participation to specific entities.
- **Permissioned versus Permissionless Access**: Permissioned blockchains grant access and participation rights to known and authenticated participants, whereas permissionless blockchains allow anyone to join without prior approval.
- **Use Cases**: Permissioning is crucial in scenarios where confidentiality, compliance, or regulatory requirements dictate strict control over network access. It ensures that only authorized participants can interact with sensitive data and processes.

The key principles of blockchain security–cryptography, consensus algorithms, immutability, and permissioning–form the bedrock of secure and trustful blockchain systems. Together, these principles enable blockchain technology to revolutionize digital transactions, data integrity, and decentralized trust. In the following sections, we will explore best practices for implementing and enhancing blockchain security, building upon these fundamental principles.

Best Practices for Blockchain Development

Developing secure and robust blockchain applications is essential to harness the full potential of this transformative technology. Blockchain development, whether for cryptocurrencies, smart contracts, or decentralized applications, demands a meticulous approach to security. In this section, we will explore best practices that developers should adhere to when building blockchain solutions.

Threat Modeling

Threat modeling includes identifying potential attack vectors and designing security measures accordingly.

Understanding Threat Modeling

Threat modeling is a systematic process that helps developers anticipate potential security threats and vulnerabilities in their blockchain applications. It involves:

- **Identifying Assets:** Determining what needs protection, such as data, digital assets, and smart contracts.
- **Identifying Threats:** Recognizing potential threats, including cyberattacks, fraud, and data breaches.
- **Assessing Vulnerabilities**: Evaluating weaknesses in the system that might be exploited by attackers.
- **Designing Countermeasures:** Creating security measures and safeguards to mitigate risks.

Role of Threat Modeling in Blockchain Development

Threat modeling is especially critical in blockchain development because:

- **Immutable Data:** Once data is recorded on the blockchain, it cannot be changed. Identifying and addressing security threats proactively is essential to prevent costly mistakes.
- **Smart Contracts:** Smart contracts are self-executing and irreversible. Flaws in smart contract logic can result in irreversible financial losses.

- **Evolving Threat Landscape**: The blockchain space is dynamic, with new threats emerging regularly. Threat modeling helps developers stay ahead of potential risks.

Secure Coding Practices

It includes avoiding common vulnerabilities such as SQL injection, buffer overflows, integer overflows, and race conditions.

Secure Coding Principles

Writing secure code is paramount in blockchain development. Secure coding practices include:

- **Input Validation:** Ensuring that input data is properly validated to prevent injection attacks like SQL injection.
- **Buffer Overflow Mitigation**: Implementing safeguards to prevent buffer overflows, which can lead to code execution vulnerabilities.
- **Integer Overflow Prevention**: Using proper data types and checks to prevent integer overflows that can result in unexpected behaviors.
- **Race Condition Avoidance:** Identifying and mitigating race conditions that may occur when multiple processes access shared data concurrently.

Importance of Secure Code

In the blockchain context, secure coding is crucial because:

- **Irreversible Transactions**: Once a transaction is executed, it cannot be undone. Flaws in smart contracts or transaction scripts can lead to permanent losses.
- **Financial Implications:** Many blockchain applications involve financial assets. Vulnerabilities can result in significant financial losses.
- **Smart Contracts:** Secure coding practices are essential for writing reliable and secure smart contracts, which automate processes and agreements.

Smart Contract Security

It includes auditing smart contracts for vulnerabilities, testing, and verification of contract logic.

Smart Contract Vulnerabilities

Smart contracts are self-executing agreements with predefined rules. Ensuring their security is vital, as vulnerabilities can have far-reaching consequences. Common smart contract vulnerabilities include:

- **Reentrancy Attacks**: Malicious contracts can repeatedly call other contracts, potentially draining funds.
- **Unchecked External Calls**: Failing to check the results of external contract calls can lead to unexpected behaviors.

Unchecked external calls can allow reentrancy attacks to occur, as the callee contract can execute arbitrary code before the caller contract finishes its execution. To prevent this, it is advisable to use the checks-effects-interactions pattern, which ensures that all state changes and effects are done before calling external contracts.

Another common vulnerability in smart contracts is the lack of input validation and access control. Input validation means verifying that the inputs to a function are valid and within the expected range. Access control means restricting access to certain functions or variables based on predefined rules. Failing to implement these mechanisms can result in unauthorized actions or a corrupted state.

For example, input validation can prevent integer overflows or underflows by checking that the inputs do not exceed the maximum or minimum values of the data type. Access control can prevent malicious actors from calling functions that are meant to be private or restricted to specific roles.

Therefore, to secure smart contracts, developers should always validate their inputs and implement proper access control mechanisms. Additionally, they should follow coding standards and best practices, such as using the latest compiler version, avoiding low-level calls, and testing and auditing their code thoroughly.

- Integer Overflows/Underflows: Mishandling numeric operations can result in unintended outcomes.

Best Practices for Smart Contract Security

The best practices to secure smart contracts:

- **Code Auditing**: Have your smart contracts audited by security experts to identify vulnerabilities.
- **Testing:** Thoroughly test contracts in different scenarios to identify potential issues.

- **Formal Verification**: Use formal methods to mathematically verify contract logic.

Smart contract auditing is a crucial step to ensure the security and reliability of your contracts. By hiring security experts to review your code, you can identify and fix any vulnerabilities that could compromise your assets or functionality. Testing is another essential practice to ensure your contracts work as intended in different situations. You should test your contracts for edge cases, such as unexpected inputs, low gas limits, or malicious attacks. Formal verification is a more advanced technique that uses mathematical logic to prove the correctness of your contract code.

Auditing, testing, and formal verification are important ways to secure your smart contracts and prevent costly errors. Smart contract auditing involves having your code reviewed by professionals who can spot and fix any flaws or weaknesses. Testing involves simulating different scenarios and inputs to check how your contracts behave and handle errors. Formal verification involves using rigorous mathematical methods to verify that your contracts match your specifications and logic.

To ensure the safety and quality of your smart contracts, you need to audit, test, and formally verify them. Smart contract auditing is the process of having your code checked by experts who can find and correct any bugs or vulnerabilities. Testing is the process of running your code in various conditions and inputs to see how it performs and handles errors. Formal verification is the process of using mathematical proofs to confirm that your code meets your requirements and logic.

Open-source and Community Involvement

It involves leveraging the community to identify and fix security issues.

Strength of Open Source

Blockchain projects often involve open-source development, which encourages transparency and collaboration. Leveraging the community and open-source tools is advantageous:

- **Peer Review**: Open-source projects benefit from peer review, which helps identify and address security vulnerabilities.
- **Community Knowledge**: The collective knowledge of the community can provide insights into best practices and emerging threats.

- **Faster Fixes**: When security issues arise, the open-source community can often respond quickly with fixes.

Best practices for blockchain development are integral to creating secure, reliable, and efficient blockchain applications. Threat modeling helps anticipate and mitigate risks, secure coding practices prevent vulnerabilities, and rigorous smart contract security ensures the integrity of self-executing agreements. Open-source collaboration with the blockchain community enhances the security and quality of blockchain projects. By adhering to these best practices, developers can harness the full potential of blockchain technology while minimizing security risks and ensuring the trust of users and stakeholders.

Best Practices for Blockchain Deployment and Operations

Once a blockchain application is developed, the focus shifts to deployment and operational management. Effective deployment and operation practices are essential to ensure the security, availability, and efficiency of a blockchain network. In this section, we will explore the best practices for deploying and managing blockchain systems.

Access Control

It involves controlling who can access the blockchain network and what actions they can perform.

Access Control Policies

Access control in blockchain systems is crucial for governing network interactions. It involves:

- **Identity Verification**: Verifying the identity of participants to prevent unauthorized access.
- **Authorization:** Specifying what actions users or nodes are allowed to perform within the network.
- **Role-Based Access Control (RBAC):** Assigning roles and permissions based on users' responsibilities and needs.

Role of Access Control in Blockchain Security

Access control is vital because:

- **Confidentiality**: It prevents unauthorized parties from viewing sensitive data or executing unauthorized transactions.
- **Regulatory Compliance**: In regulated industries, access control helps ensure compliance with data protection laws.
- **Preventing Unauthorized Changes**: It prevents malicious or unauthorized modifications to the blockchain's state.

Network and System Hardening

It involves securing network and system infrastructure, minimizing attack surface.

Network Security

Securing the network infrastructure is critical to blockchain security:

- **Firewalls**: Implementing firewalls to filter incoming and outgoing traffic and protect against unauthorized access.
- **Intrusion Detection Systems (IDS) and Intrusion Prevention Systems (IPS):** Deploying IDS and IPS to detect and prevent malicious activities.
- **Encryption**: Encrypting data in transit to protect it from eavesdropping.

System Hardening

System hardening focuses on securing individual nodes and devices:

- **Regular Updates:** Keeping software, including operating systems and blockchain client software, up-to-date with security patches.
- **Minimal Installations**: Only installing the necessary software to reduce the attack surface.
- **Security Configuration**: Configuring systems to follow security best practices, such as disabling unnecessary services and using strong authentication.

Data Protection

It involves securing sensitive data both in transit and at rest, implementing secure backups and disaster recovery plans.

Data Encryption

- **In Transit**: Encrypting data as it travels between nodes or over networks to protect it from interception.

- **At Rest**: Encrypting data stored on disk or in databases to safeguard it from unauthorized access.

Backups and Disaster Recovery

- **Regular Backups:** Creating regular backups of blockchain data and configurations to prevent data loss.
- **Disaster Recovery Plans:** Developing comprehensive plans to recover from various disasters, including data breaches or hardware failures.
- **Testing and Verification:** Regularly testing backup and recovery processes to ensure their effectiveness.

Incident Response

It includes developing a plan for responding to security incidents and mitigating their impact.

Incident Response Framework

Developing an incident response plan is crucial for:

- **Detection**: Detecting and identifying security incidents as they occur.
- **Containment**: Containing the incident to prevent it from spreading and causing further damage.
- **Eradication**: Identifying the root cause of the incident and eliminating it.
- **Recovery**: Restoring affected systems and services to normal operation.
- **Lessons Learned**: Analyzing the incident to improve security measures and prevent future occurrences.

Importance of Incident Response

- **Minimizing Downtime**: A well-executed incident response plan can minimize the downtime caused by security incidents.
- **Reducing Damage:** Timely containment and eradication can reduce the extent of damage caused by security breaches.
- **Preserving Reputation:** A prompt and effective response can help maintain trust and reputation with users and stakeholders.

Best practices for blockchain deployment and operations are pivotal to maintaining a secure and efficient blockchain network. Effective access control policies ensure that only authorized entities interact with the blockchain, while network and system hardening protect against external threats. Data protection measures safeguard sensitive information, and incident response plans help mitigate the impact of security incidents. By following these best practices, blockchain operators can ensure the continued reliability and security of their networks, fostering trust among users and stakeholders.

Continuous Monitoring and Improvement of Blockchain Security

Blockchain security is an ongoing process that requires constant vigilance and adaptation to emerging threats. Continuous monitoring and improvement are essential aspects of maintaining a secure blockchain network. In this section, we will explore the best practices for keeping a blockchain system secure over time.

Threat Intelligence

It involves keeping up to date with new and emerging security threats and vulnerabilities.

Understanding Threat Intelligence

Threat intelligence is the process of gathering, analyzing, and disseminating information about current and potential cybersecurity threats. This includes:

- **Monitoring Threat Sources**: Continuously monitoring sources of threat intelligence, such as cybersecurity news, reports, and forums.
- **Analyzing Threat Data**: Analyzing data to identify trends, tactics, and vulnerabilities exploited by attackers.
- **Sharing Information**: Collaborating with the broader cybersecurity community to share threat intelligence and best practices.

Role of Threat Intelligence in Blockchain Security

Threat intelligence is crucial for blockchain security because:

- **Evolving Threat Landscape:** The cybersecurity landscape is constantly evolving, with new attack techniques and vulnerabilities emerging regularly. Threat intelligence helps blockchain operators stay informed about the latest threats.
- **Proactive Defense**: By anticipating potential threats, organizations can take proactive measures to prevent security breaches rather than merely reacting to them.

- **Strategic Decision-Making:** Threat intelligence informs strategic decisions about security investments and measures.

Regular Security Assessments

It involves conducting regular security assessments and penetration testing to identify and remediate vulnerabilities.

Security Assessments

Security assessments involve the systematic evaluation of a blockchain network's security posture. Key components of security assessments include:

- **Vulnerability Scanning:** Using automated tools to identify known vulnerabilities in the network's infrastructure and applications.
- **Penetration Testing:** Conducting controlled attacks on the network to uncover weaknesses that may not be identified through automated scanning.
- **Security Audits**: Reviewing the network's configuration, policies, and procedures to ensure compliance with security best practices.

Importance of Regular Security Assessments

Regular security assessments are essential because:

- **Risk Mitigation:** Identifying vulnerabilities and weaknesses allows organizations to proactively mitigate risks before they can be exploited by malicious actors.
- **Compliance Requirements**: Many industries and regulatory frameworks require regular security assessments to ensure data protection and compliance.
- **Continuous Improvement:** Security assessments help organizations continually improve their security posture based on the changing threat landscape.

Security Awareness Training

It involves educating developers, operators, and users on security best practices and how to avoid common security pitfalls.

Security Awareness Programs

Security awareness training programs educate individuals within an organization about cybersecurity best practices, including:

- **Phishing Awareness**: Teaching individuals to recognize and avoid phishing attempts, which are common in blockchain-related attacks.
- **Password Hygiene:** Promoting the use of strong, unique passwords and multi-factor authentication.
- **Safe Browsing Habits:** Advising users on how to browse securely and avoid suspicious websites and downloads.

Role of Security Awareness in Blockchain Security

Security awareness is vital because:

- **Human Element:** Many security breaches result from human error or lack of awareness. Educating users and operators helps reduce these risks.
- **First Line of Defense:** Users and operators are often the first line of defense against cyber threats. Their ability to recognize and respond to threats can prevent security incidents.
- **Culture of Security:** Fostering a culture of security within an organization ensures that security is a shared responsibility.

Iterative Security Improvement

It involves continuously improving security measures based on new threats and emerging best practices.

Continuous Improvement Cycle

Continuous improvement is an iterative process that involves:

- **Monitoring**: Continuously monitoring the blockchain network for security events and anomalies.
- **Assessment:** Regularly assessing the effectiveness of existing security measures.
- **Adaptation:** Adapting security measures to address new threats and vulnerabilities as they emerge.
- **Feedback Loop:** Incorporating lessons learned from security incidents and assessments into future security strategies.

Necessity of Continuous Improvement

Continuous improvement is essential because:

- **Adaptive Threats:** Cyber threats are dynamic and adaptable. Security measures must evolve to counter new tactics and techniques.

- **Regulatory Changes**: Changes in regulations and compliance requirements may necessitate adjustments to security measures.
- **Technological Advancements:** The evolution of technology, including blockchain technology itself, may introduce new security considerations.

Continuous monitoring and improvement of blockchain security are paramount in today's evolving threat landscape. Threat intelligence keeps blockchain operators informed about emerging threats, while regular security assessments identify vulnerabilities and weaknesses. Security awareness training educates users and operators to recognize and mitigate risks, and iterative security improvement ensures that security measures stay effective in the face of evolving threats. By embracing these practices, organizations can maintain the trust and security of their blockchain networks over time.

Best Practices for Blockchain Security

In an era defined by digital innovation and decentralized trust, blockchain technology has emerged as a transformative force. Its potential to revolutionize industries, streamline processes, and enhance security is undeniable. Yet, to fully unlock the benefits of blockchain, one must navigate the intricate landscape of blockchain security.

Cryptography, Consensus, Immutability, and Permissioning form the bedrock upon which secure blockchain systems are built. Cryptography secures data and transactions, while consensus mechanisms ensure agreement in a decentralized network. Immutability guarantees the integrity of data, and permissioning governs access, shaping the nature of blockchain networks.

Best Practices for Blockchain Development

Threat modeling sets the stage by identifying vulnerabilities and potential threats, allowing developers to design robust security measures. Secure coding practices safeguard against common pitfalls like SQL injection and buffer overflows, ensuring the reliability of smart contracts and transactions. Smart contract security calls for rigorous audits and verification to prevent irrevocable losses. The open-source collaboration leverages the strength of the community, strengthening security through transparency.

Best Practices for Blockchain Deployment and Operations

Access control stands as the sentinel, guarding the entry points to blockchain networks, ensuring that only authorized entities traverse its corridors. Network and system hardening armor the infrastructure, minimizing vulnerabilities, and safeguarding against external threats. Data protection ensures that sensitive information remains secure in transit and at rest, with comprehensive backup and recovery strategies for business continuity. Incident response strategies stand ready to contain and mitigate the impact of unforeseen security breaches.

Continuous Monitoring and Improvement of Blockchain Security

In an ever-evolving digital landscape, threat intelligence acts as our eyes and ears, keeping us attuned to the shifting tides of cyber threats. Regular security assessments shine a spotlight on vulnerabilities, offering the chance to remediate risks proactively. Security awareness training imbues the human element with the knowledge and vigilance to recognize and combat threats. Iterative security improvement reminds us that security is not static; it's a dynamic process that adapts to emerging threats and changing landscapes.

In the grand tapestry of blockchain security, each thread—whether cryptography or continuous monitoring—plays an integral role. Security is not a destination but a journey—a journey defined by resilience, adaptability, and a commitment to maintaining trust in a decentralized world. As blockchain technology continues to evolve, so too must our dedication to safeguarding its promise. With these best practices in hand, we embark on that journey, confident in our ability to secure the future of blockchain.

Conclusion

As blockchain technology continues to evolve and shape the future of digital transactions, ensuring its security is paramount. By following the best practices outlined in this chapter, you'll be well-equipped to navigate the intricate landscape of blockchain security, mitigate risks, and build a robust and resilient blockchain ecosystem. So, let's embark on this journey to fortify the foundations of your blockchain endeavors.

Key Terms

Key Principles of Blockchain Security

- **Cryptography Basics**:
    - Fundamental cryptographic principles vital to blockchain security, including hash functions, digital signatures, and public and private keys.
- **Consensus Algorithms**:
    - Different mechanisms like Proof of Work (PoW), Proof of Stake (PoS), Practical Byzantine Fault Tolerance (PBFT), and Delegated Proof of Stake (DPoS) that contribute to the security of blockchain systems.
- **Immutable Ledger**:
    - The concept of immutability in blockchain that ensures data integrity and security against tampering.
- **Permissioning**:
    - Distinguishes between public and private blockchains, and explores permissioned versus permissionless access models.

Best Practices for Blockchain Development

- **Threat Modeling**:
    - Identifying potential attack vectors and designing appropriate security measures.
- **Secure Coding Practices**:
    - Guidelines to avoid common vulnerabilities like SQL injection, buffer overflows, integer overflows, and race conditions.
- **Smart Contract Security**:
    - Importance of auditing, testing, and verifying smart contracts for vulnerabilities.
- **Open-source and Community Involvement**:
    - Utilizing the blockchain community for identifying and addressing security issues, and the role of transparency and collaboration in enhancing security.

Best Practices for Blockchain Deployment and Operations

- **Access Control**:
    - Managing who can access the blockchain network and implementing access control policies.

- **Network and System Hardening**:
  - Securing network and system infrastructure and minimizing attack surfaces.
- **Data Protection**:
  - Securing sensitive data in transit and at rest, and developing secure backup and disaster recovery plans.
- **Incident Response**:
  - Developing comprehensive plans for detecting, mitigating, and recovering from security incidents.

Continuous Monitoring and Improvement of Blockchain Security

- **Threat Intelligence**:
  - Staying informed about emerging security threats and vulnerabilities.
- **Regular Security Assessments**:
  - Conducting routine security assessments, audits, and penetration testing.
- **Security Awareness Training**:
  - Educating on security best practices and raising awareness about common security pitfalls.
- **Iterative Security Improvement**:
  - Continuously enhancing security measures and adapting to new threats and best practices.

Index

C

D

E

G

I

L

N

O

P

R

S

T

V